MW01615500

15

Celebrating the

125th Birthday of
H.P. Lovecraft

and recognizing the

75th Anniversary of the
Street & Smith Comics

Compiled and edited by Tom Roberts

BLACK DOG BOOKS

2015
Normal, IL

"My First Lovecraft," by F. Paul Wilson © 2015 the author.

"Lovecraft and Pseudo-Mathematics," by Robert Weinberg © 2015 the author.

"How Great Britain 'Discovered' Lovecraft," by Stephen Jones © 2015 the author. All rights reserved

"The Call of Khalk'ru and Other Speculations," by Will Murray © 1991, 2015 the author.

"Lovecraft and *Weird Tales*," by S.T. Joshi © 2015 the author.

"The Truth About *The Shunned House* Hardcover," by Robert Weinberg © 2015 the author.

"Chant," by Robert Weinberg © 2001 the author.

"Sydney Taine vs. The Slime God," by Robert Weinberg © 2015 the author.

"The Art of H.P. Lovecraft," by Will Murray © 1981, 2015 the author.

"The Look of Lovecraft," by Randy Broecker © 2015 the author.

"Street & Smith In Four Colors," by Anthony Tollin © 2015 the author.

"The Street & Smith Comics," by Michelle Nolan © 2015 the author.

"From Pulp to the Silver Screen, 2015," by Ed Hulse © 2015 the author.

The publisher wishes to thank the following individuals for additional contributions made to this volume: Val Edwards, Robert Weinberg, Gene Christie, Doug Ellis and John Gunnison.

This edition, editing, arrangement and presentation © 2015 by Black Dog Books. All rights reserved. Except for brief passages for critical articles or reviews, no portion of this book may be reproduced in any form or by any mechanical, electronic or other means, now known or hereafter invented including photocopying, xerography, and recording, or in any information retrieval and storage system without the express written permission of the publisher.

ISBN 978-1-884449-61-1

Cover art by Les Edwards © 2007 the artist. All rights reserved. Reprinted by permission.

Editing, book layout and design: Tom Roberts.
Proofreading: Doug Ellis, Gene Christie.

Black Dog Books, 1115 Pine Meadows Ct., Normal, IL 61761-5432.
www.blackdogbooks.net / info@blackdogbooks.net

CONTENTS

H.P. Lovecraft Celebration

Special Fiction Section
Stories by H.P. Lovecraft

The Lasting Influence of Lovecraft
Fiction inspired by the work by HPL

Art Focus

The Street & Smith Comics

Film Focus

About the cover

"LOVECRAFT IN BRITAIN" (2007) BY LES EDWARDS

Born in 1949 in Walthamstow, East London, Les Edwards began his illustration career immediately on leaving the notorious Hornsey College of Art in 1972. In the years that followed he became a stalwart of the UK illustration scene. He has worked for all the major UK publishing houses and for many in the US, and his work has also encompassed advertising, gaming, record and CD covers, and film posters, while his paintings are to be found in private collections world-wide. He also paints under the pseudonym "Edward Miller" in order to do a different kind of work and use a more romantic style. Edwards has been voted Best Artist by the British Fantasy Society on seven occasions, been nominated for five Chesley Awards, and been nominated for the World Fantasy Award for Best Artist five times (his alter-ego, Edward Miller, won it in 2008).

"This was the cover for a monograph by Stephen Jones and published by the British Fantasy Society," explains the artist. "Like my dust-jacket painting for *Weirder Shadows Over Innsmouth*, it shows London invaded by Lovecraftain beasts. There are not that many photos of Lovecraft to work from, and the brief was to paint him in *Famous Monsters* colors."

To learn more about Les, visit his website at *www.lesedwards.com*.

Shadows Over Lovecraft

DAVID H. KELLER, M.D.

During the last of February and the first half of March 1937, a gentleman of the old school lay in a bed at the Jane Brown Memorial Hospital of Providence, Rhode Island, and daily wrote his last weird tale. This story, written solely for his own pleasure and the information of his physician, has not been published, but there can be no doubt as to its plot and style. Like so many of his other compositions, it must have been told in the first person singular, and narrated the story of a hero struggling against one of the great and constantly threatening enemies of the human race.

Against this enemy, which has existed for ages, modern science has battled without too great success. For centuries, physicians have known about these malignant gods from the universal nowhere. To them, syphilis, cancer, leprosy, tuberculosis and pneumonia are as much feared as any fancied demons called Cthulhu, Yuggoth or Yog-Sothoth.

This conflict of man against terrible and unconquerable powers of darkness was a favorite motif in Lovecraft's stories. The older gods, prisoned in the earth, under the oceans, on remote planets, were battling constantly for the freedom that would enable them to destroy humanity. Occasionally, some of them, for a short time, crossed the barrier, but were always driven back and, for a time, rendered harmless. The hero of such tales was frequently destroyed, while the narrator became so mentally shattered by his participation in the horror that he either contemplated suicide or became helplessly psychotic.

This man not only wrote, but lived, his last tale in a pattern very so familiar to him. It was simply one more conflict between a man and one of the elder gods in which the man was defeated—destined by fate to fight on hopelessly, doomed from the beginning to certain failure. In this last battle, no courageous state police routed the foe with dynamite, no providential typhoon temporarily sealed the ocean home of the enemy. There was no one to destroy it with great carboys of acid, or carefully close, with stone and cement, the opening from which it had escaped.

While writing this last story he must have felt the utter futility of the struggle. He was very much alone. If any of his intimate friends visited him then, they have never spoken of it. There is no record that he obtained consolation and strength from any minister of a God supposedly friendly to mankind. His doctor visited him; the nurses cared for him. Otherwise, he spent his last days as he had spent much of his life, very much alone.

Sheer physical disability, without loss of the keen mentality that had been,

Reprinted from *Fantasy Commentator,* Summer 1948.

through all his life, such a prominent part of his personality, forced him to stop writing. He came to the end of the story and wrote Finis without complaint, and, perhaps, without regret. Without understanding why Fate had made him what he was, he was determined to do the best he could with what he had. He could have said, as did William Ernest Hanley, during his last days:

> *In the fell clutch of circumstance*
> *I have not winced or cried aloud.*
> *Under the bludgeonings of chance*
> *My head is bloody, but unbowed.*

Thus ended the literary career of Howard Phillips Lovecraft.

There are certain facets of his personality that deserve comment. Preeminently, he was a gentle soul. There is no evidence that he ever spoke or wrote unkindly to anyone. He was fond of calling himself a gentleman, and his entire life proved him such a one that even Lord Chesterfield would have been pleased. While shunning formal society to a marked degree, he gave of himself freely, without thought of personal gain, to all who called on him for help.

His various biographies—all short, and, at times, lacking in vital details— show him to have been a man who never admitted defeat. Handicapped as he was by family circumstances and lifelong disabilities, he rarely if ever complained. He continued fighting against heavy odds for the attainment of a lifelong goal: that of becoming a force in literature.

The fact that his ability was not fully recognized until after his death is nothing new in the history of great authors. Those famous lines can aptly be quoted, "Seven cities claimed poor Homer dead, through which the living Homer begged his bread." Thoreau's first edition of Walden remained unsold while he supported himself by making and selling lead pencils, or depended on the charity of friends. Poe's greatness was unrecognized, except in France, for years after he died an alcoholic pauper in Baltimore. Melville's *Moby Dick* attracted little attention during his lifetime; but years later it was acclaimed a great saga of man's battle against his destiny.

The realization that much of the world did not appreciate his stories probably made no impression on him. He wrote for the pleasure of writing because of a super-active, creative mind. Undoubtedly, he was pleased when he sold a story and saw it printed, but he willingly lived on fifteen cents a day for food, devoting long hours to correspondence, ghost-writing and revising stories others had written. Had he composed fewer letters, spent fewer hours on revisions and ghost-writing, he would have had more time to produce and sell his own stories.

A desire to write was his primary objective; the thought of sale was an entirely secondary consideration. While in high school, he hectographed a small magazine, *The Rhode Island Journal of Astronomy*. In 1914, he became a member of the United Amateur Press Association, and from that time contributed generously to such publications as *The Unified Amateur, The Vagrant, Science-Fantasy Correspondent* and *Marvel Tales.* It was not until he was thirty-two years old that his first story was published professionally. This was a horror serial, "Herbert West: Reanimator," and appeared in 1922 in *Home Brew* magazine.

In 1923, he became one of the authors who contributed to the newly-formed *Weird Tales,* which, under the able editorship of Farnsworth Wright, rapidly gained eminence in the pulp field. Lovecraft's contribution to its fame is shown by the fact that of the fifty-two titles listed in the bibliography in *HPL: A Memoir,* forty-six were first published in *Weird Tales.* However, it must be noted that, of this total number, sixteen did not appear there until after his death in 1937. Five of those sixteen were reprinted from smaller or amateur publications. Thus, from 1922 until his death in 1937, Lovecraft had but thirty-four stories professionally printed—an average of a little more than two a year. Had this been his only source of income, he would indeed have been a very poor man.

Some of the thirty-six sonnets titled "Fungi from Yuggoth" also first appeared in *Weird Tales,* though many of them were originally donated to such fan magazines as *The Fantasy Fan* during the period 1931–37, and some did not see print till as late as 1945. Besides stories and poems, Lovecraft wrote essays, among which are "Heritage or Modernisms" and "Some Causes of Self-Immolation." His very complete "Guide to Charleston, South Carolina" first was in letter form.

Thousands of letters comprise the rest of his literary work; he was a tireless correspondent. For nearly twelve years, he wrote one friend, weekly, letters from one to thirty pages in length, each page covered with almost microscopic words written in longhand. All this was a labor of love to a man he never met, who was a boy of fourteen when the first letter was written. These letters, thousands in number, simply flowed from his pen. There could have been no time for thoughtful composition or hour-consuming revision. When these letters are finally published, they will reveal, far more than his stories, his real creative ability.

Early in life, he became interested in literature. At the age of four, he was reading Grimm, at five, *The Arabian Nights,* and when six absorbing Greek and Roman mythology. His first horror story was written at the age of seven, influenced by Dante's *Inferno* and Coleridge's "Ancient Mariner," both illustrated by Doré. In later years, many of his somber descriptions of landscapes give the impression that he was also acquainted with Doré's illustrations for Cervantes' Don Quixote.

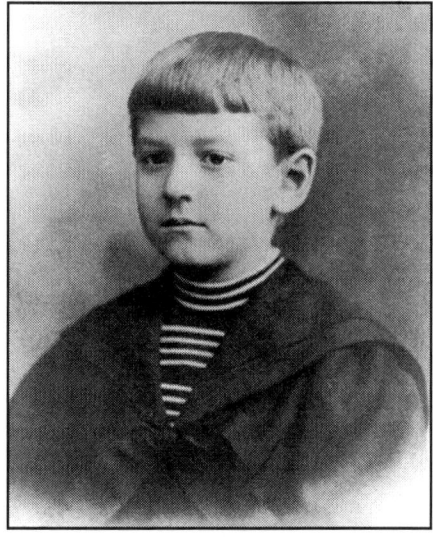

H.P. Lovecraft, about 1900.

A view of Providence, Rhode Island, 1905.

Not content with reading these books, he often acted them, thus becoming the hero of the tale. Beyond question, the time came when, as narrator, he felt that he personally experienced the horrors he so vividly and carefully described.

From early childhood, he manifested the same desire to live in the past that was evidenced in much of his mature conduct. Rather than play baseball with other boys, he would in solitude erect altars on the banks of the Seekonk River, and there offer sacrifices to the Greek and Roman gods. In his autobiography, he wrote, "I had a happy childhood," but he says later in the same work ("Some Notes on a Non-entity"), "Among my few playmates I was very unpopular, since I would insist on playing out events in history, or acting according to consistent plots. Thus repelled by humans I sought refuge and companionship in books." If he was a happy child, it was only because no adult trained him to be a normal one and instead gave him full liberty to follow his own fantastic, antisocial inclinations.

His educational history is interesting. When eight years of age, his mother took him from public school, considering him too frail to continue mingling with masses of other children. Private tutors instructed him till he was fourteen years old. From 1904 to 1908, he attended the Hope High School. Some unnamed illness prevented the fulfillment of his wish to enter Brown University. It is probable that this illness was induced, or at least aggravated, by the same over-solicitous

mother-love that played such an important part in Lovecraft's earlier life.

In spite of never receiving a formal, cultural university education, he acquired, surprisingly early in life, a fund of knowledge derived almost entirely from reading real literature. He absorbed the works of Dunsany, Machen, Poe, Blackwood, Chambers and de la Mare. The reading of these masters of the weird was an important influence on the development of his style. In addition, he became well acquainted with the traditions and early history of New England, especially as these pertained to the psychological traits of both Puritan and agnostic. His retentive memory enabled him to make all this acquired knowledge instantly available. Although surrounded by books, his real and most valuable library remained, carefully card-indexed, in his memory.

While he must have written letters without revision and probably sent them without rereading, his method of story-writing was entirely different; according to his own outline in the essay, "Notes on the Writing of Weird Fiction." Seeking for perfection, he wrote, and re-wrote the same story many tines, and, even at the end, was never satisfied with the results. The fact that he enjoyed this did not make it any less laborious. This constant effort to find the exact way to tell a story with the use of precise phrases and proper vocabulary is certainly indicative of a personality which he could not escape from and deserves further consideration.

Definitely, Lovecraft was a profound neurasthenic; but it is unnecessary to cite his love of solitude, antisocial tendencies, the constant desire to avoid the present by living in the past and the dietary peculiarities to make such a diagnosis. His style and manner of writing are definitely those of a psycho-neurotic. His stories did not flow like his letters but were slowly and carefully built, with constant changes, seeking to obtain the correct form and the exact word. In his effort to include everything he considered vital, the final tale gives the impression that he was never certain either of beginning or ending. He comes to what seems to be a logical ending and then writes on and on in an unnecessary and un-called-for anticlimax. This is particularly obvious in "The Shadow over Innsmouth."

Lovecraft has been named one of the great writers of the horror story. He certainly felt the terror of the situations he created, and tried to communicate this fear to the reader by making use of a vocabulary that is unique in its multitude of what can best be described as "dark" words. Despite his effort to create a mood, he leaves little to the reader's imagination. Such criticism may be resented by his admirers, and even considered iconoclastic, but as an illustration, study this one paragraph from "The Lurking Fear":

> Shrieking, slithering torrential shadows of red viscous madness chasing one another through endless ensanguined corridors of purple fulgurous sky . . . formless phantasms and kaleidoscopic mutations of a ghoulish, remembered scene. Forests of monstrous over-nourished oaks with serpent roots twisting and sucking unnameable juices from an earth verminous with millions of cannibal devils; mound-like tentacles groping from underground nuclei of polypous perversion . . . insane lightning over malignant ivied walls and demon arcades choked with fungous vegetation.

There are exactly seventy-three words in this paragraph, and forty-six of them can be classed as dark words. In his stories, vegetation, landscapes, buildings and characters alike are lavishly described in similar vocabulary. Ultimately, the reader becomes surfeited with such carefully described horror scenes and situations, and becomes physically exhausted instead of morbidly thrilled or depressed.

Heredity is an important factor in many Lovecraft stories, and is always of a degenerative type. His families deteriorate both mentally and physically; become shiftless paupers, and, in at least two stories, develop cannibalism. Whatever taint the original ancestors had becomes greatly magnified in a very few generations. Nowhere does the human race give promise of reaching toward the stars. There is always family decadence. In several of those stories, the taint is produced by intermarriage with the elder gods, and the offspring resemble their celestial ancestors in body and personality. In such descriptions, Lovecraft gives many excellent case histories that are duplicated in actual life in the records of any psychiatrist, especially in studies of patients bearing the stigma of hereditary syphilis.

This fear of heredity is apparent in the fact that Lovecraft, late in life, married a woman ten years older than himself. Obviously, there never was any intent or desire on his part to procreate a child. It was as though he said, "This is the end of the curse!" In marrying a widow with a mature daughter, he may have hoped that he would vicariously have a child and grandchildren, but there is nothing to indicate that such hopes came to fruition. Yet the hope of immortality through descendants is obvious, for he was fond of signing his letters "Yr. Obt. Grandsire," and "Grandpa H.P." He had genuine affection for many of the young men he met and corresponded with and looked upon them as his sons. He may have often wondered what life would have been like had his house been filled with children and grandchildren, and had Fate permitted him to write a "Children's Hour."

The main action of his tales occurs during the dark hours of night. If the tale runs into the daytime the sky is usually overcast or the ground drenched by streaming rain. Since the beginning of time, mankind has dreaded the dark hours when witches ride through the black night to attend the Sabbath and devils lurk behind every tree, awaiting a chance to mutilate and kill the body and steal the soul of their victim. In using night scenes for most of the story action, Lovecraft followed the most ancient and universal pattern of human thought. However, he not only wrote of the darkness, but lived in it and loved it. Only at night did he take his long, solitary walks, and if he wrote during the day, it was usually by artificial light, with shades drawn to exclude all sunshine.

A distinctive feature of his writing that so far has not attracted attention (and therefore has not been given any particular significance) is the fact that there are few, if any, references to his narrators or heroes eating. His villains eat, but he does not deem it necessary to describe in any way the nourishment of his decent characters. In this, he differs from other authors, some of whom—like Dickens—fill pages with accounts of hearty meals, beef steaks and kidney pies. To him, eating was merely a physiological function necessary to prolong life. The only exception was his fondness for cheese, candy and ice cream. He detested seafood. Indeed, a psychoanalytical study could readily be made from his dietary peculiarities. The important point is that, as he took no special interest in food, few if any of his good characters did either. In "The Lurker at the Threshold," there are references to eating and the preparation of meals, but these were written by Derleth and not Lovecraft. In "The Shadow Over Innsmouth," the narrator mentions a meal in a cheap restaurant, a typical Lovecraft meal: "a bowl of tomato soup and crackers was enough for me." That could never have been written by an author accustomed to three hearty meals a day.

As far as the record shows, Lovecraft was a total abstainer. Therefore, there are no references to alcohol in his tales. Even under the greatest stress, his narrators never resort to liquor to release their nervous tension. One of his characters is deliberately made drunk to loosen his tongue, but old Zadok Allen is the only drunkard that I have found in a Lovecraft story.

Living as he did, thinking as he did, he found little in life to laugh at. Occasionally, he wrote with tongue in cheek, as when he produced "Ibid," or that remarkable version of old melodrama, "Sweet Ermingarde." These writings are whimsical, clever and show craftsmanship in the use of different styles, but they do not seem to be provocative of much laughter. They represent an insignificant

Howard Phillips Lovecraft, 1934

portion of his collected writings. Nor do the various imitative, Victorian verses of humor particularly increase the sum total of humor there. Lovecraft may have smiled at times, and there is one statement made to the effect that he laughed on one occasion; but there is nothing to show that he often indulged in hearty, side-splitting mirth. Deliberately, he lived the part of an old gentleman as described by Lord Chesterfield in his *Sciences and Maxims:* "Loud laughter is the mirth of the mob, who are only pleased with silly things. . . . A man of parts and fashion is therefore only seen to smile, but never heard to laugh."

Though women dominated his entire life, he never understood them, and therefore never wrote of them. Uninterested in sex because of his neurasthenia, shyness and strong belief in heredity, he lived a life as devoid of feminine interest as that of St. Anthony. If he were ever tormented by such dreams as Gustave Flaubert said that saint suffered, he never mentioned it in conversation or correspondence. Thus, there is a definite absence of femininity in all of Lovecraft's tales. Rarely, except when it is necessary to continue a family and its curse, are females mentioned. Women being absent, there is also a complete omission of sex or love interest. "Medusa's Coil" is an exception—but this story was only revised, not written, by Lovecraft. His antipathy to the female, especially when pictured almost or entirely in the nude, is emphasized by the testimony of friends that he carefully tore off and destroyed magazine covers thus decorated. He wanted the sales appeal to lie in the stories, not the pictures.

Lovecraft compensated for the absence of wicked females by presenting as choice a collection of evil-minded males as can be found in weird literature. It is interesting that so gentle and kindly a man could deliberately create such demons, supernatural and human characters and endow them with such a diversity of cruel and sadistic manifestations. His gods from Beyond never seemed to be without many ardent worshippers, and these earthly followers indulged freely in torture, mutilation and murder. In at least two stories ("The Lurking Fear" and "The Rats in the Walls"), cannibalism is stressed.

His admirers, and they are many, say that Lovecraft, in his special field, was a literary genius. Certainly, he excelled in the horror story. If you examine the medical histories of other authors and poets elevated to the hall of fame, we find that many suffered from some form of toxemia. Such a poison, irrespective of its source, contributed towards their productivity. Stevenson, a tubercular invalid, could write only when at the height of his fever. DeQuincey and other noted Englishmen took opium. Poe, Burns and London were alcoholics, as are some well-known writers now living. Nietzsche, Beardsley and Gautier were syphilitics and died paretics, as did Guy de Maupassant. It is evident that if a man has creative ability, these varied toxins in some way make it possible for him to so write that he is called a genius.

It seems necessary, therefore, to consider such factors in the development of Lovecraft's genius as a writer of the horror story. The main facts of his life are but partly documented, and there are large segments that can never be studied from the medico-scientific viewpoint they deserve. However, as with prehistoric animals, the entire structure can be surmised from a few remaining bones.

Lovecraft's father was born in 1853. The date of his marriage to Sarah Susan Phillips is not available, but their only son was born in 1890, when the father was thirty-seven years old and the mother thirty-three. Shortly after the birth of this child, the father became psychotic; and when Howard was three years old, Albert A. Baker was appointed his guardian because of the father's mental incompetency. The father died in 1898, and little is known concerning his final years. It is even uncertain where he died, and thus no hospital records are available. All that is definitely known is that in the death certificate demise was attributed to "an advanced stage of paresis." At that time, the relation between paresis and syphilis was not clearly understood. It was not until some years later that the spirochete *pallada* was discovered. We now know that it takes from fifteen to twenty years for a syphilitic to develop paresis. Lovecraft Sr. was not a paretic when he married and procreated a son, but at that time, he was definitely syphilitic, in the communicable stage of that disease.

Sarah Lovecraft was a confirmed neurasthenic. We do not know whether she had any knowledge or even suspicion of the cause of her illness. There is, however, ample evidence that she feared the hereditary influence of her husband's mental condition on her son and was obsessed with the idea that he was destined to a life of invalidism, that he could grow to manhood only by the most intense protection. Several of the essays collected in *Marginalia* show her constant anxiety clearly. It is certain that this fear was constantly being communicated to the son, not only by the mother, but also by his two aunts and by those who taught and cared for him, such as Miss Ella Sweeney. All this insistent solicitude and all the overwhelming anxiety concerning his health could not help but make a profound impression on the little child. Just when or how he learned that this maternal fear was created by the circumstances surrounding his father's illness and death is not known, but the constant references in Lovecraft's stories to the unfortunate influences of heredity show positively that he had some idea of the relationship between his father's illness and his own invalidism.

This problem of heredity becomes more acute in 1919, when the mother entered a hospital for the psychotic. There, her physician, Dr. F.J. Farnell, made the interesting statement that her disorder "had been evidenced for fifteen years"; that, in all probability, "abnormality had existed for at least twenty-five years"— which definitely places the beginning of her recognized mental illness five years before her husband's death. The same physician notes his belief that mother and son combined to form an Oedipus complex.

With the definite knowledge that his mother was psychotic and was considered to have been so since he was three years old, Lovecraft had additional reason to be interested in problems of heredity. Both of his parents had probably been psychotic before he was born! Irrespective of what he thought of this sudden realization, he continued the same kindly, uncomplaining gentleman he had been. After his mother's hospitalization, he frequently visited her, but never entered the buildings or saw her in her room; and absolutely avoided all contact with the other patients. The author who wrote in great detail about the mental abnormalities of the human race could not face them in actual life. In May 1921, it became necessary to operate on Sarah Lovecraft. The gall-bladder surgery resulted in her death on May 24, 1921, a little over two years after her hospitalization. During her final illness, she was visited by her sister, Mrs. Lillian Clark, but, there is no record that her son saw her in this period. Torn between conflicting emotions—one an intense love for his mother, the other a dread of seeing the changes produced in her by the operation—he deliberately remained away from her bedside. He could not force himself to suffer further mental anguish.

Thus was Howard Lovecraft released from a part of the influence this Oedipus complex had on him. However, his aunts at once assumed his care. With the exception of the months spent in New York and a few short trips, he lived with one or the other of them until his death. Probably a subconscious attempt to escape from this vicarious complex was one of the reasons for his marriage to Mrs. Sonia Greene of Brooklyn. This marriage is a type familiar in the case histories of men involved in an Oedipus complex following the death of the mother. In marriage, always with an older woman, they seek a mother-substitute.

It is difficult for anyone save a psychiatrist to determine why Lovecraft married Mrs. Greene; but it is not hard to understand why she married him. Receiving an adequate income in a mercantile establishment, she was at the same time an amateur writer. Lovecraft had helped revise her manuscripts, and she may have felt that, with his assistance, she could become a professional author. Just prior to his arrival in the metropolis, she issued the first number of an amateur periodical, *The Rainbow,* filling it with poems, pictures and articles by and about Howard Lovecraft and his friends. She believed, and correctly so, that he gave promise of becoming a successful author and a celebrity—if whip and spur were applied so that he would write more stories and fewer letters.

Photo of Lovecraft as printed in *The Rainbow,* July 5, 1921.

Considering all the factors involved, the marriage was doomed to failure. Lovecraft wrote a few frank but kind lines concerning this period of his life. In refraining from bitter criticism, he demonstrated fully that he was a gentleman, and lived up to his own statement, "A gentleman always makes himself at home no matter where he happens to be."

His experience in New York was not a happy one. Fond of solitude, dreading crowds, constantly feeling the pressure of poverty, it is no wonder that he brooded over some form of escape. Fortunately, he did not use the vial of poison that Samuel Loveman says he always carried. His mental condition worried such a true friend as Frank Belknap Long, who wrote, "Howard became increasingly miserable and I feared he might go off the deep end."

Fortunately, he returned to his beloved Providence to live with his aunt, Mrs. Lillian Clark. And when she died in 1932, he occupied an apartment with the other aunt, Mrs. Annie Gamwell. Now, at last, he had a semblance of liberty, and spent some of his time traveling. He was poor still, and continued to budget only fifteen cents a day for food, thus enabling him to save dollars for postage that enabled him to continue his beloved correspondence. These written contacts were a substitute for the personal associations that he more and more avoided, except with a select few. He continued to love cats, any kind of cat, and preferred a diet of cheese and ice cream. He became "gaunt and pale." It is evident that he was beginning to show the early symptoms of the final shadow, cancer, which caused him to pass into the unknown on March 15, 1937.

Prior to Freud, psychiatrists were content to record the history and symptomology of their patients. Freud introduced the word why into psychiatry. Therefore, it is pertinent to ask the question: Why did Lovecraft become one of the great writers of the horror story?

There were shadows over Lovecraft, shadows from which he could not escape. There is medical evidence to show that these shadows were all caused by one large cloud that resulted in much of his life being spent in twilight and often the blackest night.

Now, there are certain axioms in medical science. Three of these are: (1) Cerebral insults, in men forty or younger, are almost always the result of syphilis, (2) The wife of a syphilitic is a syphilitic. (3) The child of a paretic is a syphilitic.

Winfield Scott Lovecraft was born in 1853. The day of his marriage to Sarah Susan Phillips, while indefinite, was certainly before 1889, as their son was born in 1890. Winfield Lovecraft was evidently not markedly psychotic when he married sometime before the age of thirty-six, but he was hospitalized four years later, and died at the age of forty-five. Beyond the death certificate, we have no medical testimony concerning his illness and its cause. But his son unknowingly contributed very vital information that throws light on the problem.

In 1915, Maurice W. Moe, a member of the United Amateur Press Association, asked Lovecraft to write an autobiography. In this autobiography, we find the following statement:

> In 1903 my father was seized with a complete paralytic stroke, due to insomnia and an overstrained nervous system, which took him to the hospital for the remaining five years of his life. He was never thereafter conscious and my image of him is vague.

As Howard Lovecraft was but three when his father was hospitalized, and eight when he died, he could have obtained such information only from members of the family. They told him merely enough to satisfy his curiosity; but from that little, a psychiatrist can obtain a partial picture of the father's last ten years of life. For an uncertain time, he had insomnia and an overstrained nervous system. Lovecraft was in error in saying that these were the cause of the illness; they were, instead, simply clear symptoms of a condition already existing. Then he had "a complete paralytic stroke," and was placed in a hospital. In other words, there was a period of some years when he was deteriorating mentally, and this period of mild psychosis terminated in a cerebral insult. "He was never thereafter conscious." Lovecraft's use of this adjective is interesting. Certainly, he did not mean that his father was in a state of complete stupor or coma for five years. What he did mean was that he was not oriented or aware of his surroundings—which corresponds perfectly with Webster's definition of the word conscious: "mentally awake, psychically active or acute. . . ." Lovecraft's phrase gives a perfect description of the mental condition of a paretic in the last stages. The evidence is admittedly incomplete, neurological and serological factors are absent, but from the available data, it can nevertheless be stated: Winfield Scott Lovecraft was positively a syphilitic for years before marriage.

It therefore follows that his wife was a syphilitic also, even though in an attenuated form, as shown by her ability to bear a living child. It has been positively stated that she was abnormal mentally from the time this child was three years old, and that this had been evidenced for fifteen years before her hospitalization, which occurred two years before her death. While the hospital failed to give a true psychiatric diagnosis of her mental illness, it seems necessary only to refer to axiom two, as stated above.

Finally, if both Lovecraft Sr. and wife were syphilitic, then the son was a case of hereditary syphilis. It was in a still more attenuated form, for otherwise he would never have been born, or born, survived; but syphilis was nonetheless present if we consider axiom three. Winfield Townley Scott, in his excellent biographical essay, "His Most Fantastic Creation," shows that this question of hereditary syphilis has been considered and discarded by Lovecraftians. "There is no indication at all that his son inherited his father's disease," he writes. This is the opinion of a layman. The neuro-psychiatrist, familiar with syphilis of the central nervous system, is forced to differ.

Lovecraft seems seldom to have mentioned his father. It is probable that he and his illness were seldom spoken of by the family. His aunt's husband, Dr. Franklyn C. Clark, was a man of no small education. To him, Lovecraft may have talked about his father, but the physician may have deliberately concealed the facts to shield the sensibilities of his nephew.

Whatever Lovecraft knew or guessed about this shadow, he carefully kept to himself. Naturally, it was a subject no gentleman would care to talk or write about. At the same time, he was a scientist, as his interest in astronomy shows. In later years, as a scientist, especially after the mental illness and the hospitalization of his mother, he must have

Lovecraft, Brooklyn, New York, 1922.

considered the relation of his own illness to that of his parents.

Consciously or subconsciously, the thought of heredity must always have been present. He thoroughly believed in it and his stories are filled with references to it. His descriptions of mental and physical deteriorations of families and the individual members of those families show many of the symptoms of hereditary syphilis. His stories seem to convey the impression that he was always covered by the shadow of a threatening psychosis. Reading his stories told in the first person, and remembering that he loved to consider himself the chief character in any drama, we are forced to conclude that while writing these stories, he was, as the narrator, actually living them and experiencing all the horror of the situations he so carefully described. And those stories, we should bear in mind, usually concluded with the narrator either becoming insane or considering suicide, driven to such extremities by the horrors from the Beyond, and unable to endure even the memory of witnessed events after the actual danger had passed. There was a constant repetition of this theme song—the terror of heredity, the mental and physical degeneration, the hopelessness of struggle, the ultimate, unavoidable end. Lovecraft not only wrote this song again and again, but he lived it, under a shadow from which he could not escape.

That he had such a fear finally became evident to his friends. They began to have the same fears regarding him. This they show by referring to the vial of poison Lovecraft carried with him, by writing that he was morbidly depressed: "Howard became increasingly miserable; I feared he might go off the deep end." Fortunately, he died, as far as the evidence shows, from cancer and Bright's disease, and remained to the end of his life the keen intelligence he was so noted for.

Such, then, were the shadows over Lovecraft.

Had his parentage been different, his childhood and adolescence those of the usual boy, his health normal, his mother as wise as she was loving; had he eaten three hearty meals a day, become a soldier, or fallen in love and married early in life, had children, joined the Rotary Club and occasionally become intoxicated, he might not have become a master writer of the horror tale. But with his heritage, his share in the Oedipus complex, his poverty and meager living and the early development of an introverted personality, he could write nothing else.

It is greatly to his credit that he lived and died a brave, kindly, uncomplaining gentleman. I fancy I can envision his reception into the heaven of St. John. There he would be given a spacious house with Venetian blinds shielding all the windows, for "there is no night there," and it would take him some time to become accustomed to the constant sunshine. In one room would be deep-freeze units filled with every variety of ice cream. Cats would roam through the house. The largest room would be a library, the shelves packed with complete editions of all noted writers of the weird, including the fabulous *Necronomicon* of the mad Arab, Abdul Alhazred. His first assignment would be to write a travel book on Hell, and when this, illustrated by Doré, was published, it would be so terrible that Dante, reading it, would grow green with envy. In his spare time, he would compose horror stories, perfectly plotted, with proper vocabulary and exquisite style. Oc-

casionally, he would read these to carefully selected groups of weird tale fans.
I am sure he would be happy in such a life.
Eventually he might wish to open the Venetian blinds.

David H. Keller, MD
Underwood,
Stroudsburg, Pennsylvania
April 1948

Acknowledgement by David H. Keller: In the preparation of the above article I have made full use of *H.P.L.: A Memoir,* and the short biographical articles in *Marginalia, Rhode Island on Lovecraft* and *The Arkham Sampler.* Without the information found there, this work could never have been written. I wish to thank August Derleth and Donald Wandrei for their permission to quote verbatim one paragraph from "The Lurking Fear." And, finally, I wish to express my appreciation to August Derleth for his many letters to me which have been of the greatest help in arriving at an understanding of Lovecraft.

DAVID H. KELLER (1880–1966) obtained his medical degree from the University of Pennsylvania and practiced psychiatry from 1915 through 1945, serving as assistant superintendent at state hospitals for the mentally ill in Louisiana, Illinois,

Portrait of David H. Keller from *Science Wonder Stories,* July 1929

Tennessee and Pennsylvania. He joined the U.S. Army Medical Reserve as a First Lieutenant during the First World War and retired from that organization as a Lieutenant Colonel following World War II.

Keller brought a new psychological depth to popular fiction, beginning with "The Revolt of the Pedestrians," in the February 1928 issue of *Amazing Stories.* From then until his death, he contributed many tales of fantasy, horror and science fiction to *Weird Tales,* the Gernsback magazines and other pulps. He was also involved in science fiction fandom, writing extensively about it, encouraging fanzine editors, and supplying them with original stories and articles, including "Shadows Over Lovecraft."

COMING MAY 2015

MYSTERIOUS   IMAGINATIVE   FANTASTIC

A COMPLETE WEIRD TALES PULP COLLECTION. PART OF OUR AUCTION #49, CLOSING ON MAY 1ST, 2015 STARTING AT 7:00 PM. COME BY OUR BOOTH TO LOOK AT KEY ISSUES OF THE SET, AND THE REMARKABLE TRAYCASES THAT REALLY HIGHLIGHT THIS WEIRD TALES COLLECTION.

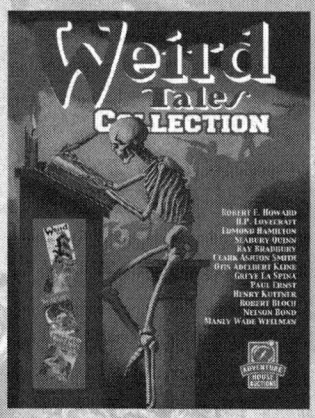

WEIRD TALES COLLECTION MAGAZINE
40 FULL COLOR PAGES - $10

ADVENTURE HOUSE AUCTIONS
914 LAREDO RD - SILVER SPRING MD 20901
WWW.ADVENTUREHOUSE.COM
GUNNISON@ADVENTUREHOUSE.COM

DYING COMES HARD

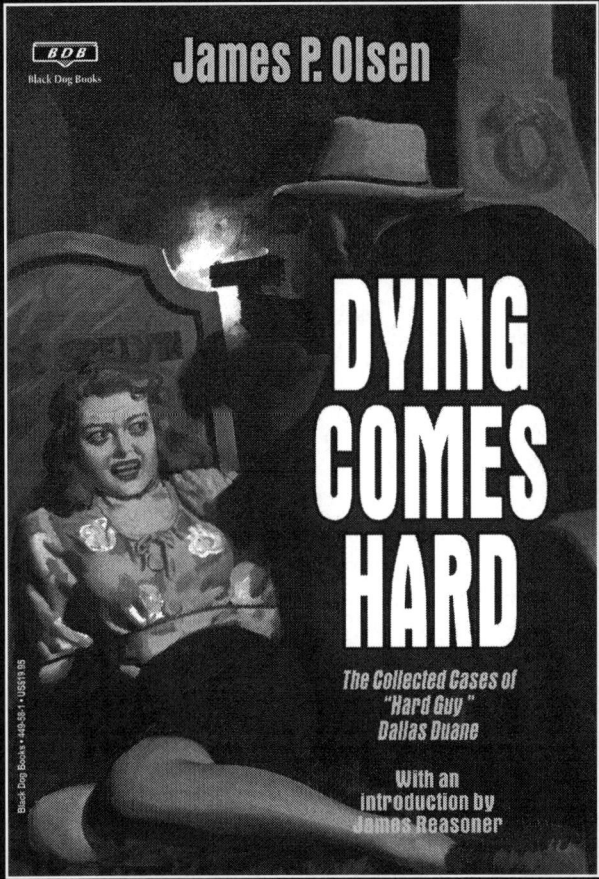

They don't call him Hard Guy for nothin'!

Into the rough and tumble oil fields of Texas and the
American southwest of the 1930s comes Dallas Duane,
troubleshooter, freelance private dick and undercover
investigator for the oil companies.

"Hard and fast" is his motto! Watch as he works
his way in and out of trouble—both with the wildcatters and
wild women—knuckling a path through a series of bank robberies
and payroll heists, murder and corrupt officials, crooked
gambling and haunted graveyards.

With an introduction by James Reasoner.

BDB

BLACK DOG BOOKS
1115 Pine Meadows Ct.
Normal, IL 61761-5432

www.blackdogbooks.net I info@blackdogbooks.net

Follow us!

Twitter.com/blackdogbooks1
Facebook.com/blackdogbooks1

My First Lovecraft

F. PAUL WILSON

"The Thing on the Doorstep."

What a title, conjuring a gallimaufry of images, all of them unsettling.

This was my first Lovecraft story, the one that started me down the road to ruin. Had I but known . . .

Never mind.

According to the de Camp biography, this was one of H.P.'s last stories, written in longhand in August of 1933, but not typed up until the winter of 1934. After *Weird Tales'* rejection of "At The Mountains of Madness" (due more to its length than to its story values), he was apparently so unsure of himself and of what he perceived to be a waning talent, that he did not have the courage to send "The Thing on the Doorstep" off to *Weird Tales* until the summer of 1936—two years after he'd written it. Farnsworth Wright, no dummy, snapped it up immediately.

Good thing he did. H.P. had less than two years to live.

The story was finally published in 1936.

Twenty-three years later it found me.

Donald A. Wollheim is to blame. He started me on Lovecraft. In 1959 I was just a kid, a mere thirteen years old when he slipped me my first fix. I was a good kid up till then, reading Ace Doubles and clean, wholesome science fiction stories by the likes of Heinlein, E.E. Smith, Poul Anderson, Fred Pohl, and the rest. But he brought me down with one anthology. He knew what he was doing. He called it *The Macabre Reader* and slapped this lurid neato-cool Ed Emshwiller cover on it. I couldn't resist. I had to open it, look for pictures (there weren't any), and check out the table of contents. I hadn't heard of any of the authors, but the titles—good Lord, the titles were fabulous. "The Crawling Horror" by Thorp McClusky, "The Opener of the Way" by Robert Bloch, "The Curse of Yig" by Zelia Bishop, "The Hollow Man" by Thomas Burke, "The Hunters from Beyond" by Clark Ashton Smith, "It will Grow on You" by Donald Wandrei, and others. But the title that really promised to bring the horror home (literally and figuratively) was "The Thing on the Doorstep" by someone who didn't use a first name, just initials—H.P. Lovecraft. I bought it. I read it. And that was it. The beginning of my end.

You've got to understand where I was coming from. This was the late Fifties. No one was publishing horror fiction—*no one*. We had plenty of horror to watch—Universal had sold its horror library to TV and Hammer was putting out some great Technicolor remakes—but after you'd read the original *Dracula* and *Frankenstein*, and the too-rare Bradbury or Matheson collections, what was left? Forry Ackerman's *Famous Monsters of Filmland* was the only thing coming out on a regular basis, and that was all pictures. I wanted to be scared, to be chilled,

I wanted to gasp, wanted my skin to crawl.

The Macabre Reader did it all. Here were the stories I'd been looking for. Creepy tales—dark, eerie, intense, the emotions jumping right off the page—like nothing I'd ever read before. But the one that grabbed me by the throat was "The Thing on the Doorstep."

I was dragged into the story by the opening line ("It is true I have sent six bullets through the head of my best friend, and yet I hope to show by this statement that I am not his murderer."), captivated by the setting (". . . witch-cursed, legend-haunted Arkham, whose huddled, sagging gambrel roofs and crumbling Georgian balustrades brood out the centuries beside the darkly muttering Miskatonic"), blown away by the dense prose that tossed off words like eldritch and foetor and Cyclopean and nacreous, that casually mentioned strange, forbidden books and towns like Innsmouth (where even Arkhamites fear to go) as if I should be familiar with them.

All this was old hat, I suppose, to Lovecraft devotees, and must have been par for the course for *Weird Tales* regulars in the Thirties, but it was a revelation for me.

"The Thing on the Doorstep" delivered on the up-close, breath-clogging horror that *The Macabre Reader*'s cover had promised, but it also served as my Cthulhu Mythos primer, my introduction to what would come to be known as Cosmic Horror.

The story

Since this seems to be something of a forgotten Lovecraft story, let me refresh your memory.

The narrator, Daniel Upton, tells us of his longtime friend, the brilliant, precocious Edward Pickman Derby, a young man of good family who was born in frail health and overly coddled by his parents. He has "Poe-like talents," immerses himself in weird literature, and while still a teenager publishes a book of poems— "collected nightmare-lyrics"—called *Azathoth and Other Horrors*. He enters Miskatonic University in Arkham at 16 and graduates at 19. He's a withdrawn sort and remains single into his late thirties—"more through shyness, inertia, and parental protectiveness than inclination."

Then Derby meets and falls for Asenath Waite, of the Innsmouth Waites, who is "dark, smallish, and very good-looking except for over-protuberant eyes." Asenath is the daughter of Ephraim Waite, a deceased wizard, and has a talent for hypnotism; such a deep talent that her subjects have come away with the sensation that they'd actually changed places with Asenath while under her spell. Asenath has been heard to say that she wishes she were a man because the male brain has unique cosmic powers. Edward Derby and Asenath marry, and slowly a change comes over our friend Derby. He starts acting out of character—he never learned to drive yet with increasing frequency he's seen handling Asenath's Packard like a racecar driver.

During his third year of marriage, Derby is found wandering in the Maine woods, rambling about "the pit of the shaggoths" and how his wife switches bodies with him, locking her own body in the library while she wears his and attends foul rites; but she occasionally loses contact, and when that happens he suddenly finds himself back in his own skin, confronting mind-numbing horrors.

But months later Derby comes to our narrator and tells him that he has sent Asenath away, that he found some spells of his own that he used to lock her out of his body before she could take it over for good, which had been her plan since marrying him. He's free.

But instead of recovering, Derby continues to deteriorate, screaming about how she's trying to take him over again, and that she really isn't a she, but old Ephraim himself! He says the aging wizard took over his daughter's body and poisoned his own. For years now Ephraim has been inhabiting Asenath's body, but all the while he's longed to be back in a male body—and he is taking Edward's!

Edward is finally committed to Arkham Sanatorium where he raves on for weeks . . . and then is abruptly sane again. But our narrator is alerted now, and he's got a pretty good idea that the suddenly rational mind in his friend's body does not belong to Edward Derby.

Now the real horrors begin.

Our narrator gets a midnight phone call but all he hears is "a sort of half-liquid bubbling noise—'glub . . . glub . . . glub-glub.'" Two hours later there's this shabby, dwarfed, humped, foul-smelling . . . *thing* standing in the shadows on his doorstep. It wears a low-pulled slouch hat and is draped in an oversized overcoat the narrator recognizes as Edward's. The thing says, "glub . . . glub." A pencil protrudes from one of the sleeves; and stuck on it is a note written in something that resembles Edward Derby's hand. The note tells the final truth.

Edward writes that he lied about sending Asenath away; the truth is that during one of the increasingly rare moments when he controlled his own body he crushed her skull with a candlestick and buried her in the basement of their home. But Asenath—or actually old Ephraim, for that's who was inhabiting Asenath's body—could still exert control from the grave. He continued to pry into Edward's body, and eventually succeeded in making the final switch while Edward was confined in the sanatorium. Edward suddenly found himself inhabiting Asenath's rotting corpse. He clawed his way out of the basement floor, and has now come to our narrator for help. Since he's inhabiting a rotting corpse, he can't speak and can barely write. So our narrator must save him. He must go to the sanatorium and shoot the man who is calling himself Edward Derby. For he is not Edward Derby. He's really Ephraim Waite.

The narrator faints, but eventually does as he's bid, thus bringing us full circle to the story's opening hook. The final paragraph describes the nature of the *thing*.

"What they finally found inside Edward's oddly assorted clothes was mostly liquescent horror. There were bones, too—and a crushed-in skull. Some dental work positively identified the skull as Asenath's."

Blown Away

In order to write the above, I reread "The Thing on the Doorstep" for the first time since 1959. All that I clearly remembered from back then was the lurid image of that putrescent *thing* on Daniel Upton's doorstep, and an intense craving for more of this sort of fiction.

Today I see a lot more. I see striking parallels between Edward Derby's social, intellectual, literary, and family history and those of his creator, H.P. Lovecraft.

I remain amazed at Lovecraft's toss-offs—the hints he drops with such apparent carelessness. Other writers would be tempted to dwell on them, or repeat them, but H.P. drops them once and then goes on. He knows what he's doing, though. The toss-offs have a cumulative effect that works in the subconscious, depositing thin layers of eeriness on everything until nothing seems quite safe or sane anymore.

Here are a few from "The Thing on the Doorstep":

- Edward Derby "was a close correspondent of the notorious Baudelairean poet Justin Geoffrey, who wrote *The People of the Monolith* and died screaming in a madhouse in 1926 after a visit to a sinister, ill-regarded village in Hungary."

- Asenath "was Ephraim Waite's daughter—the child of his old age by an unknown wife who always went veiled."

- One of Asenath Waite's servants is "a swarthy young wench who had marked anomalies of feature and seemed to exude a perpetual odor of fish."

But most of all, I'm struck by the intricacies of the plot, and by the subtle kinkiness of Edward marrying—and presumably bedding—a woman housing the personality of a man. Edward's body was being usurped by Asenath, but Asenath wasn't really Asenath because she'd been kicked out of her body by her father, Ephraim. We're dealing with a hideous form of child abuse *cum* transsexualism here. Talk about kinky! But the implications of this clever double-switch went right over my teenage head. (Although perhaps not completely. I'm more than a little taken aback by the switch aspect of the story: My novel *Sibs* hinges on an uncomfortably similar switcheroo. I remember congratulating myself on being such a clever fellow to come up with that final twist. But now, upon rereading "The Thing on the Doorstep," I realize the seed was planted decades before by old H.P. himself.)

The Legacy
But after the image of the *thing* faded, the heart of the tale that lingered in my teenage mind long after I'd finished the story: the concept of another reality impinging on ours, knowledge of which could drive you stark raving mad; a dimension of perverse logic and bizarre geometry, full of godlike creatures with unpronounceable names, aloof and yet decidedly inimical.

"There are black zones of shadow close to our daily paths, and now and then some evil soul breaks a passage through."

My thirteen-year-old world did not seem quite so safe and sane, my reality seemed a tad less real.

After that first fix, I started mainlining Lovecraft. The local pushers—excuse me, *book dealers*—introduced me to Arkham House and I nearly died of an overdose. Eventually I went cold turkey and kicked the habit. (Well, not completely. Occasionally I'll reread a favorite story. I can handle it now. Really.) But the Cosmic Horror concept still fascinates me. I used it in *The Keep* and I used it in "The Barrens," and it's the engine that powers the larger arc of the Repairman Jack novels.

Thanks, H.P.

F. PAUL WILSON is the author of forty-plus books and numerous short stories spanning science fiction, horror, adventure, medical thrillers, and virtually everything between. His novels regularly appear on The New York Times Bestsellers List. He was voted Grand Master by the World Horror Convention and received the Lifetime Achievement Award from the Horror Writers of America. He has also received the Stoker Award, the Porgie Award, the Prometheus and Prometheus Hall of Fame Awards, the Pioneer Award from the RT Booklovers Convention, the Inkpot Award from San Diego ComiCon, and is listed in the 50th anniversary edition of *Who's Who in America.*

Over eight million copies of his books are in print in the U.S. and his work has been translated into twenty-four languages. He also has written for the stage, screen, and interactive media. His latest thriller, *Fear City,* stars his urban mercenary, Repairman Jack, and *The Dead World: A Pellucidar novelette based on the works of Edgar Rice Burroughs* is now available for Kindle. Paul resides at the Jersey Shore and can be found on the Web at www.repairmanjack.com.

The Voice of the Night
by Hugh Pendexter

A series of baffling robberies strike the high society of New York. Jefferson Fanchon, Inquirer, has been called in to decipher the events. Immediately he recognizes the hand of his old European adversary, Bouchard. But never before has Bouchard's influence spanned the Atlantic. Why now?

The game is afoot as the great Inquirer's legendary powers of deduction are put to the test in this series of astounding cases!

In the grand tradition of Sherlock Holmes, uncover the startling answers in *The Voice of the Night*.

With an introduction by award-winning author Evan Lewis.

BLACK DOG BOOKS
1115 Pine Meadows Ct.
Normal, IL 61761-5432
www.blackdogbooks.net | info@blackdogbooks.net

Follow us!
Twitter.com/blackdogbooks1
Facebook.com/blackdogbooks1

Collecting Lovecraft: A Gallery

GENE CHRISTIE

The early works of H.P. Lovecraft—in fanzines, magazines and books—are among the most expensive and sought-after items in the realm of fantasy collectibles. Following is a selection of the rarest examples of his work, including *The Outsider and Others* (1939), the first publication issued by Arkham House—a company formed specifically to preserve HPL's writings in book form.

Marvel Tales, Vol.1, No.1, May 1934 (Fantasy Publications).
A short-lived magazine published by Lloyd A. Eshbach (1910-2003),
with contributions by his *Weird Tales* associates.

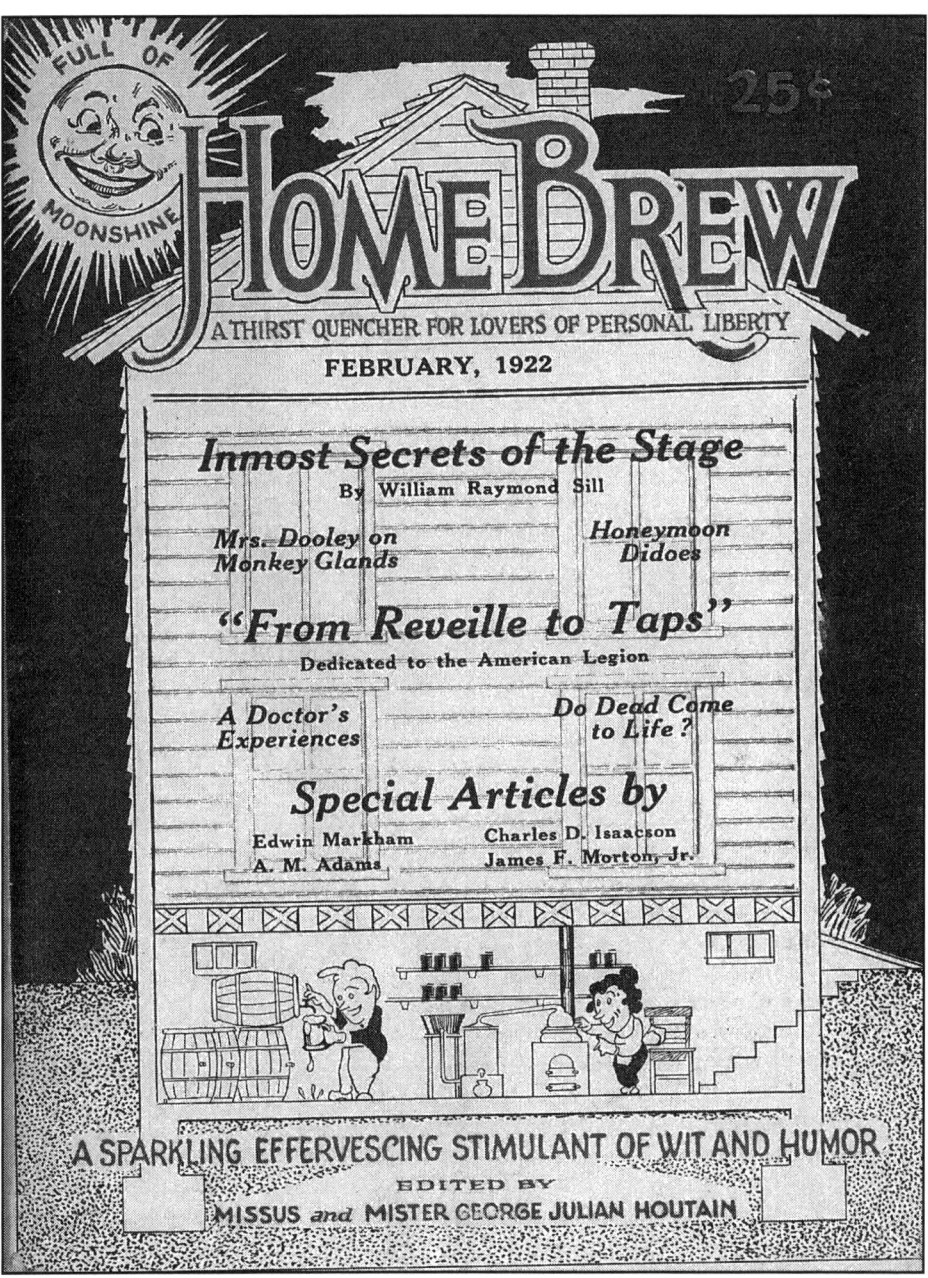

Home Brew Vol.1 No.1, February 1922 (E. D. Houtain).
Contains "From the Dark," part one of "Herbert West—Reanimator."

Weird Tales, October 1923 (The Rural Publishing Corporation).
This issue contains the first contributions to *Weird Tales*
of both H.P. Lovecraft and Seabury Quinn.

Fanciful Tales of Time and Space Magazine, Fall 1936 (Shepherd & Wollheim).
"The Nameless City," is considered to be Lovecraft's first Cthulhu Mythos story.
It had first appeared in 1921, in the amateur journal *Wolverine*.

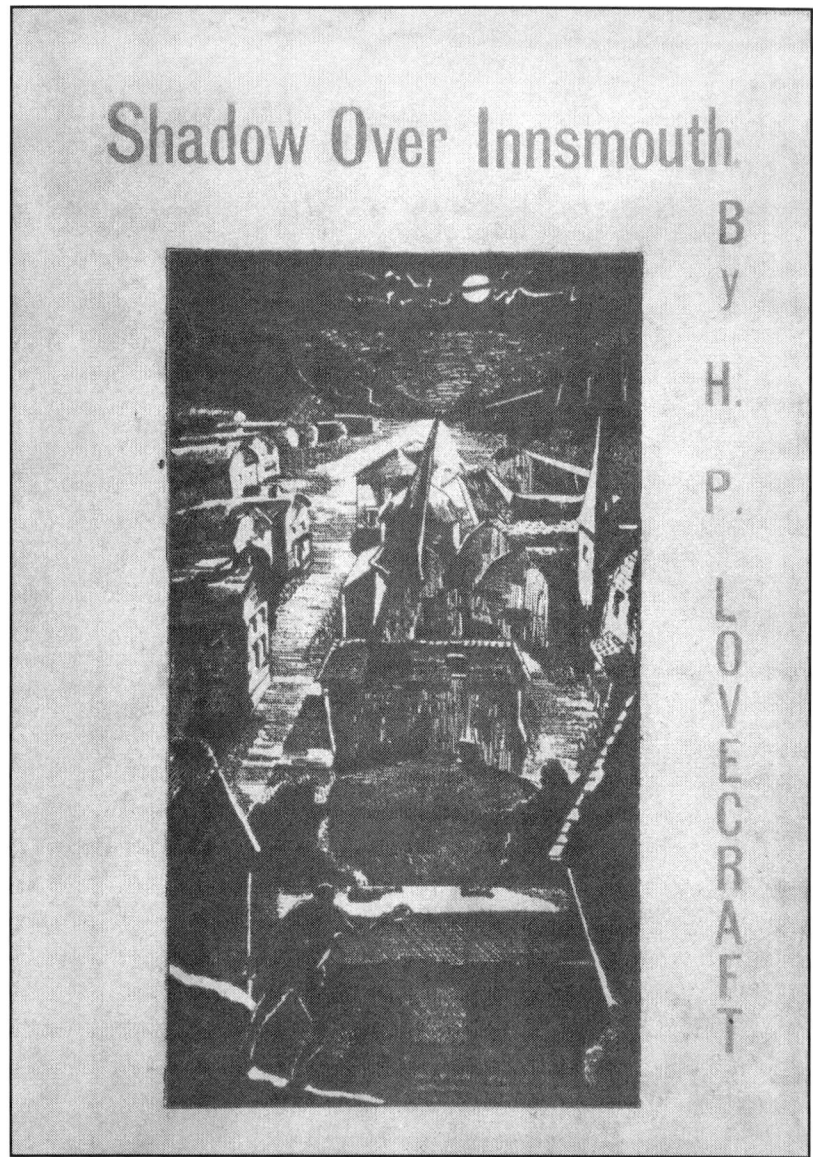

Shadow Over Innsmouth (Visionary Publishing Co.) 1936.
This is the only book of Lovecraft's fiction to be published during the author's lifetime.
Says Robert Weinberg: "Crawford printed 400 copies, but only bound 200; the unbound
sheets were later destroyed. Very few copies of the book were actually were sold."
Sadly, the book was marred by a rash of typographical errors.

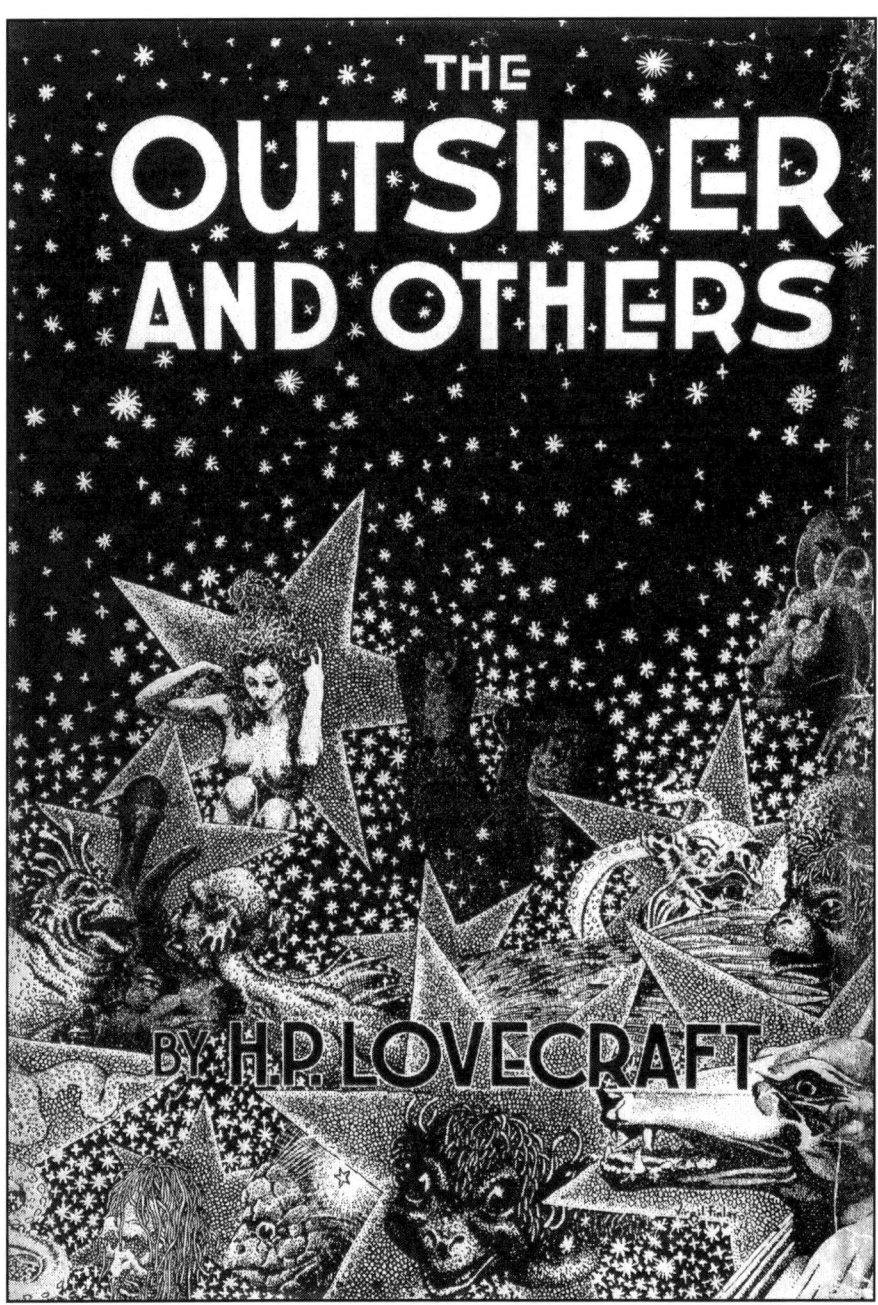

The Outsider and Others (Arkham House, 1939)
The first publication printed by Arkham House, with cover art
by Virgil Finlay, in an edition of 1,268 copies.

Beyond the Wall of Sleep (Arkham House) 1943.

Issued in a edition of 1,217 copies, this is the second collection of Lovecraft's work, and only the fourth publication by Arkham House.

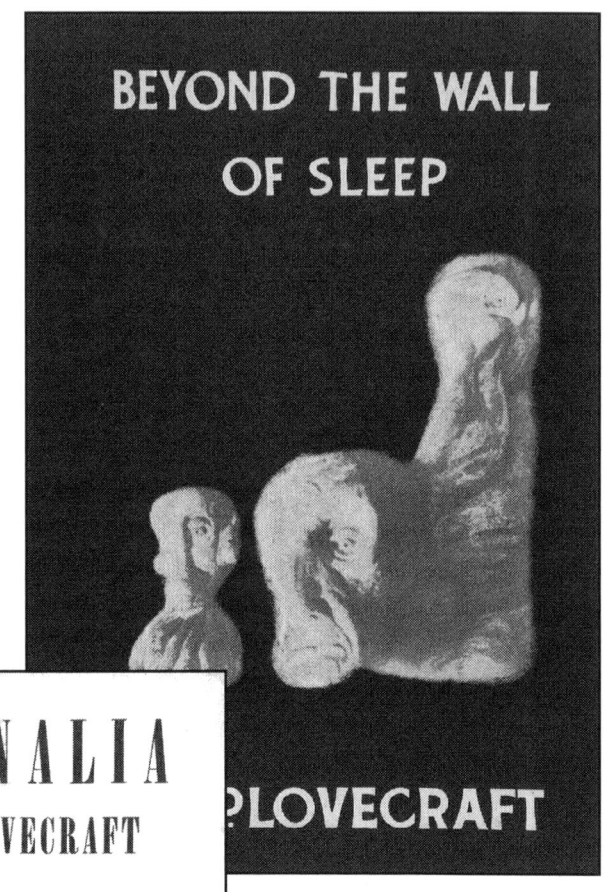

Marginalia (Arkham House) 1944.

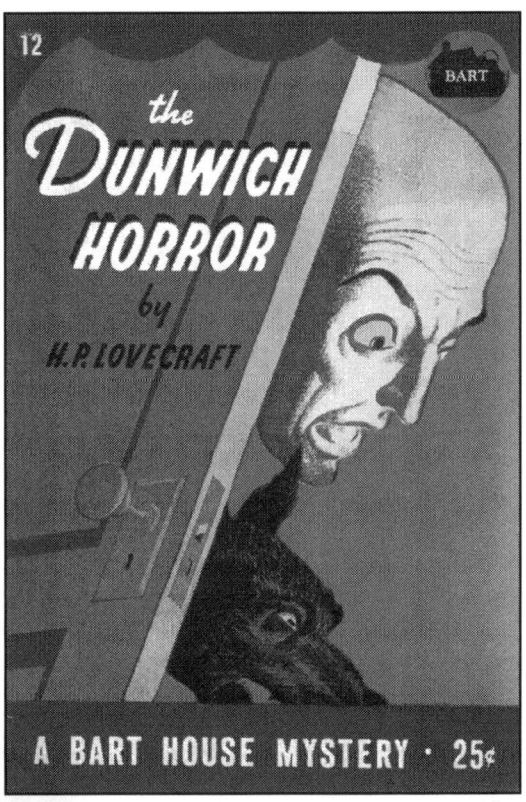

The Dunwich Horror
(Bartholomew House, Inc.) 1945.

The Weird Shadow Over Innsmouth.
(Bartholomew House, Inc.) 1944.

Early paperback editions.

Best Supernatural Stories of H.P. Lovecraft (World) 1946.
Another collection assembled by August Derleth.

TARABA ILLUSTRATION ART

Walter Baumhofer:
At the drafting table, 1924.

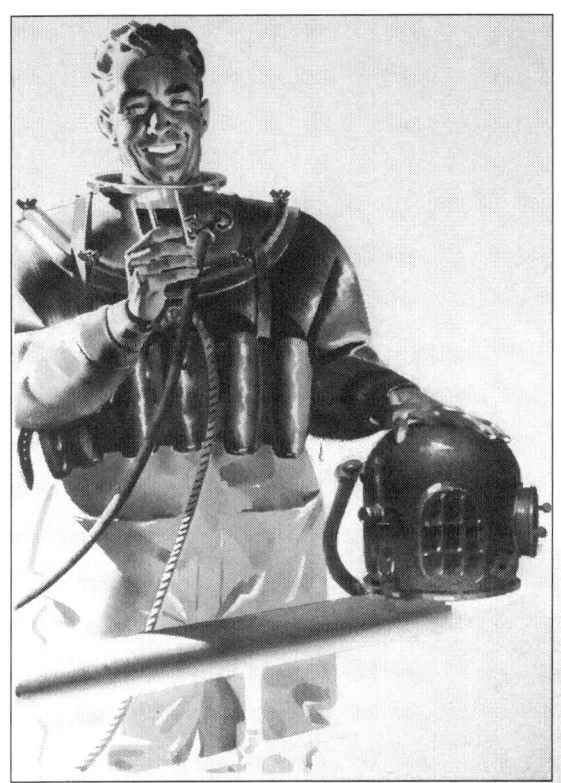

W.J. Heffron: Advertisement

Victor Prezio:
Man's Life cover,
1970

Fred Taraba • P.O. Box 1438 • Casper, WY 82602
307/333-2517 landline • 307/251-8345 mobile

H.P. Lovecraft and Pseudo-Mathematics

ROBERT WEINBERG

One of the strongest points in the Cthulhu stories by H.P. Lovecraft is the skill-ful blending of the unreal and the real. True and false are juggled together until one is undistinguishable from the other. Probably the most mentioned example of this work is Lovecraft's invention of a number of fictitious books complete with quotes, mysterious authors and histories. However, little attention has ever been given to the mathematics, or in reality, the pseudo-mathematics used in several of the Cthulhu tales. In this piece, I hope to cover this area however briefly.

In the period that Lovecraft did his writing (1920–1935) science was just emerging from the greatest traumatic period in all history. At the turn of the century, the Michaelson-Morley experiment had all but destroyed the notion of an all-pervasive ether. Einstein and Planck had completely disrupted all of classical physics with the theory of General Relativity and their restructuring of the physical universe. Heisenberg's Uncertainty Principle had completely reshaped the idea of what we know, and more important, of what we can learn. Research done by half-a-dozen famous scientists had determined the structure of the atom. For the first time in history, modern man was exposed to what is now being called "Future Shock." Man tried, with little success, to grasp *all* that was occurring about him. Popular science articles in the Sunday papers were quite common, as well as many books proclaiming "Mathematics for the Millions" and "Relativity Made Easy." The unfortunate fact is that without a strong background and training such concepts are not easy. Nor are they simple. Most simplistic views of the subjects were no more than a thin gloss of a much deeper idea.

Most of the writers in the fantasy-science fiction field of this time were not scientists. The few that were, were not associated with the fields of major advances. There were exceptions, of course, like John Campbell, but even he did not use a strong straight science background in his stories. Most of the tales in the period employed what can be loosely called pseudo-science. That is, made-up science which had very little or no relation to the real work of the period. The speed of light, which was just then being recognized as an absolute upper bound on speed, was ignored by every writer who used a FTL drive. Structural impossibilities in construction of super cities were common (and still are). Biological impossibilities (such as violations of the square-cube law) were the order of the day. Though the claim has been made that this was the period of *science* fiction (i.e., the science emphasized while the fiction was not), this statement is not true. Anyone competent in the sciences could tell otherwise. It was a time of *pseudo-science* fiction. In other words, a time when impossible science was emphasized. Not speculative science, with a possibility of reality someday (as in *Ralph 124C41+)*, but just sheer nonsense masquerading as science. This is not to say that some of these stories were not entertaining, but just to point out that they were straight fantasy. Any speculation they contained was false and misleading. (A fine example of such work is Ray Cummings' stories about "The Girl in the Golden Atom." These are fairly entertaining tales, but Cummings' basic premise that the structure of an atom is somewhat similar to a solar system is utter nonsense, and was known to be nonsense long before most of the series appeared.)

The revolution in mathematics had taken place sometime before the revolution in physics, though the two events are closely interrelated. Cantor's work with infinite sets was a major breakthrough from finite to infinite mathematics. Work in non-Euclidean geometry, showing that structure was possible as long as an axiomatic system was maintained, produced a minor breakthrough. Again, popular science articles tried, with little success, to convey the meanings of such breakthroughs to the public. Misconceptions immediately arose.

Lovecraft's misunderstandings in both geometry and quantum physics are therefore nothing uncommon for the time he wrote. Even if he had (or did) consulted various reference works of the period for information, it is doubtful that the references to mathematics in his stories would have been very different.

In nearly all of the Cthulhu stories, some mention is made to the alien geometry encountered (as in "The Call of Cthulhu," "The Shadow Out of Time," and others). Instead of going over every story, I will attempt to note the pseudo-mathematics used in one story, and thus avoid repetition. The mistakes in one are common throughout all of the mythos stories (including work by others, such as "The Hounds of Tindalos" by Frank Belknap Long). The story I have chosen to study is "Dreams in the Witch House."

The story is the one in which HPL makes his greatest use of mathematics. The protagonist of the story is Walter Gilman, a mathematics student at Miskatonic University. Gilman is very interested in non-Euclidean calculus, we are told, as well as quantum physics. Needless to say, no such subject as non-Euclidean calculus exists, nor does such a name make any real sense. While calculus does have a strong background in geometry, an in-depth study of the subject reveals the relative unimportance of the field in which the actual limit process takes place. The name of the subject sounds good, but means nothing. Quantum physics is a fancy name for the study of quantum mechanics, i.e., the motion of the universe as related by the theory developed by Planck and Einstein.

Lovecraft's pseudo-mathematics we might call pseudo-geometry. That is, the notion that certain geometric shapes could be constructed that might not be entirely of this dimension. In the story itself, Gilman speculates on the possibility of creating a hole in the space-time continuum by a geometric construction, so that a person could step in through the hole at one place and emerge in another. It is much the same idea that was popular around the same time and after about a space warp. Space, we know, is curved. If, as we are told by the pseudo-scientists, we were able to bend space, then we could step from one spot in space to another without traveling the intervening distance.

This idea, unfortunately, is not quite true. The existence of higher dimensions should be of little concern to this world as any contact with such dimensions is impossible. Lovecraft's angles and curves that vanish into some other space is absolute nonsense. The reason for this is that geometry is a closed system. It is impossible (not unlikely or not yet possible, but impossible, actually shown to be never possible) to construct a higher dimension from a lower one. A quick reading of *Flatland* by Abbott will suffice to convince the reader. A two-dimensional being which lives on a flat surface cannot grasp the concept of "up" and "down." Such flatworlders cannot understand the meaning of height, or depth, or thickness, as no such thing exists, nor can it exist, in their two-dimensional world. As I do not want to belabor this point, I would strongly advise all of those interested to read *Flatland,* a book quite easy to understand and readily available in most libraries.

The same facts, thus, also apply to a three-dimensional world. There is no way that we can construct a four-dimensional object. Nor can such a thing even exist in our world. Since our perceptions are only three-dimensional, we could not see the fourth dimension extension of the object even if it had one. As all of our building material is only three dimensional, it would be impossible to construct anything of a higher dimension out of it. A quick way to grasp this impossibility is this. A straight line segment defines one dimension. Put another line segment perpendicular to this first line segment (getting something in the form of an L) and you have defined two dimensions (length and width). A third line sticking out from the paper at a right angle, defines depth. Now, to define a fourth dimension of measurement (as we are talking of instantaneous occurrences, we ignore time measurements in our argument) take another line segment and put it at right angles to all of the other three. This will give you a fourth dimension. This is also quite impossible in our physical universe.

We are also told in the story of Gilman stating that time could not exist in certain belts of space, so that one could live forever in such regions. This fact would surprise a number of scientists.

In conclusion, Lovecraft was a master craftsman who used whatever knowledge he could in the furtherance of his story. Unfortunately, while his grasp of science and mathematics might have been greater than the average layman, it was not strong enough to present a convincing picture to the careful reader. Further, Lovecraft made the cardinal mistake of speculation of the impossible. While to the non-scientist, this may not sound like much of a sin, it is the cardinal mistake of the uninformed.

An authority on genre fiction, **ROBERT WEINBERG** has edited over a hundred and fifty books in the science fiction, fantasy, horror, mystery, young adult, and western fields. He has written columns on all these branches of fiction and is a well-known lecturer at conventions and seminars. He has acted as consultant on genre fiction for publishers and is widely regarded as one of the leading experts on horror and dark fantasy fiction in the world. Bob is a two-time recipient of the World Fantasy Award. In 2007, Bob won the Lifetime Achievement Award from the Horror Writers Association.

FANTASY
I L L U S T R A T E D

PULPS FOR SALE!

Thousands of pulps in stock. We love
servicing your want lists.

■

Contact DAVE SMITH
(425)745-0229 • (425)750-4513
rocketbat@msn.com

■

40 years experience in
the paper collectibles field.

Prompt professional service.

Specializing in Pulp Magazines,
Vintage Comic Books, BLBs,
Pin-up material and Houdini.

■

Pulps wanted!

High prices paid. All genres wanted.
One piece or a lifetime collection. No
collection is too large or small.

P.O. Box 13443
Mill Creek, WA 98082

FANTASY
I L L U S T R A T E D

How Great Britain "Discovered" H.P. Lovecraft

STEPHEN JONES

The story always goes that, during his lifetime, H.P. Lovecraft's fiction was all but ignored by the mainstream media. This may certainly be true in America, where his stories were mostly relegated to amateur press journals or such cheaply produced pulp magazines such as *Weird Tales* and *Astounding Stories*.

However, the same cannot be said for Britain.

Ironically, since Lovecraft was an avowed anglophile (perhaps best exemplified by Virgil Finlay's famous portrait of him as an 18th century gentleman), who preferred to use archaic English spelling and phrases, it is only fitting that his work was taken much more seriously in the land of his ancestors—not only regularly appearing between hardcovers for the first time, but also being showcased for the populace of one of the most dynamic cities in the world.

For fans of classic horror fiction, and collectors of the American pulp magazine *Weird Tales* in particular, the "Not at Night" series of anthologies is one of the genre's best-kept secrets.

You'll Need a Night Light, 1927

Beginning with the book from which the series took its collective name, *Not at Night*, published in October 1925, literary agent and author Christine Campbell Thomson (1897–1985) edited twelve volumes which appeared from British publisher Selwyn & Blount during the 1920s and '30s.

As she later recalled: "The idea had been conceived on the top of a bus (they were open-decked buses in those days) just as it pulled away from its Oxford Circus stop about six o'clock one evening. I was on that bus with the then Director of Selwyn & Blount, Ltd. He was, I remember, lamenting, like every other publisher, that he wanted something new and couldn't find it . . . and something popular. I believe that he claims the bright moment when *Not at Night* took birth, but I think that it was a case of two minds on the same thought at the same moment—at any rate, I know that I am responsible for the title of the series!"

Although the original book had initially been conceived as a stand-alone volume, it was an immediate success, going through eleven printings in five years. As a result, over the next decade Thomson went on to edit *More Not at Night* (1926), *You'll Need a Night Light* (1927), *Gruesome Cargoes* (1928), *By Daylight Only* (1929), *Switch on the Light* (1931), *At Dead of Night* (1931), *Grim Death* (1932), *Keep on the Light* (1933), *Terror By Night* (1934), and *Nightmare By Daylight* (1936).

One of the major claims to fame of Thomson's anthology series is that it included early hardcover appearances by such *Weird Tales* alumni as H.P. Lovecraft, Robert E. Howard, Clark Ashton Smith, Seabury Quinn, Edmond Hamilton, August W. Derleth, Frank Belknap Long, Jr., Hugh B. Cave, H. Warner Munn, Hazel Heald, David H. Keller, and Mary Elizabeth Counselman, among its contributors.

In fact, more than half of the stories collected by the editor came from the pages of "The Unique Magazine"—often soon after their initial appearance in the legendary American pulp because of an arrangement between the publisher and *Weird Tales* editor Farnsworth Wright.

Wright took over at the helm of the near-bankrupt magazine in the summer of 1925 and, as previously noted, Thomson's first volume appeared in October that same year. However, Lovecraft did not make his first appearance in the series until the third volume, *You'll Need a Night Light*, was published in 1927.

In a letter to Wright, dated July 16th that same year, Lovecraft told his editor: "A third pleasure is given me by the news of [The Horror at] Red Hook's anthological reprinting; and I'd like to see the book if you can get me a copy later on."

It may have taken five months before Wright could forward a copy, but writing to correspondent Donald Wandrei on December 19th, 1927, Lovecraft revealed: "I've just received the 3rd of the Selwyn & Blount 'Not at Night' series with my 'Horror at Red Hook' as the last story in the book. This is my first—if not my last—appearance between cloth covers."

Although he had described the book as "Not half bad!" in a letter to Wright written on December 22, 1927, by January 20 the following year, the author was already disparaging his appearance in *You'll Need a Night Light* in a further letter to Wandrei: "As for that 'Not at Night'— that's a mere lowbrow hash of absolutely no taste or significance. Aesthetically speaking, it doesn't exist."

Unfortunately, Lovecraft did not pay much attention to retaining the rights to his stories, and consequently he received little or nothing for reprints from *Weird Tales*. Never concerned with the demands of commercial writing, he defended his attitude by exclaiming: "If this is 'poor business', then I say damn business!"

However, even Lovecraft was outraged when journalist and editor Herbert Asbury, best remembered for his nonfiction study *The Gangs of New York: An Informal His-*

By Daylight Only, 1929

tory of The Underworld (1927), apparently pirated stories from several volumes of Christine Campbell Thomson's anthologies and published an illegal American edition entitled *Not at Night!* (note the added exclamation mark) from Macy-Masius in 1928.

Switch on the Light, 1931

The book included "The Horror at Red Hook," and in a letter dated February 15, 1929, Lovecraft wrote to Wright: "I am indeed interested to hear of the proposed action regarding *Not at Night*, and certainly hope the matter can be properly straightened out."

In the same letter, Lovecraft seemed somewhat confused about who owned the books, claiming that Hutchinson & Co. had bought the rights to *You'll Need a Night Light* and other titles in the series from Selwyn & Blount, who he appeared to have mistakenly believed had gone out of business. Grudgingly, Lovecraft continued: "As to including me on the list of plaintiffs—I suppose it's all right so long as there is positively no obligation for expense on my part in case of defeat . . . If, however, the guarantee of non-assessment on your part is to be taken literally as covering all possible expenses both principal and incidental, I suppose it would be foolish not to stand behind the action and reap whatever royalties might be due me in case of victory. I certainly need all such things that human ingenuity can collect."

He concluded the letter by saying that he would pass the information on to friend and fellow contributor Frank Belknap Long, whom he believed would extend similar authorization. As it turned out, Macy-Masius subsequently withdrew the book rather than pay any royalties or damages to *Weird Tales*.

Meanwhile, despite his previously harsh criticism of the series, Lovecraft seemed happy to announce to Donald Wandrei in September 1929 that "My 'Pickman's Model' will appear in a new volume of the British 'Not at Night' anthology."

The story was published in *By Daylight Only* that year, and was followed in

1931 by a third tale, "The Rats in the Walls," in *Switch on the Light.*

Apparently not all writers were as lucky as Lovecraft when it came to obtaining copies of their appearances in the "Not at Night" series. In November 1932, Lovecraft wrote to Robert E. Howard: "I suppose you know that your 'Black Stone' is in the new 'Not at Night' anthology?"

Howard, who lived in rural Texas with his parents, admitted that he was unaware of his first British hardcover appearance in *Grim Death.* "No, I didn't know my 'Black Stone' had landed in the 'Not At Night' anthology," he wrote to Lovecraft in December. "I'm so far off the beaten track of literature, that I get only vague hints of what goes on in the world of pen and ink."

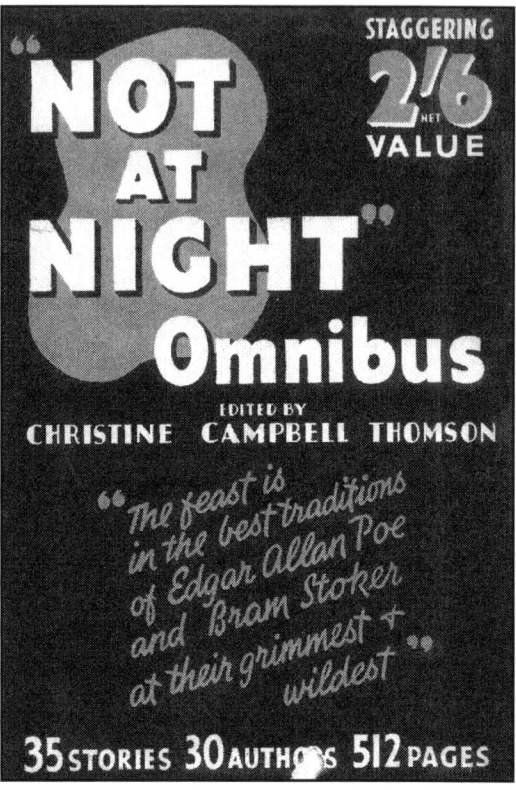

Not at Night, 1937 edition

Lovecraft was quick to offer his friend some helpful advice. "So you didn't know 'The Black Stone' had landed in the 'Not at Night' anthology?" he wrote in a letter dated January 21, 1933. "That's odd, for you ought to have received a small cheque from Charles Lovell [sic] *(W.T.'s* London agent) for the reprint rights. Better ask Wright about it." He then went on to provide Howard with the London address for Selwyn & Blount.

With money tight, Howard admitted in a letter written to Lovecraft in September 1933 that he had been saving up for a copy of *Grim Death*: "I've been laying off to get the book that published my 'Black Stone' but haven't ever got around to it."

Howard was also able to inform Lovecraft about another of his stories which Thomson was reprinting: "I understand that 'Worms of the Earth' is to appear in the 'Not at Night' series." The story was published later that year in *Keep on the Light.*

By now, Howard was obviously keen to obtain copies of these hardcover printings of his stories, which he probably believed would raise his prestige among the local townsfolk, who considered the young writer to be something of an eccentric.

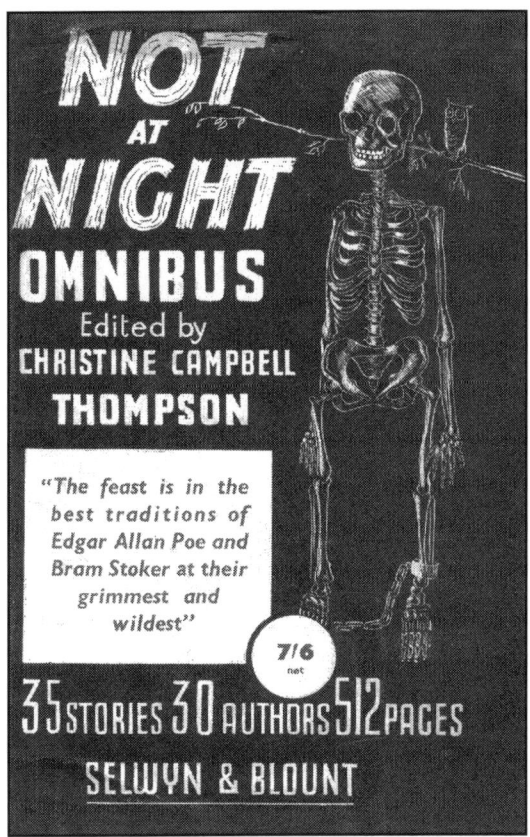

Not at Night, Reprint edition

In a P.S. to a March 1934 letter to Clark Ashton Smith, Howard asked, "Where do you get your 'Not at Night' anthologies? I've been trying to locate a firm that handled them, but without success."

In a reply, Smith—whose own story, "Isle of the Torturers," had also appeared in *Keep on the Light*—told his friend and fellow *Weird Tales* contributor where he could obtain his copies from. However, in a letter to Smith dated May 21, Howard admitted that he had encountered a problem: "I ordered the 'Not at Night' books I wanted, but they were out of them, and had to send to England for them. I haven't yet received them."

That same year, Howard's Conan story "Rogues in the House" appeared in the tenth "Not at Night" volume. As the author revealed to August Derleth in a letter dated October, 1934: "I haven't yet gotten a copy of the *Terror by Night*, but intend to do so shortly."

At least Lovecraft was apparently still being kept apprised of his reprints three years later. In his very last letter, written to James F. Morton but unfinished and unmailed, Lovecraft wrote: "Wright informs me that 'Pickman's Model' is about to be reprinted again—in a Special Coronation Omnibus of the 'Not at Night' series. The material reward will be only £1 sterling—but it will gratify me to be in any way connected with the enthronement of our new Sovereign. God Save the King!"

Whether or not it actually had anything to do with George IV's ascension to the British throne in December the previous year is debatable, but the final volume in the series appeared in 1937 under the title *The "Not at Night" Omnibus*. It reprinted thirty-five stories from the earlier books, including Lovecraft's "Pickman's Model."

Over the years, a number of variations have come to light in the dustjackets for various reprintings of the "Not at Night" books. Yet the most striking difference is that found between the two states known for the *Omnibus*.

One version is completely typographical with a big orange blob and a 2/6 (two shillings and sixpence) price. The other (and much more common) version features a very distinctive black and white scratchboard illustration of a skeleton with its feet shackled, standing in front of a tree branch with an owl sitting on it. This variant is priced at 7/6 (seven shillings and sixpence)—three times more expensive than on the alternate cover!

Every edition of this title has exactly the same number of stories and pages, and they are all first printings according to the indicia page. So the question arises as to whether one book is a first printing and the price was subsequently increased (quite a lot), or if the publisher later reissued the same edition in a cheaper format with a new dust-jacket?

With *The "Not at Night" Omnibus* Christine Campbell Thomson decided to bring the series to an end because, she claimed, of a lack of good enough material.

"The *Not at Night* series of horror stories has become such a universal favourite that, with eleven volumes already published, it seemed a good moment to collect some of the best stories into a bumper-sized twelfth volume," she explained. "All the stories in this *Omnibus* have been published in one or another of the eleven previous volumes of the series, and it must be confessed that it has been extraordinarily interesting to make this selection—to choose one's own favourites and include the work of as many authors as possible, to remember especially those which have been commented upon in the past."

What this brief history reveals is that some authors—notably Robert E. Howard, and most probably others—had problems getting hold of copies of their own work in the "Not at Night" series.

H.P. Lovecraft may have had his editions forwarded to him by *Weird Tales*, but even Clark Ashton Smith apparently had to order his volumes from an import dealer. Whether this was the fault of editor Thomson, British literary agent Charles Lavelle, or even Farnsworth Wright, we will probably never know.

By the late 1930s, Selwyn & Blount was in financial difficulties and the imprint was finally sold to Hutchinson & Co. In 1939, illness and economics forced Wright to sell *Weird Tales*. Although he stayed on for a brief time as editor, he finally had to relinquish control when the debilitations of Parkinson's disease took their toll. No longer able to walk without assistance, he died in 1940 as a result of an operation designed to alleviate his condition.

Thomson herself went on to become a successful literary agent and novelist. She retired in 1970 and died at her Hampshire home on September 29, 1985, at the age of eighty-eight.

Although none of the contributors to the "Not at Night" series are with us any longer, there was one author who was around long enough to shed some light on whether or not authors were sent copies of the volumes with their stories in them.

Veteran pulp author Hugh B. Cave (1910–2004) had the rare distinction of having been one of the original contributors to Christine Campbell Thomson's "Not at Night" anthologies. "The original series reprinted stories by many now-famous pulp writers," explained Cave, "and I'm happy to say, two of my tales were so honored. My 'Cult of the White Ape' appeared in *Keep on the Light* and 'The Watcher in the Green Room' was in *Terror By Night* and was also included in the remarkable *'Not at Night' Omnibus*, in which were collected what the editor considered the 'best' of the 'Not at Night' stories."

Regrettably, the author could no longer remember how or when he acquired his copies of the books: "I presume they were sent to me either by the publisher or my agent, who at the time was Lurton Blassingame," Cave recalled. "I carefully kept all such information in notebook files—even listing what magazines rejected a story before it finally sold!—and then lost everything when, needing more space in my workroom, I moved some files into a wooden garden house and the darned thing burned down—struck by lightning, we think—when my wife and I were away from home one weekend.

"I don't remember whether I was paid for my stories or not. If the money came through Farnsworth Wright, we probably were paid eventually, though Wright was often rather slow in paying for work in *Weird Tales*. One thing I'm fairly certain of: I didn't buy my three books. Someone must have sent them to me."

With the passing of time, it now seems unlikely that we will ever know if contributors other than Lovecraft were sent copies of their "Not at Night" appearances or not.

H.P. Lovecraft's other, uniquely British, appearance during his lifetime came around Halloween 1932.

Written in 1921 and originally published the following year in the March edition of *The National Amateur*, the author's story "The Music of Erich Zann"

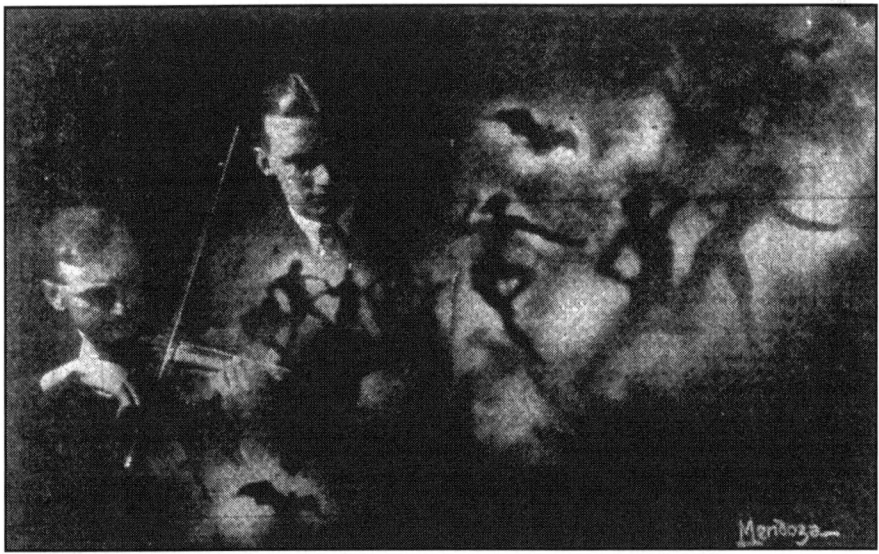

Illustration for "The Music of Erich Zann," *The Evening Standard,* October 24, 1932

was selected by editor Dashiell Hammett for his 1931 anthology *Creeps by Night: Chills and Thrills*, which was reprinted in Britain by Gollancz the following year as *Modern Tales of Horror*.

It was most probably from that source that the editors of the London newspaper *The Evening Stan"'* in the Monday, October 24th, 1932 edition, along with the shout line "Chaos & Pandemonium Before Me" and a suitably atmospheric illustration by Montague Phillip Mendoza (1898–1973).

Once again, it is unknown if Lovecraft was ever aware that he was being read by the multitude of London as they hurried home during the rush-hour on a cold winter's night, or if he was ever paid a royalty for the use of the story in the popular newspaper.

Four years later, Brooklyn fan (and later literary agent and legendary comic book editor) Julius Schwartz (1915–2004)—who had already successfully sold the author's novella "At the Mountains of Madness" to *Astounding Stories*—attempted to place a collection of Lovecraft's work with a British book publisher, as the author informed Farnsworth Wright in a backhanded submission letter dated July 1st, 1936:

Julius Schwartz in 1945.

"Young Schwartz has persuaded me to send him a lot of manuscripts for possible placement in Great Britain," wrote the author, "and it occurs to me that I'd better exhaust their cisatlantic possibilities before turning them over to him. Accordingly I am going through the formality of obtaining your official rejection of the enclosed—so that I won't feel I've overlooked any theoretical source of badly-needed revenue. In the absence of other American markets for purely weird material, I won't need to try them elsewhere—hence, if you don't mind, you might send them on after rejection to Julius Schwartz, 255 East 188th St., New York, N.Y., instead of returning them to me."

As it turned out, Wright bought both stories on offer—"The Thing on the Doorstep" and "The Haunter of the Dark"—for publication in *Weird Tales*, while Schwartz's efforts to sell a Lovecraft collection in Britain eventually came to nothing.

Although it is not known which publisher Schwartz approached with Lovecraft's fiction, it is interesting to speculate that it may have been Denis Archer Ltd.—then a part of the Hutchinson group—who had contacted Robert E. Howard three years earlier and were "exceedingly interested" in publishing a book of the author's work, only to reject it eight months later because there was a "prejudice that is very strong over here just now against collections of short stories."

One can only speculate how different Lovecraft's career may have been if such a book had been published during his lifetime. Maybe it would have finally given him the valediction and financial stability that he always craved—perhaps even inspiring him to turn out more memorable stories than he did before his untimely death at the age of forty-six, just nine months after he had written to Wright.

And if proof were needed that Lovecraft was a well-known name among the British science fiction and fantasy community, the country's first fanzine, *Novae Terrae* (which listed Edward J. Carnell and Arthur C. Clarke as its Associate Editors), marked the author's passing in its October 1937 issue.

There is no doubt that H.P. Lovecraft was a relatively well-respected author in Britain during the 1930s, even if his chosen genre was not so much. It is unfortunate that the writer—probably due to a lack of funds more than a disinclination to travel—never got to cross the Atlantic, even if some of his best work did.

As the man himself observed in the 1920s: "If I could create an ideal world, it would be an England with the fire of the Elizabethans, the correct taste of the Georgians, and the refinement and pure ideals of the Victorians."

William Shakespeare couldn't have said it better.

STEPHEN JONES was born in London, England, just across the River Thames from where his hapless namesake met a grisly fate in Hazel Heald's story "The Horror in the Museum." A Hugo Award nominee, he is the winner of three World Fantasy Awards, three International Horror Guild Awards, four Bram Stoker Awards, twenty-one British Fantasy Awards and a Lifetime Achievement Award from the World Horror Association. One of Britain's most acclaimed horror and dark fantasy writers and editors, he has more than 135 books to his credit, including *Shadows Over Innsmouth*, *Weird Shadows Over Innsmouth* and *Weirder Shadows Over Innsmouth*, *H.P. Lovecraft's Book of Horror* (with Dave Carson), *H.P. Lovecraft's Book of the Supernatural*, *Hallowe'en in a Suburb & Others: The Complete Poems from* Weird Tales, *Necronomicon: The Best Weird Tales of H.P. Lovecraft* and *Eldritch Tales: A Miscellany of the Macabre*, along with such author collections as *The Complete Chronicles of Conan* and *Conan's Brethren* by Robert E. Howard and *Curious Warnings: The Great Ghost Stories of M.R. James*. His many anthologies include *Fearie Tales: Stories of the Grimm and Gruesome*, *A Book of Horrors*, *The Mammoth Book of Vampires*, the *Zombie Apocalypse!* series, and twenty-five volumes of *The Mammoth Book of Best New Horror*. You can visit his web site at: www.stephenjoneseditor.com

Copyright © Stephen Jones 2015. All rights reserved.

The Call of Khalk'ru and Other Speculations

WILL MURRAY

As far as I know, no one has ever quoted A. Merritt on the source of Khalk'ru, the octopus demon from another dimension who is the malignant foe of American Leif Langdon in Merritt's novel, *Dwellers in the Mirage.* Nevertheless, most historians of fantasy agree that the source could be none other than H.P. Lovecraft's Great Cthulhu. Merely the similarity between their phonetically-difficult names is persuasive enough to dispel doubt.

Lovecraft was long a fan of Merritt's work in *Argosy,* and in later years both writers contributed sections of the round-robin story, "The Challenge from Beyond." But Merritt's reading of HPL's fiction is only supposition—but very likely supposition. Merritt, as a lover of fantasy and contributor to *Weird Tales,* could hardly have escaped Lovecraft's work. For my part, I've always felt that the opening paragraph of Merritt's *The Metal Monster* was inspired in language and cosmic theme from the fragment from the *Necronomicon* included in "The Dunwich Horror."

Merritt's opening runs: "In this great crucible of life we call the world—in the vaster one we call the universe—the mysteries lie close packed, uncountable as grains of sand on ocean shores. They thread, gigantic, the star-flung spaces; they creep, atomic, beneath the microscope's peering eye. They walk beside us, unseen and unheard, calling out to us, asking why we are deaf to their crying, blind to their wonder."

Compare that to: "Nor is it to be thought that man is either the oldest or the last of earth's masters, or that the common bulk of life and substance walks alone. The Old Ones were, the Old Ones are, and the Old shall be. Not in the spaces we know, but *between* them. They walk serene and primal, undimensioned and unseen. . . . They walk unseen and foul in lonely places where the Words have been spoken and the Rites howled through at their seasons. The wind gibbers with Their voices, and the earth mutters with Their consciousness. . . ."

In truth, the magazine version of *The Metal Monster* was written several years before HPL penned "The Dunwich Horror." While Merritt did later revise the story for book publication, the original 1920 text featured that distinctly Lovecraftian passage at the head of Chapter III. Therefore, it strongly suggests that Lovecraft got his inspiration from Merritt, and not the other way around.

But there's no question but that Khalk'ru is out of Cthulhu—probably by way of Yog-Sothoth. Like Cthulhu, Khalk'ru is known to various cultures. As one of the characters in *Dwellers* blurts: "Don't you know what this is? It's

Reprinted from *Nyctalops,* No.19, April 1991.

the Kraken—that super-wise, malignant, and mythical sea-monster of the old Norsemen. . . . It symbolized the principle that is inimical to Life—not Death precisely, more accurately annihilation, The Kraken—and here in Mongolia! . . . And the ancient legend of the South Seas told of the Great Octopus, dozing on and biding his time till he felt like destroying the world and all its life. And three miles up in the air the Black Octopus is cut into the cliffs of the Andes! And the same symbol—here!"

Merritt's reference to the Great Octopus of the South Seas is straight out of "The Call of Cthulhu," it would seem. There are many South Seas octopus myths, such as the Maori legend of Wheke-toro, known as "Crawling Octopus" and the Samoan legends of the primeval octopus who crawled up from the rocks and from whose burst ink-sack the seas came, but I've yet to come across anything such as Merritt describes. In "The Call of Cthulhu," Cthulhu is closely associated with the

Argosy, January 23, 1932

Pacific area, which is where sunken R'lyeh lies.

Khalk'ru, on the other hand, is not imprisoned in an undersea city, but exists in another dimension and can only enter ours by a gateway. In this way, Khalk'ru is more like Yog-Sothoth than Cthulhu. But, like both of Lovecraft's entities, Khalk'ru needs human help to enter our world. In *Dwellers in the Mirage,* Khalk'ru "calls" to Leif Langdon and manipulates him into helping bridge the gate of Khalk'ru in a way not far removed from Cthulhu's influencing of susceptible dreamers. ("He whose call Khalk'ru has answered must answer when Khalk'ru calls him.") Langdon is susceptible because he is the reincarnation of an ancient warrior, Dwayanu.

Khalk'ru is no mere other-dimensional entity. Described as a huge, black, cloudy octopus, Merritt implies that this Kraken shape may not be its real form, but rather one forced upon it by its passing into our dimension. Further, Merritt says Khalk'ru is ". . . the Beginning-without-Beginning, as he would be the End-without-End. He was the Lightless Time-less Void. The Destroyer. The Eater-up of Life. The Annihilator. The Dissolver. He was not Death—Death was only a part of him. He was alive, very much so, but his quality of living was the antithesis of Life as we know it. Life was an invader, troubling Khalk'ru's ageless calm. Gods and man, animals and birds and all creatures, vegetation and water and air and fire, sun and stars and moon—all were his to dissolve into Himself, the Living Nothing-ness, if he so willed. But he let them go on a little longer. Why should Khalk'ru care when in the end there would be only—Khalk'ru! Let him withdraw from the barren places so life could enter and cause them to blossom again; let him

Abraham Merritt (1884–1943)

touch only those who were the enemies of his worshipers, so that his worshippers would be great and powerful, evidence that Khalk'ru was the All in All. It was only for a breath in the span of his eternity. Let Khalk'ru make himself manifest in the form of his symbol and take what was offered him as evidence he has listened and consented."

Parallels between Khalk'ru and Lovecraft's Great Old Ones are rife. Khalk'ru is "the All in All" to Lovecraft's "One-in-All and All-in-One," Yog-Sothoth. He is as unconcerned with humanity (with the exception of helpful adherents) as any of the Old Ones. His life is akin to death. Lovecraft tells us in "The Call of Cthulhu" that although the Great Old Ones "no longer lived. They could never really die." Cthulhu spoke to the first man and so established the cult that perpetuated his worship. Similarly, Khalk'ru taught the ritual of bridging the gate to human ancestors a "forgotten age" ago.

That ritual involves a ring bearing a yellow stone in which the nebulous symbol of the Kraken resides—something of a counterpart to the Cthulhu image in Lovecraft's story. Khalk'ru's patient waiting for his time to come easily echoes the line from that *Necronomicon* fragment that goes: "They wait patient and potent, for here shall They reign again."

Merritt calls Khalk'ru "the Soul of the Void," and in one sense, he is like Azathoth, the mindless entity which rules in Chaos, to which Walter Gilman is repeatedly drawn in Lovecraft's "The Dreams in the Witch House." According to Merritt, "Khalk'ru was nothing but the second law of thermodynamics expressed in terms of anthropomorphism. Life *was* an intrusion upon Chaos, using that word to describe the unformed, primal state of the universe. An invasion. An accident. In time all energy would be changed to static heat, impotent to give birth to any life whatsoever. The dead universes would float lifelessly in the illimitable void. The void *was* eternal, life was not. Therefore the void would absorb it. Suns, worlds, gods, gods, men, all things animate, would return to the void. Go back to Chaos. Back to Nothingness. Back to Khalk'ru."

This is perilously close to Lovecraft's contention in "At the Mountains of Madness" that human life is an accident, if not a joke.

All in all, *Dwellers in the Mirage* is so riddled with uniquely Lovecraftian concepts that it beggars belief to think they weren't drawn directly from HPL's stories. Even the ending is right out of "The Dunwich Horror." About to come through the gate, which is in the form of a screen, Leif Langdon shatters it—forever forbidding Khalk'ru from gaining a tentacle-hold on earth.

According to a letter Lovecraft wrote to Robert H. Barlow, dated January 13, 1934, HPL read *Dwellers* in its magazine form. Curiously, none of his published letters comment on it in any detail—curious because Lovecraft couldn't help but notice his own malign concepts staring back from the printed page in unfamiliar dress. As much of an admirer of Merritt as he was, Lovecraft should have been flattered by the borrowings. Perhaps he felt Merritt borrowed *too* much and kept a gentlemanly silence on his personal thoughts, out of respect for the author of one of Lovecraft's favorite fantasies, "The Moon Pool."

It's interesting that Merritt emphasized the Kraken as the atavistic symbol of Khalk'ru. Lovecraft liked to hint that our familiar myths were symbolic of the deeper horror of his Great Old Ones. Both Khalk'ru and Cthulhu seem to be names designed to evoke such South Sea gods as Ru-Taki-Nunu and others, but none of this has anything to do with the Kraken. In my article, "The Dunwich Horror and Other Inversions" *(Lovecraft Studies*, Vol.II, No.2), I speculated that a probable source for Cthulhu was Alfred Lord Tennyson's monstrous poem, "The Kraken." I still think this might be the case, but recently I came across something in Lovecraft's *Selected Letters I* which may also have a bearing on Cthulhu's genesis.

In a letter to Clark Ashton Smith, dated March 25, 1923, Lovecraft praises Smith effusively for his poem, "The Hashish-Eater." Quoting lines from that work, Lovecraft informs Smith that:

> "I delight in your use of the cosmos instead of merely the *world* as a
> background; you can't imagine—or then again, you probably *can*—the pic-
> tures that flit through my mind at lines like
> ". . . The blind
> And worm-shap'd monsters of a sunless world,
> With krakens of the ultimate abyss,
> And demigorgons of the outer dark. . . ."

Could the nascent inspiration for Cthulhu have come from the pen of Clark Ashton Smith?

WILL MURRAY is the author of over 60 novels, including several posthumous Doc Savage collaborations with Lester Dent under the name Kenneth Robeson, and 40 in the long-running Destroyer series. His 2000 book, *Nick Fury Agent of S.H.I.E.L.D.: Empyre,* reads like a blueprint for the 9/11 terrorist attacks.

His latest novel, *The Sinister Shadow,* pits Doc Savage and his aides against The Shadow and his agents in 1933 New York.

A contributor to many anthologies, Murray has written stories about such classic characters as Superman, Batman, Wonder Woman, Spider-Man, Ant-Man, The Hulk, The Spider, The Avenger, and Lee Falk's immortal Ghost Who Walks, The Phantom.

Other stories have appeared in anthologies such as: *100 Crooked Little Crime Stories, 100 Creepy Little Creature Stories, The Cthulhu Cycle, Miskatonic University, Disciples of Cthulhu II, Dead But Dreaming 2, Horror fur the Holidays, Black Wings IV, That is Not Dead, Worlds of Cthulhu, The Shub-Niggurath Cycle, 365 Scary Stories, 100 Vicious Little Vampire Stories, 100 Wicked Little Witch Stories, 100 Clever Little Cat Crimes, 100 Clever Little Cat Crimes, The Yig Cycle, Weird Trails, The UFO Files, Future Crime, Rehearsals for Oblivion, Mammoth Book of Roaring 20s Whodunnits, Mammoth Book of Perfect Crimes & Impossible Mysteries, Tales of Masks and Mayhem,* and *Astounding Hero Tales.*

For many years, Murray was a frequent contributor to the leading Lovecraftian fanzines, *Crypt of Cthulhu* and *Lovecraft Studies.* He was one of the principals who organized the Friends of H.P. Lovecraft, which placed the H.P. Lovecraft memorial plaque on the grounds of the John Hay Library during the Lovecraft Centennial in August 1990.

Will is a recognized authority on the pulp magazine era, particularly the hero pulp characters such as Doc Savage, The Shadow and The Spider. He contributes new historical essays on Doc Savage, The Shadow, The Whisperer and The Avenger for the current series of reprint editions published by Sanctum Books.

For Radio Archives, he produces the Will Murray Pulp Classics lines of audio and ebooks.

Lovecraft and *Weird Tales*

S. T. JOSHI

"In the days of Senf's covers, monthly Jules de Grandins, Henry S. Whitehead and Dunwich Horrors, into Rankin's era with his clouded, evil, misty illustrations, bursting into Howard's pulsating epics, Depression days and bi-monthly issues—terrible time of famine—and so on into the present day. *Per ardua ad astra!*" So one reader (Reginald A. Pryke in the October 1937 issue) saw the development of *Weird Tales* and its minor if distinctive place in American civilisation. In spite of the reams of drivel and hackwork that cluttered every issue, in spite of its rejecting the best tales of Lovecraft, Whitehead, Moore, and other serious fantaisistes, in spite of the shaky financial foundations on which it managed to run for an astonishing thirty years, the "unique magazine" has remained exactly that to its current followers (whose number is now far greater than its original readership), and in spite of all shall always have a small place in the study of history and letters; for among its achievements can be named two in particular: its enlivening the confused third and fourth decades of this century with its familiar red covers, thereby becoming an authentic element of American popular culture; and its publishing many of the important works of Howard Phillips Lovecraft, now universally acknowledged as the twentieth century's premier fantaisiste and a figure of growing importance in world literature.

But it would be an error to say that these blessings are unmixed, as it would be presumptuous to assume that Lovecraft would never have reached his present status in weird fiction had he never appeared in *Weird Tales.* Second-guessing history is a tricky proposition for the historian or critic, but in this case some hypotheses can be made on certain effects that *Weird Tales* had on Lovecraft's writing—effects that, had he never submitted there, might not have occurred.

Lovecraft was the first to admit that his habit of writing specifically for *Weird Tales* resulted in a corrupting of his style so that it became more explicit, less suggestive, and more "pulpish." Despite his statements that he never wrote with a particular audience in mind, we have other remarks that attest to his desire to cater to the readership of the magazine—or, at any rate, to gain some needed revenue by placing tales there.[1] By the time Lovecraft realized the results of this cheapening effect, it was too late. It is clear that such tales as "The Horror at Red Hook," with its hackneyed use of traditional occultism, and "The Dunwich Horror," with its naive confrontation of good vs. evil (Armitage vs. Whateley), were written with *Weird Tales* in mind. Whether Lovecraft could have retained the subtlety of "The Music of Erich Zann" or the delicate prose-poetry of "The Quest of Iranon" in his later years is open to question, since regardless of *Weird Tales* he seemed

---

1 "I shall [soon] devote myself to the composition of more stories to submit to *Weird Tales"* (*SL* 2.37).

to be moving toward the cosmic horror of "At the Mountains of Madness" in the course of his development as a weird writer. If it is true, as H. Warner Munn remarked in the magazine's letter column, "The Eyrie" (March 1925), that *Weird Tales* "discovered" Lovecraft, then it must be noted (as Lovecraft often did) that in its discovery it produced a writer significant different from the one who, from 1917 to 1923, was writing solely for "self-expression" and publishing solely in amateur journals.

But *Weird Tales* affected Lovecraft's writing in another way, through its repeated and capricious rejections of his best tales. Ever sensitive to criticism, Lovecraft could not fail to be bothered when his tales were rejected, not on lack of merit, but on their failure to conform to the artificial and hackneyed standards of *Weird Tales* and other pulps. It is ironic, however, that some of his rejected stories were, when later accepted and published, praised more highly than those that editor Farnsworth Wright considered more in tune with *Weird Tales'* audience. Wright knew that Lovecraft was a powerfully original writer, but he made the mistake of underestimating the intelligence and tastes of his readership: like the Valetudinarian of Addison (*Spectator* 25, 29 March 1711) who was so concerned about his health that he became the more ill, Wright was so hesitant to inflict his public with work that departed from the conventional ghost story or "scientifiction" tale (or, as Lovecraft more aptly termed it, "boys' wild west stuff given an interplanetary setting, with

Editor Farnsworth Wright

handsome young space-pilots instead of cowboys and sheriffs, and 'Martians' and 'moonmen' instead of Indians and outlaws" [*SL* 5.302–3]) that he dared not publish such tales as "The Call of Cthulhu" or "Through the Gates of the Silver Key" without first rejecting them. It is chilling to read Lovecraft's remark that the rejection of "At the Mountains of Madness" by Wright "did more than anything else to end my effective fictional career" (*SL* 5.224).

Wright, however, was not the only one who underestimated his readership: it must be admitted that Lovecraft may have done so as well. When he called the *Weird Tales* audience a "herd of crude and unimaginative illiterates" (*SL* 4.53) he seemed not to consider the numerous readers who, in "The Eyrie," praised Lovecraft's own tales and analyzed the sources of their horror quite ably. Indeed, as time passed his views became more and more jaundiced, to such a degree that in 1935 he felt obliged to let loose this jeremiad:

> [Pulp magazine editors] aim to please the very lowest grade of readers— probably because these constitute a large numerical majority. When you glance at the advertisements in these cheap magazines (and they wouldn't

continue to be inserted if they weren't answered) you can see what a hope-lessly vulgar and stupid rabble comprise the bulk of the clientele. These yaps and nitwits probably can't grasp anything even remotely approaching sub-tlety. *Suggestion*—the most artistic way to present any marvellous event—means absolutely nothing to them. One has to draw a full diagram and drive the idea into their heads with a hammer before they "get" it.[2]

While it cannot be denied that many readers were puerile and had undevel-oped tastes in weird fiction (the inane praises of such hacks as E. Hoffmann Price, Edmond Hamilton, Seabury Quinn, and others prove it), there were a good many others whose levels of appreciation were somewhat higher. Lovecraft himself had an inkling of this when he tried to plead with Wright that the "Eyrie-bombarding proletariat" (*SL* 4.322) was not representative of the total readership of the maga-zine; but this had little effect on Wright, who told Lovecraft "that his index to popular whim is, almost exclusively, the flood of semi-illiterate Eyrie mail which pours in upon him" (*SL* 3.194). A number of current critics have deemed Farns-worth Wright a capable editor; but to hold such an opinion is to ignore his treat-ment of the writer who, aside from being the most important contributor to the magazine, is now largely responsible for the continuing consideration of the mag-azine at all. Wright, it is true, managed to keep *Weird Tales* on its feet through the Depression; but it was at the expense of rejecting the best work of its best writers and publishing torrents of pulpish hackwork whose permanent inhumation can only be a blessing to weird fiction.

Who read *Weird Tales* and why? It is an interesting social commentary that a number of them turned to the "unique magazine" simply to escape the "mass of literary farce that we are treated to in the other magazines" ("The Eyrie," August 1929). Lovecraft too recognized that the material published in what H. Warner Munn ("The Eyrie," March 1925) called the "ultraconservative" magazines was becoming "increasingly lifeless, sterile, mannered, preoccupied with form, and obviously linked with obsolescent attitudes and interests and perspectives" (*SL* 5.399). Both *Weird Tales* and the "ultraconservatives" represented two sides of the cultural havoc of American (and European) civilization between the two World Wars: the latter opted for a blind return to conventionalism, while the former chose imaginative (or sometimes not so imaginative) escape from the hideous realities of Al Capone and the Great Depression. *Weird Tales* was still serving this function in the late 1930s, as a comment in "The Eyrie" of June 1937 (which al-most anticipates the decade of the 1950s and Joe McCarthy) shows: "In these days of stark realism of wars and rumors of wars, of cracked politics and politicians, of 200% Americans and enemies that bore from within, it was more than relief to turn to a Lovecraft story."

Here is only one reader of many who identified Lovecraft with *Weird Tales*. Donald A. Wollheim (October 1937) did the same when he said that Lovecraft's

2 Lovecraft to Duane W. Rimel, 16 April 1935 (ms., JHL).

Lovecraft in Brooklyn, New York, 1931.

myth-cycle (particularly such elements as the *Necronomicon)* "was one of the factors contributing to the making of *WT's* vivid and unique personality." It is a delicate question whether Lovecraft or such other writers as Seabury Quinn or Edmond
Hamilton were actually the most "popular" contributors to the magazine. To be
sure, these latter writers, experienced and businesslike pulpsters that they were,
contributed far more voluminously to *Weird Tales* than Lovecraft; but readers were
constantly clamoring for the latter's work (especially in the 1930s, when the relative sparsity of his original fiction, as well as his reluctance to submit to the magazine and risk additional rejections, caused Wright to appease readers with the feeble
expedient of reprinting earlier tales by Lovecraft), and I think it can safely be said
that even the magazine's cruder readers recognized that Lovecraft was on a higher
plane than Quinn or Hamilton.

Nor was it the case (as with other such accidentally popular geniuses as

Beethoven, Virgil, and Shakespeare) that readers failed to appreciate Lovecraft's true merits and enjoyed him for some coincidentally appealing feature of his work. In several letters to "The Eyrie" (many from Lovecraft's own correspondents) we note a vague and confused awareness of the philosophical bases of his work; a few of the letters, indeed, may represent some of the more astute early vignettes of Lovecraft criticism. Robert E. Howard, even before he began corresponding with the Providence writer, grasped that his "range is cosmic" (May 1928); and while we may smile at his remark that Lovecraft "touches peaks in his tales which no modern or ancient writer has ever hinted," we nonetheless must be impressed at Howard's perception of the central doctrine of Lovecraft's work (expressed by Lovecraft himself in his letter to Farnsworth Wright of July 5,1927, published in the February 1928 issue of *Weird Tales*). A good number of readers were captivated by Lovecraft's polished, erudite, and slightly archaic style, and Ray Cummings expressed the feelings of many when he said, "Never have I encountered any purer, more beautiful diction. [His tales] sing; the true poetry of prose" (June 1926). Harold Farnese maintained that Lovecraft's "weird and eldritch atmosphere has yet to be equalled by other writers" (August 1931), while a comment by E. Hoffmann Price hints at a major philosophical concept in Lovecraft's later work:

> In his utter unreality and impossibility, he is like a non-Euclidean geometer who, though working on physically impossible axioms, reasons truly from them and produces theorems, and subsequent Q.E.D.'s, which are as true as if they actually were true; or as one who reasons of the inconceivable fourth dimension and by self-consistent hypotheses and logic deals logically with impossibility. (April 1926)

The "self-consistency" that Price notes is equivalent, more or less, to what Lovecraft felt must now be the basis for true fantasy: "The time has come when the normal revolt against time, space, and matter must assume a form not overtly incompatible with what is known of reality—when it must be gratified by images forming *supplements* rather than *contradictions* to the visible and mensurable universe" (*SL* 3.295–96).

Not all of Lovecraft's fans in "The Eyrie," however, were so astute. Several writers (despite their assertions that they had read Shakespeare and other such writers) confirmed Lovecraft's opinion of their "semi-illiteracy"—or, at any rate, their lack of judgment—by proclaiming him and *Weird Tales* among the best works in world literature. We know through Lovecraft's letters that he censured many of his younger correspondents (R.H. Barlow, J. Vernon Shea, Willis Conover) for holding such views as *"Weird Tales* is the best magazine ever published" (October 1926) or that "Lovecraft is as great a writer as ever lived" (June 1929) or that "The Outsider" is "the greatest weird story ever written" (September 1931). And we can only laugh at the puerility of J. Wasso (February 1930), who wished to form an H.P. Lovecraft fan club. These opinions reflect the difference between true critical appreciation and that immature adulation which regrettably casts a dubious shadow on the author himself. Indeed, it may have been precisely such remarks that caused Edmund Wilson, in 1945, to condemn "the Lovecraft cult" as "on even a more infantile level than the Baker Street irregulars and the cult of Sherlock Holmes" (Wilson 49). Lovecraft has had to wait too long to escape the pathetic talons of fandom.

Not only was Lovecraft praised to the skies in *Weird Tales,* but many championed his poorer stories—"The Hound," "The Lurking Fear," "The Horror at Red Hook." The phenomenal response to "The Dunwich Horror" is a virtual index to its (unconscious) conformity to pulp standards. Still more amusing are those fans who were so taken with Lovecraft that they (unconsciously?) imitated his erudite writing style when writing their letters:

> "The Dunwich Horror" transported me, upon the wings of imagination, to the uttermost depths of vast caverns in the bowels of the earth—caverns which are swept by foul, moaning winds laden with the breath of the grave and which contain cosmic cesspools wherein the corruption, filth and evil of millions of centuries have accumulated; from there I traveled, in an instant, to far-off worlds or places where only a brief glimpse of unnamable horrors and formless, space-filling alien entities send me scurrying and screaming (mentally) with terror back to my warm fireside. (April 1930)

Then there were the truly eccentric readers whose minds were somehow ignited by Lovecraft's tales: one tells us that "The Outsider" is a true story founded on an incident in Germany; another notes some mysterious essays on Shakespeare written by Lovecraft during his involvement with amateur journalism; yet another, quoting Ibsen in the process, wishes the *Necronomicon* to be serialized in *Weird Tales.*

This brings up one of the more amusing aspects of Lovecraft's popularity in *Weird Tales:* the remarkably widespread belief that the *Necronomicon* was an actual book, and that his myth-cycle of Cthulhu and Yog-Sothoth had an actual basis in fact or was an authentic cycle of folklore. The hoax was obviously aided by Lovecraft's correspondents, who in their own tales used these very elements as if out of a common pool of esoteric knowledge. Indeed, virtually all of his newer correspondents—Derleth, Conover, Howard, Shea, Rimel, and others—had to be disabused as to the reality of the myth-cycle. The game was of course carried on after Lovecraft's death: in one of the most famous letters in "The Eyrie," one J.H. Stewart, Jr, tells how Manly Wade Wellman nearly stumbled upon a copy of the *Necronomicon* in a bookstore presided over by an ancient crone (July 1952).

What is also interesting is the use of the term "Elder Gods" by readers to describe the gods of Lovecraft's mythos. It was, of course, August Derleth who, after Lovecraft's death (and initially in the story "The Return of Hastur"), launched his own myth-cycle where "Elder Gods" battled the "Great Old Ones" in a puerile struggle of good vs. evil. Derleth, indeed, took every opportunity to foster his myth-cycle and to claim that it represented the development of the mythos as Lovecraft himself would have done had he lived (cf. his letter in the May 1941 issue). The "Elder Gods" have no existence in Lovecraft's tales (certainly not the all-powerful one that Derleth gave them), and even in "The Strange High House in the Mist" there are mentions only of strange, unexplained entities called "Elder Ones." *Weird Tales* readers seem to have confused them with the Great Old Ones (Cthulhu, Nyarlathotep, Yog-Sothoth, et al.), for Bernard Austin Dwyer (June 1930) makes reference to "Other Gods in the Elder World." Another writer, B.M. Reynolds (October 1936), mentions the Elder Gods themselves—this being the earliest mention of them in a quasi-Derlethian sense that I have found. Robert Leonard Russell makes note of "Cthulhu, Azathoth and the other Elder Gods" (August 1937), and Jacques Bergier speaks of Lovecraft's "cycle of the Elder Gods and strange civilisations" (September 1937). It is tempting to wonder whether these mentions in any way helped to shape Derleth's perverted conception of Lovecraft's myth-cycle.

The facility with which many readers noticed the Lovecraftian flavour of some of his revisions published in *Weird Tales* is striking. Hazel Heald's tales in particular were called out for mention, one reader soberly informing us that "Even Lovecraft . . . could hardly . . . have surpassed the grotesque scene" that served as the climax to "The Horror in the Museum" (May 1934). Aside from Heald, this "female Lovecraft" (June 1935), William Lumley's "The Diary of Alonzo Typer" was praised, Paul S. Smith claiming that Lumley had a fair chance of being "a worthy successor to the late master" (August 1938). Lovecraft himself wryly remarked that "some of my revision clients congratulate *themselves* when the readers praise stories (like 'The Last Test,' 'The Curse of Yig,' 'The Horror in the Museum,' 'Winged Death,' etc.) that *I* wrote" (*SL* 4.394).

Not all readers expressed favorable views, of course: despite the obviously sensible policy that only letters of praise were allowed, in the main, to appear in "The Eyrie," some dissenting letters emerged; interestingly, these came largely during the editorships of Edwin Baird (1923–24) and Dorothy McIlwraith (1940–54), and their absence during Wright's tenure can only be another sign of his paranoiac insecurity. Toward the latter days of the magazine, when the end was perhaps visible, there flared up a minor debate about Lovecraft's worth as a writer which is interesting not so much for the arguments expressed (being on both sides basically subjective and irrelevant), but for the fact that a majority of adverse critics have taken precisely the view here adopted by Joseph V. Wilcox, who put forth the claim that Lovecraft's style was "turgid"[3] and not suitable for the weird tale.

The number of Lovecraft's correspondents who wrote letters praising him in "The Eyrie" (many of these letters appearing before their writers even began corresponding with him) is interesting. These included not merely his fellow fantaisistes—Derleth, Munn, Wandrei (although only after Lovecraft's demise), Bloch, Kuttner, Price, Clark Ashton Smith, and others—but associates only marginally involved in weird fiction—James F. Morton, Harold S. Farnese, J. Vernon Shea,

---

3 This is curiously echoed by the classical scholar and critic Gilbert Highet in his idiosyncratic snipe at Lovecraft in *A Clerk of Oxenford* (New York: Oxford University Press, 1954), p.9.

Bernard Austin Dwyer, Paul J. Campbell, and the like. Several writers, in fact, became associates of Lovecraft through "The Eyrie" itself—Derleth, Howard, and perhaps Jacques Bergier. On the other hand, it is odd that such colleagues as Frank Belknap Long, Robert H. Barlow, and others, who were both Lovecraft's close friends and significantly involved in either *Weird Tales* itself or fantasy fandom, never sent letters to "The Eyrie"—or, at any rate, never had them published.

Lovecraft's death in March 1937 produced the most overwhelming tide of letters of comment ever found in "The Eyrie," and far exceeded the amount for other such deceased writers as Robert E. Howard or Henry S. Whitehead. A great many of Lovecraft's correspondents, from those who had known him in the 1920s (Smith) to those who had corresponded with him only a few months before his death (Robert A.W. Lowndes, Earl Peirce), sent letters of regret, while other associates (particularly Henry George Weiss and Kenneth Sterling) extolled him as a great writer, thinker, and epistolarian. Those who had known Lovecraft only through his work were as moved by his death as they had been by his stories: "I feel," writes Robert Leonard Russell, "as will many other readers of *Weird Tales,* that I have lost a real friend" (August 1937). But Lovecraft's work by no means stopped appearing upon his demise: many tales previously rejected were now printed, and when these ran out poems were used to satiate the readers' demands. But, as L. Sprague de Camp (435) has pointed out, Lovecraft's death, so closely following that of Robert E. Howard and the virtual surcease of Clark

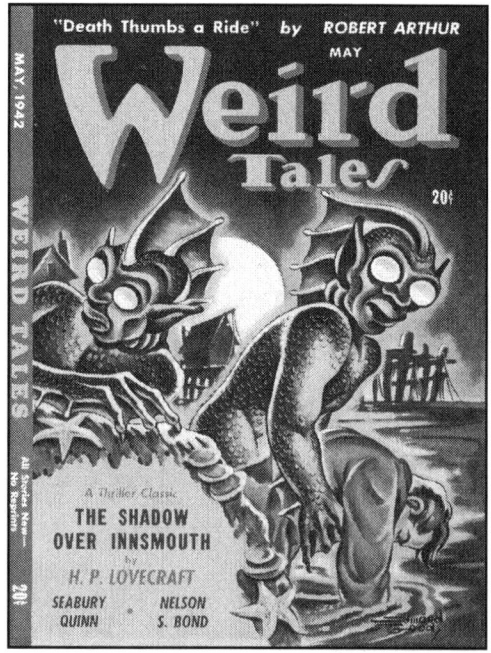

The Canadian version of *Weird Tales,* May 1942, featuring a Lovecraft cover story.

Dorothy McIlwraith

Ashton Smith's fictional output, dealt a fatal blow to *Weird Tales,* caused it to lose much of its "vivid and unique personality," and heralded a death that, though staved off for some seventeen years, was as inevitable as Lovecraft's own. There were still, under the none too competent guidance of Dorothy McIlwraith, some fine writers appearing in its pages—Bloch, Bradbury, Wellman, and others—but the lack of any writer of the stature of a Lovecraft or a Howard, plus the rising competition of the science fiction magazines and the emergence of the paperback book as an alternative to the pulp magazine, ensured *Weird Tales'* collapse. In its decline "The Eyrie" too dwindled from the lively readers' column of the 1920s and 1930s to the dry editorial ramblings of the 1940s and 1950s. From a full 160 pages to a small digest size—such was the ignominious end of a magazine that had seen in its pages the work of Lovecraft, Whitehead, Smith, Long, Wandrei, Bloch, and so many of the most important figures in modern weird fiction; but perhaps it could have met no other fate, for it was very much a product of its time, very much a part of the Roaring Twenties and Depression Thirties from which it had sprung.

It is needless to say that both Lovecraft and *Weird Tales* would have been very different without each other; but whether for better or for worse, their fortuitous joining helped to bring about what is probably the finest weird fiction that the twentieth century has ever seen. In view of this, the crudities and absurdities of *Weird Tales* become trivial, just as refulgent gold outshines its dross.

Works Cited

de Camp, L. Sprague. *Lovecraft: A Biography.* Garden City, NY: Doubleday, 1975.

Wilson, Edmund. "Tales of the Marvellous and the Ridiculous" (1945). Rpt. in S.T. Joshi, ed., *H.P. Lovecraft: Four Decades of Criticism.* Athens: Ohio University Press, 1980. 46–49.

S.T. JOSHI is a leading authority on H.P. Lovecraft, Ambrose Bierce, H.L. Mencken, and other writers, mostly in the realms of supernatural and fantasy fiction. He has edited corrected editions of the works of Lovecraft, several annotated editions of Bierce and Mencken, and has written such critical studies as *The Weird Tale* (1990) and *The Modern Weird Tale* (2001). His award-winning biography, *H.P. Lovecraft: A Life* (1996), has already become a collector's item. An expanded and updated version, *I Am Providence: The Life and Times of H.P. Lovecraft,* was published in 2 volumes in 2010. You can visit his web site at: http://stjoshi.org.

A Lovecraft Rarity:
1917 Draft Registration Card

DOUG ELLIS

"During World War I there were three registrations. The first, on June 5, 1917, was for all men between the ages of 21 and 31. . . ." —from www.archives.gov

Editor's note: This rarely seen item offers several interesting physical facts about Lovecraft as he registered with the Selective Service. It is fascinating to note that as early as 1917, Lovecraft states his occupation as a writer. Only one piece of fiction had been placed by Lovecraft at this time, although he had composed numerous essays, amateur journalism pieces and astronomy commentary works for regional publication.

Lovecraft in 1915, two years before registration.

38-1-5-A

REGISTRAR'S REPORT

1 | Tall, medium, or short (specify which)? _Tall_ Slender, medium, or stout (which)? _Medium_

2 | Color of eyes? _Dark Brown_ Color of hair? _Dark Brown_ Bald? _No_

3 | Has person lost arm, leg, hand, foot, or both eyes, or is he otherwise disabled (specify)? _No_

I certify that my answers are true, that the person registered has read his own answers, that I have witnessed his signature, and that all of his answers of which I have knowledge are true, except as follows:

Charles G. Winsor
(Signature of registrar)

Ward 2 - Dist-6
Precinct

City or County _Providence_

State _Rhode Island_ _June 5, 1917_
(Date of registration)

Lovecraft's Astronomical Notebook

DAVID H. KELLER

In my Underwood library reposes a Lovecraft document that gives most interesting information concerning his interest in astronomy. His love of the science has been noted by several of his biographers but many details contained in his notebook have not been given and should be of interest. In this small notebook, four by seven inches, Lovecraft went into detail concerning his observations of the habitants of the skies. This book, in his own handwriting (with the exception of one small printed item), also contains drawings of celestial phenomena such as Halley's and Delavan's Comets.

Laid in is a small printed notice, yellowed by time. It reads:

PRO. ASTRONOMICAL SCY.
1904. H.P. Lovecraft, Pres't.
An organization destined to encourage the study of the heavens.
All persons interested in Astronomy should at once join, as this society affords valuable instruction and cooperation.
All business transacted by mail so those far away from Providence may join.
Persons unfamiliar with the science are taught.
Members are required only to send in monthly reports. ALL FREE.
Write for directions and membership certificate NOW.
598 Angell St. Providence R.I., U.S.A.

Lovecraft was fourteen years old when this was printed.

The title page of the unbound notebook reads:

Astronomical
Observations
Made
By
H.P. Lovecraft,
598 Angell St.
Providence,
R.I.
U.S.A.
Years 1909-1910-1911-1912-1913-1914-1915

Reprinted from *The Lovecraft Collector,* No.3, October 1949.

On page 100 Lovecraft writes:

POSITION OF RESIDENCE
598 Angell St. Provo R.I.
Latitude 41° 50' 00" N.
Longtitude 71° 23' 09" W.

The rest of the page is filled with Fundamental data showing corrections in position and time. Evidently Lovecraft was not satisfied with locating his residence by number, street, city, state and nation but wished to show that he knew exactly where he lived by scientific observations. I do not know of any other author who was so careful to be completely oriented in space.

Page 99 reads:

PRINCIPAL ASTRONOMICAL WORK.

1. To keep track of all celestial phenomena month by month, as positions of planets, phases of the moon, Sign of Sun, occultations, Meteor Showers, unusual phenomena (record) also new discoveries.
2. To keep up a working knowledge of the constellations and their seasons.
3. To observe all planets, etc. with a large telescope when they are favorably situated (at 7 h 30" in winter, abt. 9 h in summer, supplemented by morning observations)
4. To observe opera or field glass objects among the stars with a low power instrument, recording results.
5. To keep a careful record of each night's work.
6. To contribute a monthly astronomical article of about 7p. Ms. or 4p. type to the *Providence Evening Journal* (begun Jan. 1, 1914.)

On the last page of the notebook is a description of Lovecraft's telescope and astronomical library.

INSTRUMENTS
Dimensions of Telescope.
Clear aperture......................3 inches
Eyepieces, 2. 50 (Ten) and 125 (Ast.)
Focus (with Astro)................44 in.
"   (" Ten) ....52 in.
Manuf. By Bardore.
Altazimuth Stand by R.L. Allen.
Purchased 1906 (Sept. 13)

The public had a growing awareness in astronomy.
Puck, November 7, 1906, the same year that Lovecraft purchased his telescope.

Accessories
Lunar Map by Wright
Year Book—Fanner's Almanack
Planispheres-Whitaker & Barrett Servis.
Atlas by Upton—Library.
Opera glasses—Prism Binoculars
Am. Exh. & Want Almanac.

Page 1 of the notebook is headed:

ASTRONOMICAL
OBSERVATIONS
1909
Begun Sept. 1, 1909.

But on an earlier date there is a record of an eclipse.

Special Observation.
June 3—1909
Moon's eclipse. Clouds interfered but several glimpses were obtained.
Total 7.58.

On September 1 and 2, 1909, Lovecraft described the occultation of Mars by the moon.

On Thursday, May 26, 1910, he wrote a lengthy description of Halley's Comet and drew three pictures of it.

Under the date 1911 there is the statement, no observations.

On February 1, 1912, he wrote concerning a lunar halo:

Observed a lunar halo at about 6.30 p.m. Moon 1 d of full. Halo was of about 46° diameter, with rather noticeable paraselenae on a horizontal line with the moon. The left hand (northern) paraselena was more or less obscur'd by clouds and appeared only at intervals. The right hand mock moon was prominent and attracted much attention. The two paraselenae were seen as diffus'd patches of light. The northern part of the halo was by far the brightest part.

Almost all of page 4 is used in an illustration of this lunar halo.

On Oct. 19, 1912, he notes the relation of Copernicus to the moon.

1913 shows no observations.

In January 1914, he observes Mars and Saturn. On February 26th of the same year he writes:

The moon's crescent very thin. Earthshine visible in strong twilight. The moon was almost at the vernal equinox. Earlier in the day the moon and Mercury had been in conjunction.

This is illustrated on page 6 and includes a house and a tree.

On March 11–12 he observed a partial eclipse of the moon.

The next and last note in this book was made on September 16th and 17th of 1914 and concerns Delavan's Comet. It includes two illustrations. One of a house and mountains with the location of the comet in the Plough and the other of the comet showing head and tail. The text is so detailed that it is given in full:

> Sept. 16—4:00 a.m. to dawn. Obs. Delavan's Comet and heavens in general. Delavan's Comet lay in R.A. 10 h. 08m 06s Dec. 49° 14" in Ursa Major, as shown in diagram. It had about the brightness of a star of the 4th magnitude, appearing to the naked eye as a blurred spot of light; rather faint, yet easily visible. In the opera glasses this blur resolved itself into a star-like nucleus, a bright coma, and a short broad tail. In the prism binoculars these details were better seen. Whilst in the 3" telescope with powers of 50 and 100 the comet was indeed a beautiful sight. A small telescope star could at that time be seen shining through the faint lumination of the tail. The best view was with 3" tel Ten, Eyepiece 50 diameters. Tail about 1° in length. Observations made from grounds of residence and somewhat hampered by electric street lights. At this same time moon was a beautiful crescent 3rd before new. Earthshine very powerful. Could see Maria Orisian, Seren Tranq. Rec. Nect. very plainly on dark part of disk. Saturn also fine object.
>
> Winter stars fully in view—Orion, Cosmis Major and Orion's nebula very beautiful in 3" with pr. 50
>
> Sept. 17—Obs Delavan's Comet 4:00–5:00 a.m. Also Moon. Earthshine on moon very strong, especially rising above house top and bright thin crescent hidden. Comet appears brighter as Moon wanes.

This notebook shows more than Lovecraft's interest in astronomy. There is an evident love of the beauty of the skies and an occasional sense of frustration. The clouds prevent a full view of the eclipse of the moon, the city lights make observation of a comet difficult. While he mentions these frustrations, he accepts them as being unavoidable. This calm reaction to the inevitable marked much of his life.

It would be interesting to correlate these notes with the monthly articles Lovecraft wrote for the Providence *Evening Journal.*

*Notes**

Dr. Keller's article with its excerpts from the astronomical notebook of H.P. Lovecraft will at once suggest several intriguing avenues of inquiry to students of the latter's life and works.

What became of HPL's telescope and other astronomical equipment?

Did the little printed invitation secure any members for the Providence Astronomical Society? Can any of those members be located today?

Did HPL's early studies of the heavens reveal to him anything that could have served as a basis for his later development of a "mythos" of beings who thrive "outside" the earthly sphere?

Did HPL give his extra-terrestrial beings any kind of definite position in space in any of his stories?

I leave these questions as seed for Lovecraft researchers.

Editorial note: The above notes are by Ray Zorn, editor and publisher of *The Lovecraft Collector*.

"The twentieth century's greatest practitioner
of the classic horror tale."
—*Stephen King, commenting on Lovecraft*

Collected Poems (Arkahm House, 1963). Cover and interior art by Frank Utpatel.

HERITAGE®

ILLUSTRATION ART

Selling the finest original pulp art, pulps, science fiction and fantasy related manuscripts, books, and rarities

VIRGIL FINLAY
Seal of the Damned, Fantastic Universe
Science Fiction digest cover, July 1957
Oil on board | 11.875 x 8.5 in. | Estimate: $10,000-$15,000

Inquiries: 877-HERITAGE (437-4824)

Todd Hignite
Ext. 1790 | ToddH@HA.com

THE WORLD'S THIRD LARGEST AUCTION HOUSE

HERITAGE HA.com
A U C T I O N S

Always Accepting
Quality Consignments
in 39 Categories.

Annual Sales Exceed $900 Million | 900,000+ Online Bidder-Members

3500 Maple Ave. | Dallas, TX 75219 | 877-HERITAGE (437-4824) | HA.com

DALLAS | NEW YORK | BEVERLY HILLS | SAN FRANCISCO | HOUSTON | PARIS | GENEVA

Paul R. Minshull #16591. BP 12-25%; see HA.com. 36281

The Truth About
The Shunned House Hardcover

ROBERT WEINBERG

Perhaps the oddest book ever published by Arkham House was the 100 copy hardcover edition of *The Shunned House*. While the basic facts regarding the book are common knowledge, the actual inspiration for its hardcover publication have never been known. This short article hopefully will serve as an answer to that question which has plagued collectors for more than fifty years.

"The Shunned House," a long horror novelette, was written by H.P. Lovecraft during the week of October 16–19, 1924. The house of the story was based in part on a real house in Providence, R.I. located at 135 Benefit Street. Lovecraft's aunt lived in the house in 1919–1920. The inspiration for the story was another house, one located in Elizabeth, New Jersey (not far from where Bob grew up, which may explain many things!) at the northeast corner of Bridge Street and Elizabeth Avenue. Of that house, Lovecraft wrote that it was a "hellish place where night-black deeds must have been done in the early seventeen-hundreds."[1] In the same letter, he further explained "its image came up again with renewed vividness, finally causing me to write a new horror story with its scene in Providence and with the Babbit House as its basis."[2]

In 1928, Lovecraft's friend, and fellow small-press enthusiast, W. Paul Cook, proposed publishing "The Shunned House," as a 250-copy Recluse Press hardcover book. Lovecraft was agreeable and Cook printed the sheets of the book. It was poorly typeset and contained a short introduction by Frank Belknap Long. However, according to August Derleth, Cook was always out of funds to pay to bind the book, and he totally abandoned the project when he moved from Massachusetts to Vermont several years later.[3] Cook gave the unbound sheets to Lovecraft. In 1936, eighteen-year-old Robert Barlow took it on himself to hand bind around a dozen sets of the sheets. One of the books was of course for Lovecraft. The others he sent out to some of Lovecraft's closest friends. The

Robert H. Barlow

1   H.P. Lovecraft, *Selected Letters Vol.I*, p. 357 (as quoted in Wikipedia, *The Shunned House*, http://en.wikipedia.org/wikifThe_Shunned_House#_note -1

2   Ibid

3   Derleth, August, "Letter to Sam Peeples," November 2, 1961

THE SHUNNED HOUSE

BY

H. P. LOVECRAFT

With a Preface by Frank Belknap Long, Jr.

ATHOL, MASS.
Published by W. Paul Cook
The Recluse Press
1928

An unbound sheet from *The Shunned House,* as printed by W. Paul Cook in 1928.

"[A] dense, richly textured story with convincing historical background and a fine sense of cumulative horror . . . " (S.T. Joshi, *H.P. Lovecraft: A Life*).

Director
AUGUST DERLETH   ARKHAM HOUSE: PUBLISHERS
                                                  SAUK CITY, WISCONSIN

2 November 1961

Dear Sam,

All thanks for yours of the 31st. I'm glad to know that the bound copy of
THE SHUNNED HOUSE reached you in good order. I had it bound uniformly with
other AH books, and, since I had a few other copies, I had them all done at
once. .... Well, now, the sheets were never bound as an edition, but a few
sets (ca. 12 - 20) were bound by hand by Barlow -- for HPL, and some of his
and Barlow's friends. TSH was done by Cook at a little press in Athol, Mass.
but Cook, like all printers, was always in straits, financial for the most
part, and always hoping for the best. However, after printing TSH he was
out of funds, a change in position loomed (he ultimately went to North
Montpelier, Vermont, and took over the Driftwind Press at Coates' death,
remaining there until his own death), and he abandoned the project, turning
over the sheets to HPL. HPL never did anything with them, and at his death
Barlow took them; when Barlow committed suicide, Barlow's friends in Mexico
City sent them on to me on the basis of our correspondence re HPL.

August Derleth letter to Sam Peeples, November 2, 1961

rest of the sheets remained unbound for the duration of Lovecraft's life. Lovecraft
died on March 15, 1937. Submitted by his friends after his death, "The Shunned
House" was finally published in the October 1937 issue of *Weird Tales.*

Robert Barlow took possession of the unbound sheets after Lovecraft's death.
He did nothing with them. On January 2, 1951, Barlow committed suicide in
Azcapotzalco, Mexico, where he had been studying early Mexican history. According to Derleth, Barlow's friends in Mexico City sent the sheets to Derleth
based on the two men's correspondence about Lovecraft.[4] Derleth received approximately 150 sets of the unbound sheets.

Derleth did nothing with the unbound sheets for the next few years. Then, in
1959, he began offering sets of the sheets for sale at $15.00 each. Despite the reasonable price, (most Arkham House books from the period were price at $3.50–
$4.00 each), not many of the sheets sold. In the 1960 catalog, Derleth advertised
the sheets again. The ad read: "THE SHUNNED HOUSE. Unbound sheets of the
rare first, never published edition, done by Cook in 1928. Only a few sets remain

---

4   Ibid

for sale. For collectors only. $15.00."[5]

It was in late 1961 that long-time fantasy book collector, Sam Peeples wrote to his friend Derleth about buying a copy of *The Shunned House*. Peeples, however, didn't want unbound sheets that would need some sort of special box or slipcase for storage. Instead, he proposed to Derleth that when the next Arkham House book was bound, Derleth would have a set of the pages of the unpublished book trimmed and bound with the press' usual binding.[6] Derleth agreed, telling Peeples by return mail, that the cost of the binding, complete with lettering on the spine of the volume, would cost an additional $10.[7]

Peeples' idea of binding the unbound sheets of *The Shunned House* in Arkham House binding obviously appealed to Derleth. In a letter to Peeples written later that year, he wrote:

> "I'm glad to know that the bound copy of *The Shunned House* reached you in good order. I had it bound uniformly with other Arkham House books, and, since I had a few other copies, I had them all done at once."[8]

In the new books announcement for 1962 Arkham House, Derleth listed the volume thusly:

> "Lovecraft collectors may like to know that we have bound the last remaining sets of the sheets of *The Shunned House* in a binding uniform with the binding of most of our books, under the Arkham House imprint, sans jacket of course, and these last copies will be sold at $17.50 a copy."[9]

According to Derleth, approximately 100 sets of the sheets were bound in hardcover. Within a year, the bound hardcover copies of *The Shunned House* were gone. By late 1962, the book was listed out of print. What hadn't sold as unbound sheets, sold fairly quickly (for an Arkham House book), in hardcover book format. Thus, it was an unusual request from a dedicated Arkham House collector that brought into existence the rarest of all Arkham House hardcovers.

5　New Books from Arkham House: Coming in 1961
6　Peeples, Sam, "Letter to August Derleth," August 1961
7　Derleth, August, "Letter to Sam Peeples," August 16, 1961
8　Derleth, August, "Letter to Sam Peeples," November 2, 1961
9　New Books from Arkham House: Coming in 1962

The Arkham House Story

AUGUST DERLETH

In 1939, the calm waters of American publishing were stirred by the introduction of a new book-publishing firm, Arkham House—the first house to be devoted solely to fantasy. Under the guidance of August Derleth and Donald Wandrei, two Daniel Boones of the fantasy scene, the House flourished until the most dubious onlooker recognized its success and solidity. Today, Arkham House is an institution. Mr. Derleth now tells us the history of that institution.

Arkham House was born out of the profound shock of H.P. Lovecraft's death in 1937, though it took two years after to bring Arkham House into being for the express purpose of publishing the hitherto virtually neglected work of one of the modern masters of the macabre, and, secondarily, to preserve the work of Clark Ashton Smith, the Rev. Henry S. Whitehead, and other writers in the genre of the fantastic—by which, let it be understood, I have referenced to all forms of fantasy, including science fiction. (There is a general tendency among devotees to separately classify science fiction as non-fantasy, which is on a par with saying that vegetable soup is, after all, not soup.)

The hiatus between the death of Lovecraft and the coming into existence of Arkham House was brought about by two factors. The initial one was the work needing to be done by Donald Wandrei and myself, with the helping hand of the late R.H. Barlow and the assistance of Lovecraft's aunt, Annie Gamwell, to put the stories and poems left by Lovecraft into their proper sequence, and to assure magazine publication for those not yet published.

Secondarily, once the first and major omnibus collection had been put into typescript as *The Outsider and Others,* we attempted to find a publisher, hesitating about establishing a business of our own. Shipping a 1,000-page manuscript from one publisher to another, however, is not easy. Moreover, Lovecraft himself had attempted to interest publishers in a less bulky collection of his stories. Both Knopf and Putnam had rejected him. Now Scribner's and Simon & Schuster rejected the omnibus we had prepared. Two years after Lovecraft's untimely death, Arkham House was born out of our exasperation with New York publishers who had rejected his work.

While my own original plan covered only the work appearing in *The Out-*

Reprinted from *Fantastic World,* Summer 1952.

Editorial note: As best as research allows, it is believed this article has never been reprinted. Full of interesting data and comments, it is fascinating to hear in Derleth's own voice the telling of the genesis of Arkham House.

August Derleth at the desk where he did his writing
and editing in his home, Place of the Hawks.

sider and Others, Donald Wandrei envisioned collecting all the work in at least three omnibus volumes and such appendix volumes as should be necessary. The decision to publish ourselves was not taken hastily. Both Wandrei and I were comparatively impecunious; in addition, I was at the time putting up a house for which a local bank had advanced a considerable loan; much to their horror, I dipped into funds loaned me for my house in order to pay for the production of *The Outsider and Others.*

It is manifest that the name "Arkham" was selected for the House because it was the most readily remembered of Lovecraft's own place-names for various east coast towns. This one was Aslem, Massachusetts, in reality. Arkham was an integral place-name in Lovecraft's remarkable Cthulhu Mythos, and seemed to us the most fitting name, one Lovecraft himself would certainly have approved. Having committed ourselves, we advertised for advance orders at $3.50 the copy, and got them to the amount of 150 before publication, at which time the cost became $5.00. Of the production costs, Donald Wandrei advanced $400.00, and I added the rest of the not inconsiderable amount; so *The Outsider and Others* was published, and so Arkham House came into being.

It took four years to sell out the 1,268-copy edition of *The Outsider and Others.* Actually, what with overhead and other costs, it took approximately that long to earn the original investment in the book. I had meanwhile gone ahead and

Donald Wandrei

collected other Lovecraft works, selling many of them without commission or charge for preparing type-scripts for the benefit of Mrs. Gamwell, who showed her appreciation of our efforts when, at her death in 1941, she willed to Donald Wandrei and myself the income from the Lovecraft writings with the sole provision that they be applied to the further publication of the work of Lovecraft. We were thus committed to the program we had outlined, without consideration of expense.

The struggle to sell *The Outsider and Others* was not encouraging. It was two years before we published another book. Then it was my own collection, *Someone In the Dark,* which William O. Weber, turning it down for Scribner's, suggested we issue under the Arkham House imprint. The press delivered 1,115 copies, to sell at $2.00 the copy. Thus our imprint was kept before the public eye while other Lovecraft works were in preparation. Soon after this publication, Donald Wandrei was forced to sever all but the most cursory connection with Arkham House (limited to the Lovecraft works), because of his induction into the U.S. Army, where he served four years.

Arkham House now went into a careful study of the cost-price problem. Readers—some of whom subsequently paid $12, $20, $30, $70, and even $100, for a copy of our first book—complained that $5.00 was too much to ask for a book. The publishers realized, after *Someone In the Dark,* that $2.00 was too little. In 1942, Arkham House experimented with a $3.00 book, the first Clark Ashton Smith collection, *Out of Space and Time,* in an edition of 1,054 copies; and in the following year came the second Lovecraft collection, *Beyond the Wall of Sleep,* again at $5.00, in an edition limited by wartime restrictions to 1,217 copies.

By the end of 1943, the slow start to Arkham House was caught up by a manifest selling spurt. It was quite clear that there was a distinct market for collections of fantastic tales, and I began to envision a programs of expanded publication embracing every aspect of fantasy, from whimsy to science fiction, but specializing in the hitherto unpublished, though not scorning works long out of print. It was clear, too, that very few of our first four titles would be left in print by the end of 1944.

In a sense, 1944 marked the first turning point for Arkham House. Before this time, the house had brought out four titles in five years. Now came four almost at once—Donald Wandrei's *The Eye and the Finger;* Henry S. Whitehead's *Jumbee and Other Uncanny Tales;* Clark Ashton Smith's *Lost Worlds;* and H.P. Lovecraft's *Marginalia.*

Henry S. Whitehead

Within yet one more year, the list had grown to include my own *Something Near;* Robert Bloch's *The Opener of the Way;* Evangeline Walton's first fantasy novel, *Witch House;* J. Sheridan Le Fanu's *Green Tea and Other Ghost Stories;* and *The Lurker At the Threshold,* a novel suggested in notes and several fragmentary portions written by Lovecraft, finished by myself in a ratio of about 1,200 words to 60,000.

The initial Le Fanu collection, of stories long out of print in America, began the importation of titles from abroad. Since many of the best writers in fantasy were British, it seemed to me necessary to add to our list such names as would bring prestige to Arkham House.

This decision was undertaken at a time when Arkham House had expanded to distribute books under two other imprints—Mycroft and Moran, specializing in off-trail sleuthing tales, the first of which was my own *"In Re: Sherlock Holmes"—The Adventures of Solar Pons,* a collection of pastiches published at the urging of Vincent Starrett, who wrote the introduction, and Ellery Queen (who later wrote the introduction for *The Memoirs of Solar Pons,* published in 1951); and of Stanton & Lee, for the publication of non-fantasy reprints and cartoon books.

In many ways, 1946 was the year of the most expanded publishing program of Arkham House. In that year we saw published Frank Belknap Long's *The Hound of Tindalos;* Robert E. Howard's *Skull Face and Others;* Henry S. Whitehead's *West India Lights;* the House's first science fiction novel, A.E. Van Vogt's *Slan,* long a popular serial in *Astounding Science Fiction;* and four British importations, one an original and the other the author's last book—Algernon Blackwood's *The Doll and One Other;* H. Russell Wakefield's *The Clock Strikes Twelve;* A.E. Coppard's *Fearful Pleasures;* and the omnibus reprint of four novels by William Hope Hodgson—*The House on the Borderland and Other Novels.*

Clark Ashton Smith in 1912.

Post-war increases in publishing costs had not yet reached Midwestern printers in 1946, but by the following year the increases were marked, though for
Arkham House standard prices of $2.50 for novels, $3.00 for short story collections, and $5.00 for omnibuses did not alter, and could not, for these were tested
prices.

The only factor that had altered was the size of Arkham House editions,
which now ranged between 2,500 and 4,000 copies per title, though only one edition of any Arkham House book was ever printed, since all books were done from
movable type and not plates, and type was not held. We had yet to learn that the
best figure for collections of fantasy was 2,000 copies; and we had to learn that
our own American writers, who were known only through magazine publication,
sold on the whole better than the famous British authors in the field.

By this time, Arkham House had inspired other small publishers to venture
into the field, and, at a time when we had just inaugurated publications in science
fiction—with *Slan*—we found a mushroom growth of competitors snatching at
titles we had hoped to bring out. Mounting costs posed a problem in 1947, but we
did publish Lady Cynthia Asquith's *This Mortal Coil;* my anthology of macabre
poetry, *Dark of the Moon;* Ray Bradbury's first distinguished collection, *Dark
Carnival;* Carl Jacobi's *Revelations In Black*; Fritz Leiber's *Night's Black Agents;*
and, under the Mycroft and Moran imprint, William Hope Hodgson's *Carnacki,
The Ghost Finder,* a far more comprehensive title than the British edition of almost four decades before, since it contained three new stories, two never before
printed, discovered among Hodgson's manuscripts.

Six more titles followed in 1948—L.P. Hartley's *The Travelling Grave and
Other Stories;* Donald Wandrei's novel, *The Web of Easter Island;* Lord Dun-
sany's *The Fourth Book of Jorkens;* Clark Ashton Smith's *Genius Loci and Other
Tales;* my own *Not Long For This World;* and the House's first illustrated book,
Seabury Quinn's *Roads*—with pictures by Virgil Finlay. The following year, how-
ever, drastically revealed the effects of steadily mounting costs—only two books
were published in 1949: Lovecraft's *Something About Cats and Other Pieces,* and
S. Fowler Wright's *The Throne of Saturn.*

The Arkham Sampler, a quarterly devoted to matters fantastic, publishing fiction,
poetry, letters, articles, bibliographical data, *et alia,* designed to sell at $1.00 the
copy, sans advertising, was begun in 1948. The magazine's first year did well,
possibly because of the serialization of the scarce Lovecraft novel, *The Dream-
Quest of Unknown Kadath;* but by mid-1949 it was apparent that the magazine
could not support itself, and, like some of our books, would not meet its production costs. With a loss running into four figures—*The Arkham Sampler* cost an
average of $0.50 the copy to produce—it was reluctantly decided to end the brief
life of the quarterly with the second volume. The eight issues of this magazine are
undoubtedly destined to join early Arkham House books as collectors' items.

The close of the first decade of Arkham House saw many of its titles out of
print and selling for fantastic prices. Many more had been reprinted in various

foreign countries, and, in addition, adjunctive anthologies prepared by the editor were being published by Rinehart & Company: *Who Knocks?, Sleep No More, The Night Side.* Pellegrini & Cudahy published *The Sleeping and The Dead, Strange Ports of Call, The Other Side of the Moon, Beyond Time and Space,* and others. Perhaps most significant of all, by 1950 almost a dozen other small houses had followed the lead of Arkham House, and several first-line publishing houses, among them some who rejected Lovecraft's work a decade and a half before, were publishing novels of science fiction.

By 1951, publishing costs had virtually tripled. It was no longer a joke to say that the typesetter of an average 2,000-copy Arkham House book could earn more money for just setting the type than either the author or the publisher of the book, it was sober reality.

True, Lovecraft's work had by this time spread far and wide; it had appeared in an Armed Service Edition; in magazines and anthologies galore; and in that same year, 1951, both an initial Lovecraft collection, *The Haunter of the Dark and Other Tales of Horror,* and *The Case of Charles Dexter Ward,* had been published by Gollancz of London, while a French edition of Lovecraft was in preparation.

Only one book was published under the Arkham House imprint in 1950, and that in a limited edition—Leah Bodine Drake's collection of fantastic poems, *A Hornbook For Witches.* In 1951, my own *The Memoirs of Solar Pons* appeared as a Mycroft and Moran book—and the poems of Clark Ashton Smith, *The Dark Chateau,* came under the Arkham House imprint.

The 1952 program has been begun with production and distribution handled by Pellegrini & Cudahy for the book trade, with my anthology of weirds, *Night's Yawning Peal,* which brings back into print the Lovecraft novel, *The Case of Charles Dexter Ward,* and Dr. David H. Keller's *Tales From Underwood.* At least one further Arkham House book is on the 1952 list—H.P. Lovecraft's collected poems, *Fungi From Yuggoth.*

Despite tribulations, Arkham House is here to stay. And the tribulations were many, for Arkham House has almost since its beginning, operated in the red—and that despite the fact that I poured into the business no less than $25,000.00 of my personal earnings from writing over a twelve-year period, leaving other debts to be carried at interest right down to the present.

Production cost rises, which have been steady without a retrogression since 1946; postage cost increases; the rising cost of overhead and clerical labor—all these factors have combined to make publishing for the small publisher far more difficult than it has ever been before. Moreover, publishing activities have encroached severely on the editor's own creative time. Yet it is an enduring pleasure to reflect that, could he have willed it so, H.P. Lovecraft would certainly have accomplished as much for those too often forgotten little classics of the strange and macabre.

Arkham House recently released its 1952 bulletin, the last to go to all its addresses now on file; henceforth, to trim costs, announcements will go only to people ordering directly from the House.

But Arkham House has survived fluctuations in both sales and costs that would have pushed another House to the wall. It has in hand a great many more projects and will go on as long as its editor goes on.

AN ARKHAM HOUSE CHECKLIST†

TITLE	DATE	COPIES PRINTED

Arkham House Imprint

* *The Outsider and Others* by H.P. Lovecraft	1939	1,268
* *Someone In the Dark* by August Derleth	1941	1,115
* *Out of Space and Time* by Clark Ashton Smith	1942	1,054
* *Beyond the Wall of Sleep* by H.P. Lovecraft	1943	1,217
* *The Eye and the Finger* by Donald Wandrei	1944	1,617
* *Jumbee and Other Uncanny Tales* by Henry S. Whitehead	1944	1,559
* *Lost Worlds* by Clark Ashton Smith	1944	2,043
* *Marginalia* by H.P. Lovecraft	1944	2,035
* *Something Near* by August Derleth	1945	2,054
Witch House by Evangeline Watson	1945	2,949
* *The Opener of the Way* by Robert Bloch	1945	2,065
* *Green Tea and Other Ghost Stories* by J. Sheridan LeFanu	1945	2,026
The Lurker At the Threshold by Lovecraft and Derleth	1945	3,041
The Hounds of Tindalos by Frank Belknap Long	1946	2,602
The Doll and One Other by Algernon Blackwood	1946	3,490
The House On the Borderland and Other Novels by Wm. Hope Hodgson	1946	3,014
Skull-Face and Others by Robert E. Howard	1946	3,004
West India Lights by H.S. Whitehead	1946	3,037
Fearful Pleasures by A.E. Coppard	1946	4,033
The Clock Strikes Twelve by H.R. Wakefield	1946	4,040
* *Slan* by A. E. Van Vogt	1947	4,051
This Mortal Coil by Cynthia Asquith	1947	2,609
Dark of the Moon ed. by August Derleth	1947	2,634
Dark Carnival by Ray Bradbury	1947	3,112
Revelations In Black by Carl Jacobi	1947	3,082
Night's Black Agents by Fritz Leiber	1947	3,084
The Travelling Grave And Other Stories by L.P. Hartley	1948	2,047
The Web of Easter Island by Donald Wandrei	1948	3,068
The Fourth Book of Jorkens by Lord Dunsany	1948	3,118
Genius Loci and Other Tales by Clark A. Smith	1948	3,047
Roads by Seabury Quinn	1948	2,137

† All information as of Summer 1952.

Not Long For This World by August Derleth .... 1948..... 2,067
Something About Cats by H.P. Lovecraft .... 1949..... 2,995
The Throne of Saturn by S. Fowler Wright .... 1949..... 3,062
A Hornbook For Witches by Leah Bodine Drake .... 1950........ 533
The Dark Chateau by Clark Ashton Smith .... 1951........ 563
Night's Yawning Peal ed. by August Derleth 1952
Tales From Underwood by David H. Keller 1952
Fungi From Yuggoth by H.P. Lovecraft 1952

Mycroft and Moran Imprint
"In Re: Sherlock Holmes" by August Derleth .... 1945..... 3,604
Carnacki, The Ghost-Finder by W.H. Hodgson .... 1947..... 3,050
The Memoirs of Solar Pons by August Derleth .... 1951..... 2,038

Released to other publishers
The World of Null-A by A.E. Van Vogt
Slan by A.E. Van Vogt
Gather, Darkness! by Fritz Leiber
Away and Beyond by A.E. Van Vogt
Conjure Wife by Fritz Leiber

Forthcoming—Arkham House Imprint
The Abominations of Yondo by Clark Ashton Smith
The Purcell Papers by J. Sheridan LeFanu
Invaders From the Dark by Grey La Spina
Xelucha and Others by M.P. Shiel
◊ *Three Tales* by Walter de la Mare
Selected Letters by H.P. Lovecraft
The Green Round by Arthur Machen
Strayers From Sheol by H.R. Wakefield
Black Medicine by Arthur J. Burks
Mr. George and Other Odd Person by Stephen Grendon
The Trail of Cthulhu by August Derleth
Pleasant Dreams by Robert Bloch
Colonel Markesan by August Derleth and Mark Schorer
Strange Gateways by E. Hoffmann Price
Kecksies and Other Twilight Tales by Marjorie Bowen
‡ *Worse Things Waiting* by Manly Wade Wellman
‡ *Orson Is Here* by Howard Wandrei
Select Poems by Clark Ashton Smith
Strange Harvest by Donald Wandrei
Portraits In Moonlight by Carl Jacobi
Lonesome Places by August Derleth

Forthcoming—Mycroft and Moran Imprint
The Phantom-Fighter by Seabury Quinn
Prince Zaleski and Cummings King Monk by M.P. Shiel
No.7 Queer Street by Margery Lawrence
The Return of Solar Pons by August Derleth

* Out of Print
◊ The announced *Three Tales* by Walter de la Mare saw print under the title *Eight Tales.*
‡ Not issued by Arkham House.

Editorial note: With the exception of two titles, Arkham House did finally release all the works on this forthcoming list, although several did require patience by anyone wishing to obtain a copy. *The Purcell Papers* by J. Sheridan LeFanu eventually saw print in 1975, and *Kecksies and Other Twilight Tales* by Marjorie Bowen was published in 1976, more than twenty years after first being announced!

Worse Things Waiting by Manly Wade Wellman was never released as an Arkham House volume, nor was *Orson Is Here* by Howard Wandrei.

A collection of fantasy and horror short stories, *Worse Things Waiting* was published under Wagner's and Drake's Carcosa imprint in 1973. It went on to win the 1975 World Fantasy Award for Best Collection/Anthology.

The title announced as *Orson Is Here* by Howard Wandrei, had begun as early as 1944 in an exchange of letters between Derleth and the author. Although included over multiple years on Arkham House's "Forthcoming" lists, the book never progressed beyond the discussion stage. "When Howard Wandrei passed away in September 1956, the contents of 'Orson Is Here' were still not set," wrote D.H. Olson in his introduction to the 1995 Wandrei collection, *Time Burial,* "and any prospect of the book's release passed away." A partial list of the possible contents of the book were included in the 1949 Arkham House list. Each of the fifteen stories listed eventually saw print in the three Fedogan & Bremer collections of Howard Wandrei's work, *Time Burial, The Last Pin* and *The Eerie Mr. Murphy.*

August Derleth

PULPFEST 2015

AUGUST 13-16

WITH FARMERCON X

—Celebrating—

H.P. LOVECRAFT & 'WEIRD TALES'

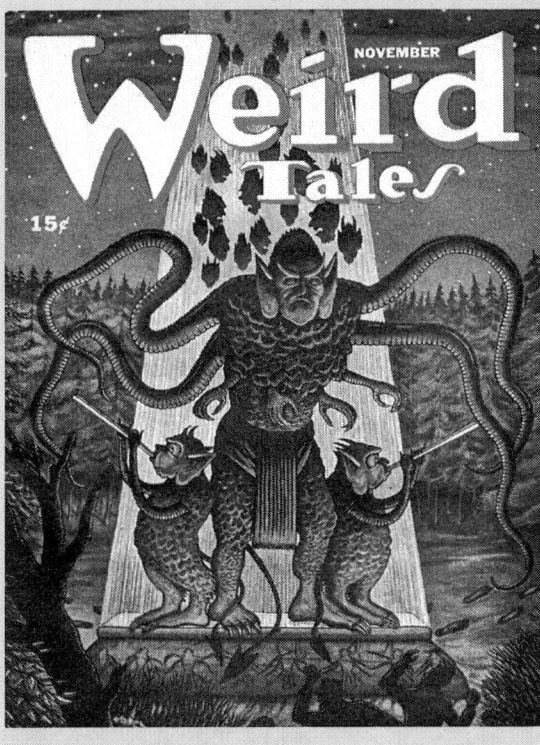

THE THRILLING GROUP — GOLDEN AGE COMICS!

AT THE **HYATT REGENCY** IN DOWNTOWN **COLUMBUS, OHIO**

TO REGISTER OR FOR MORE INFO VISIT **PULPFEST.COM**

TO RECEIVE OUR FREE NEWSLETTER OR TO REGISTER BY MAIL, WRITE
JACK CULLERS, 1272 CHEATHAM WAY, BELLBROOK, OH 45305, OR JACK@PULPFEST.COM.

The Doom That Came to Sarnath

H.P. LOVECRAFT

There is in the land of Mnar a vast still lake that is fed by no stream and out of which no stream flows. Ten thousand years ago there stood by its shore the mighty city of Sarnath, but Sarnath stands there no more.

It is told that in the immemorial years when the world was young, before ever the men of Sarnath came to the land of Mnar, another city stood beside the lake; the grey stone city of Ib, which was old as the lake itself, and peopled with beings not pleasing to behold. Very odd and ugly were these beings, as indeed are most beings of a world yet inchoate and rudely fashioned. It is written on the brick cylinders of Kadatheron that the beings of Ib were in hue as green as the lake and the mists that rise above it; that they had bulging eyes, pouting, flabby lips, and curious ears, and were without voice. It is also written that they descended one night from the moon in a mist; they and the vast still lake and grey stone city Ib. However this may be, it is certain that they worshipped a sea-green stone idol chiselled in the likeness of Bokrug, the great water-lizard; before which they danced horribly when the moon was gibbous. And it is written in the papyrus of Ilarnek, that they one day discovered fire, and thereafter kindled flames on many ceremonial occasions. But not much is written of these beings, because they lived in very ancient times, and man is young, and knows little of the very ancient living things.

After many aeons men came to the land of Mnar; dark shepherd folk with their fleecy flocks, who built Thraa, Ilarnek, and Kadatheron on the winding river Ai. And certain tribes, more hardy than the rest, pushed on to the border of the lake and built Sarnath at a spot where precious metals were found in the earth.

Not far from the grey city of Ib did the wandering tribes lay the first stones of Sarnath, and at the beings of Ib they marvelled greatly. But with their marvelling was mixed hate, for they thought it not meet that beings of such aspect should walk about the world of men at dusk. Nor did they like the strange sculptures upon the grey monoliths of Ib, for those sculptures were terrible with great antiquity. Why the beings and the sculptures lingered so late in the world, even until the coming of men, none can tell; unless it was because the land of Mnar is very still, and remote from most other lands both of waking and of dream.

As the men of Sarnath beheld more of the beings of Ib their hate grew, and it was not less because they found the beings weak, and soft as jelly to the touch of stones and spears and arrows. So one day the young warriors, the slingers and the spearmen and the bowmen, marched against Ib and slew all the inhabitants

Reprinted from *The Scot*, No.44, June 1920.

thereof, pushing the queer bodies into the lake with long spears, because they did not wish to touch them. And because they did not like the grey sculptured mono-liths of Ib they cast these also into the lake; wondering from the greatness of the labor how ever the stones were brought from afar, as they must have been, since there is naught like them in all the land of Mnar or in the lands adjacent.

Thus of the very ancient city of Ib was nothing spared save the sea-green stone idol chiselled in the likeness of Bokrug, the water-lizard. This the young warriors took back with them to Sarnath as a symbol of conquest over the old gods and beings of Ib, and a sign of leadership in Mnar. But on the night after it was set up in the temple a terrible thing must have happened, for weird lights were seen over the lake, and in the morning the people found the idol gone, and the high-priest Taran-Ish lying dead, as from some fear unspeakable. And before he died, Taran-Ish had scrawled upon the altar of chrysolite with coarse shaky strokes the sign of DOOM.

After Taran-Ish there were many high-priests in Sarnath, but never was the sea-green stone idol found. And many centuries came and went, wherein Sar-nath prospered exceedingly, so that only priests and old women remembered what Taran-Ish had scrawled upon the altar of chrysolite. Betwixt Sarnath and the city of Ilarnek arose a caravan route, and the precious metals from the earth were exchanged for other metals and rare cloths and jewels and books and tools for artificers and all things of luxury that are known to the people who dwell along the winding river Ai and beyond. So Sarnath waxed mighty and learned and beauti-ful, and sent forth conquering armies to subdue the neighboring cities; and in time there sate upon a throne in Sarnath the kings of all the land of Mnar and of many lands adjacent.

The wonder of the world and the pride of all mankind was Sarnath the mag-nificent. Of polished desert-quarried marble were its walls, in height 300 cubits and in breadth 75, so that chariots might pass each other as men drove them along the top. For full 500 stadia did they run, being open only on the side toward the lake; where a green stone sea-wall kept back the waves that rose oddly once a year at the festival of the destroying of Ib. In Sarnath were fifty streets from the lake to the gates of the caravans, and fifty more intersecting them. With onyx were they paved, save those whereon the horses and camels and elephants trod, which were paved with granite. And the gates of Sarnath were as many as the landward ends of the streets, each of bronze, and flanked by the figures of lions and elephants car-ven from some stone no longer known among men. The houses of Sarnath were of glazed brick and chalcedony, each having its walled garden and crystal lakelet. With strange art were they builded, for no other city had houses like them; and travellers from Thraa and Ilarnek and Kadatheron marvelled at the shining domes wherewith they were surmounted.

But more marvellous still were the palaces and the temples, and the gardens made by Zokkar the olden king. There were many palaces, the least of which were mightier than any in Thraa or Ilarnek or Kadatheron. So high were they that one within might sometimes fancy himself beneath only the sky; yet when lighted with torches dipt in the oil of Dothur their walls shewed vast paintings of kings and armies, of a splendor at once inspiring and stupefying to the beholder. Many were the pillars of the palaces, all of tinted marble, and carven into designs of surpassing beauty. And in most of the palaces the floors were mosaics of beryl and lapis-lazuli and sardonyx and carbuncle and other choice materials, so disposed that the beholder might fancy himself walking over beds of the rarest flowers. And there were likewise fountains, which cast scented waters about in pleasing jets arranged with cunning art. Outshining all others was the palace of the kings of Mnar and of the lands adjacent. On a pair of golden crouching lions rested the throne, many steps above the gleaming floor. And it was wrought of one piece of ivory, though no man lives who knows whence so vast a piece could have come. In that palace there were also many galleries, and many amphitheatres where lions and men and elephants battled at the pleasure of the kings. Sometimes the amphitheatres were flooded with water conveyed from the lake in mighty aqueducts, and then were enacted stirring sea-fights, or combats betwixt swimmers and deadly marine things.

Lofty and amazing were the seventeen tower-like temples of Sarnath, fashioned of a bright multi-colored stone not known elsewhere. A full thousand cubits high stood the greatest among them, wherein the high-priests dwelt with a magnificence scarce less than that of the kings. On the ground were halls as vast and splendid as those of the palaces; where gathered throngs in worship of Zo-Kalar and Tamash and Lobon, the chief gods of Sarnath, whose incense-enveloped shrines were as the thrones of monarchs. Not like the eikons of other gods were those of Zo-Kalar and Tamash and Lobon, for so close to life were they that one might swear the graceful bearded gods themselves sat on the ivory thrones. And up unending steps of shining zircon was the tower-chamber, wherefrom the high-priests looked out over the city and the plains and the lake by day; and at the cryptic moon and significant stars and planets, and their reflections in the lake, by night. Here was done the very secret and ancient rite in detestation of Bokrug, the water-lizard, and here rested the altar of chrysolite which bore the DOOM-scrawl of Taran-Ish.

Wonderful likewise were the gardens made by Zokkar the olden king. In the centre of Sarnath they lay, covering a great space and encircled by a high wall. And they were surmounted by a mighty dome of glass, through which shone the sun and moon and stars and planets when it was clear, and from which were hung fulgent images of the sun and moon and stars and planets when it was not clear. In summer the gardens were cooled with fresh odorous breezes skillfully wafted by fans, and in winter they were heated with concealed fires, so that in those gardens it was always spring. There ran little streams over bright pebbles, dividing meads of green and gardens of many hues, and spanned by a multitude of bridges. Many were the waterfalls in their courses, and many were the lilied lakelets into which they expanded. Over the streams and lakelets rode white swans, whilst the music of rare birds chimed in with the melody of the waters. In ordered terraces rose the green banks, adorned here and there with bowers of vines and sweet blossoms, and seats and benches of marble and porphyry. And there were many small shrines and temples where one might rest or pray to small gods.

Each year there was celebrated in Sarnath the feast of the destroying of Ib, at which time wine, song, dancing, and merriment of every kind abounded. Great honors were then paid to the shades of those who had annihilated the odd ancient beings, and the memory of those beings and of their elder gods was derided by dancers and lutanists crowned with roses from the gardens of Zokkar. And the kings would look out over the lake and curse the bones of the dead that lay beneath it. At first the high-priests liked not these festivals, for there had descended amongst them queer tales of how the sea-green eikon had vanished, and how Taran-Ish had died from fear and left a warning. And they said that from their high tower they sometimes saw lights beneath the waters of the lake. But as many years passed without calamity even the priests laughed and cursed and joined in the orgies of the feasters. Indeed, had they not themselves, in their high tower, often performed the very ancient and secret rite in detestation of Bokrug, the water-lizard? And a thousand years of riches and delight passed over Sarnath, wonder of the world and pride of all mankind.

Gorgeous beyond thought was the feast of the thousandth year of the destroying of Ib. For a decade had it been talked of in the land of Mnar, and as it drew nigh there came to Sarnath on horses and camels and elephants men from Thraa, Ilarnek, and Kadatheron, and all the cities of Mnar and the lands beyond. Before the marble walls on the appointed night were pitched the pavilions of princes and the tents of travellers, and all the shore resounded with the song of happy revellers. Within his banquet-hall reclined Nargis-Hei, the king, drunken with ancient wine from the vaults of conquered Pnath, and surrounded by feasting nobles and hurrying slaves. There were eaten many strange delicacies at that feast; peacocks from the isles of Nariel in the Middle Ocean, young goats from the distant hills of Implan, heels of camels from the Bnazic desert, nuts and spices from Cydathrian groves, and pearls from wave-washed Mtal dissolved in the vinegar of Thraa. Of sauces there were an untold number, prepared by the subtlest cooks in all Mnar, and suited to the palate of every feaster. But most prized of all the viands were the great fishes from the lake, each of vast size, and served up on golden platters set with rubies and diamonds.

Whilst the king and his nobles feasted within the palace, and viewed the crowning dish as it awaited them on golden platters, others feasted elsewhere. In the tower of the great temple the priests held revels, and in pavilions without the walls the princes of neighboring lands made merry. And it was the high-priest Gnai-Kah who first saw the shadows that descended from the gibbous moon into the lake, and the damnable green mists that arose from the lake to meet the moon and to shroud in a sinister haze the towers and the domes of fated Sarnath. Thereafter those in the towers and without the walls beheld strange lights on the water, and saw that the grey rock Akurion, which was wont to rear high above it near the shore, was almost submerged. And fear grew vaguely yet swiftly, so that the princes of Ilarnek and of far Rokol took down and folded their tents and pavilions and departed for the river Ai, though they scarce knew the reason for their departing.

Then, close to the hour of midnight, all the bronze gates of Sarnath burst open and emptied forth a frenzied throng that blackened the plain, so that all the visiting princes and travellers fled away in fright. For on the faces of this throng was writ a madness born of horror unendurable, and on their tongues were words so terrible that no hearer paused for proof. Men whose eyes were wild with fear shrieked aloud of the sight within the king's banquet-hall, where through the windows were seen no longer the forms of Nargis-Hei and his nobles and slaves, but a horde of indescribable green voiceless things with bulging eyes, pouting, flabby lips, and curious ears; things which danced horribly, bearing in their paws golden platters set with rubies and diamonds containing uncouth flames. And the princes and travellers, as they fled from the doomed city of Sarnath on horses and camels and elephants, looked again upon the mist-begetting lake and saw the grey rock Akurion was quite submerged.

Through all the land of Mnar and the lands adjacent spread the tales of those who had fled from Sarnath, and caravans sought that accursed city and its precious metals no more. It was long ere any traveller went thither, and even then only the brave and adventurous young men of distant Falona dared make the journey; adventurous young men of yellow hair and blue eyes, who are no kin to the men of Mnar. These men indeed went to the lake to view Sarnath; but though they found the vast still lake itself, and the grey rock Akurion which rears high above it near the shore, they beheld not the wonder of the world and pride of all mankind. Where once had risen walls of 300 cubits and towers yet higher, now stretched only the marshy shore, and where once had dwelt fifty millions of men now crawled only the detestable green water-lizard. Not even the mines of precious metal remained, for DOOM had come to Sarnath.

But half buried in the rushes was spied a curious green idol of stone; an exceedingly ancient idol coated with seaweed and chiselled in the likeness of Bokrug, the great water-lizard. That idol, enshrined in the high temple at Ilarnek, was subsequently worshipped beneath the gibbous moon throughout the land of Mnar.

• • • • •

Celephaïs

H.P. LOVECRAFT

In a dream Kuranes saw the city in the valley, and the sea-coast beyond, and the snowy peak overlooking the sea, and the gaily painted galleys that sail out of the harbor toward the distant regions where the sea meets the sky. In a dream it was also that he came by his name of Kuranes, for when awake he was called by another name. Perhaps it was natural for him to dream a new name; for he was the last of his family, and alone among the indifferent millions of London, so there were not many to speak to him and remind him who he had been. His money and lands were gone, and he did not care for the ways of people about him, but preferred to dream and write of his dreams. What he wrote was laughed at by those to whom he shewed it, so that after a time he kept his writings to himself, and finally ceased to write. The more he withdrew from the world about him, the more wonderful became his dreams; and it would have been quite futile to try to describe them on paper. Kuranes was not modern, and did not think like others who wrote. Whilst they strove to strip from life its embroidered robes of myth, and to shew in naked ugliness the foul thing that is reality, Kuranes sought for beauty alone. When truth and experience failed to reveal it, he sought it in fancy and illusion, and found it on his very doorstep, amid the nebulous memories of childhood tales and dreams.

There are not many persons who know what wonders are opened to them in the stories and visions of their youth; for when as children we listen and dream, we think but half-formed thoughts, and when as men we try to remember, we are dulled and prosaic with the poison of life. But some of us awake in the night with strange phantasms of enchanted hills and gardens, of fountains that sing in the sun, of golden cliffs overhanging murmuring seas, of plains that stretch down to sleeping cities of bronze and stone, and of shadowy companies of heroes that ride caparisoned white horses along the edges of thick forests; and then we know that we have looked back through the ivory gates into that world of wonder which was ours before we were wise and unhappy.

Kuranes came very suddenly upon his old world of childhood. He had been dreaming of the house where he was born; the great stone house covered with ivy, where thirteen generations of his ancestors had lived, and where he had hoped to die. It was moonlight, and he had stolen out into the fragrant summer night, through the gardens, down the terraces, past the great oaks of the park, and along the long white road to the village. The village seemed very old, eaten away at the edge like the moon that had commenced to wane, and Kuranes wondered whether the peaked roofs of the small houses hid sleep or death. In the streets were spears

Reprinted from *The Rainbow*, No.2, May 1922.

of long grass, and the windowpanes on either side were either broken or film-ily staring. Kuranes had not lingered, but had plodded on as though summoned toward some goal. He dared not disobey the summons for fear it might prove an illusion like the urges and aspirations of waking life, which do not lead to any goal. Then he had been drawn down a lane that led off from the village street toward the channel cliffs, and had come to the end of things—to the precipice and the abyss where all the village and all the world fell abruptly into the unechoing emptiness of infinity, and where even the sky ahead was empty and unlit by the crumbling moon and the peering stars. Faith had urged him on, over the precipice and into the gulf, where he had floated down, down, down; past dark, shapeless, undreamed dreams, faintly glowing spheres that may have been partly dreamed dreams, and laughing winged things that seemed to mock the dreamers of all the worlds. Then a rift seemed to open in the darkness before him, and he saw the city of the valley, glistening radiantly far, far below, with a background of sea and sky, and a snow-capped mountain near the shore.

Kuranes had awaked the very moment he beheld the city, yet he knew from his brief glance that it was none other than Celephaïs, in the Valley of Ooth-Nargai beyond the Tanarian Hills, where his spirit had dwelt all the eternity of an hour one summer afternoon very long ago, when he had slipt away from his nurse and let the warm sea-breeze lull him to sleep as he watched the clouds from the cliff near the village. He had protested then, when they had found him, waked him, and carried him home, for just as he was aroused he had been about to sail in a golden galley for those alluring regions where the sea meets the sky. And now he was equally resentful of awaking, for he had found his fabulous city after forty weary years.

But three nights afterward Kuranes came again to Celephaïs. As before, he dreamed first of the village that was asleep or dead, and of the abyss down which one must float silently; then the rift appeared again, and he beheld the glittering minarets of the city, and saw the graceful galleys riding at anchor in the blue harbor, and watched the gingko trees of Mount Aran swaying in the sea-breeze. But this time he was not snatched away, and like a winged being settled gradually over a grassy hillside till finally his feet rested gently on the turf. He had indeed come back to the Valley of Ooth-Nargai and the splendid city of Celephaïs.

Down the hill amid scented grasses and brilliant flowers walked Kuranes, over the bubbling Naraxa on the small wooden bridge where he had carved his name so many years ago, and through the whispering grove to the great stone bridge by the city gate. All was as of old, nor were the marble walls discolored, nor the polished bronze statues upon them tarnished. And Kuranes saw that he need not tremble, lest the things he knew be vanished; for even the sentries on the ramparts were the same, and still as young as he remembered them. When he entered the city, past the bronze gates and over the onyx pavements, the merchants and camel-drivers greeted him as if he had never been away; and it was the same at the turquoise temple of Nath-Horthath, where the orchid-wreathed priests told him that there is no time in Ooth-Nargai, but only perpetual youth. Then Kuranes

walked through the Street of Pillars to the seaward wall, where gathered the trad-
ers and sailors, and strange men from the regions where the sea meets the sky.
There he stayed long, gazing out over the bright harbor where the ripples sparkled
beneath an unknown sun, and where rode lightly the galleys from far places over
the water. And he gazed also upon Mount Aran rising regally from the shore, its
lower slopes green with swaying trees and its white summit touching the sky.

More than ever Kuranes wished to sail in a galley to the far places of which
he had heard so many strange tales, and he sought again the captain who had
agreed to carry him so long ago. He found the man, Athib, sitting on the same
chest of spices he had sat upon before, and Athib seemed not to realize that any
time had passed. Then the two rowed to a galley in the harbor, and giving orders to
the oarsmen, commenced to sail out into the billowy Cerenerian Sea that leads to
the sky. For several days they glided undulatingly over the water, till finally they
came to the horizon, where the sea meets the sky. Here the galley paused not at
all, but floated easily in the blue of the sky among fleecy clouds tinted with rose.
And far beneath the keel Kuranes could see strange lands and rivers and cities of
surpassing beauty, spread indolently in the sunshine that seemed never to lessen
or disappear. At length Athib told him that their journey was near its end, and that
they would soon enter the harbor of Serannian, the pink marble city of the clouds,
which is built on that ethereal coast where the west wind flows into the sky; but
as the highest of the city's carven towers came into sight there was a sound somewhere in space, and Kuranes awaked in his London garret.

For many months after that Kuranes sought the marvelous city of Celephaïs
and its sky-bound galleys in vain; and though his dreams carried him to many
gorgeous and unheard-of places, no one whom he met could tell him how to
find Ooth-Nargai, beyond the Tanarian Hills. One night he went flying over dark
mountains where there were faint, lone campfires at great distances apart, and
strange, shaggy herds with tinkling bells on the leaders; and in the wildest part of
this hilly country, so remote that few men could ever have seen it, he found a hideously ancient wall or causeway of stone zigzagging along the ridges and valleys;
too gigantic ever to have risen by human hands, and of such a length that neither
end of it could be seen. Beyond that wall in the grey dawn he came to a land of
quaint gardens and cherry trees, and when the sun rose he beheld such beauty of
red and white flowers, green foliage and lawns, white paths, diamond brooks,
blue lakelets, carven bridges, and red-roofed pagodas, that he for a moment forgot
Celephaïs in sheer delight. But he remembered it again when he walked down a
white path toward a red-roofed pagoda, and would have questioned the people
of that land about it, had he not found that there were no people there, but only
birds and bees and butterflies. On another night Kuranes walked up a damp stone
spiral stairway endlessly, and came to a tower window overlooking a mighty
plain and river lit by the full moon; and in the silent city that spread away from
the river-bank he thought he beheld some feature or arrangement which he had
known before. He would have descended and asked the way to Ooth-Nargai had
not a fearsome aurora sputtered up from some remote place beyond the horizon,

shewing the ruin and antiquity of the city, and the stagnation of the reedy river, and the death lying upon that land, as it had lain since King Kynaratholis came home from his conquests to find the vengeance of the gods.

So Kuranes sought fruitlessly for the marvelous city of Celephaïs and its galleys that sail to Serannian in the sky, meanwhile seeing many wonders and once barely escaping from the high-priest not to be described, which wears a yellow silken mask over its face and dwells all alone in a prehistoric stone monastery on the cold desert plateau of Leng. In time he grew so impatient of the bleak intervals of day that he began buying drugs in order to increase his periods of sleep. Hasheesh helped a great deal, and once sent him to a part of space where form does not exist, but where glowing gases study the secrets of existence. And a violet-colored gas told him that this part of space was outside what he had called infinity. The gas had not heard of planets and organisms before, but identified Kuranes merely as one from the infinity where matter, energy, and gravitation exist. Kuranes was now very anxious to return to minaret-studded Celephaïs, and increased his doses of drugs; but eventually he had no more money left, and could buy no drugs. Then one summer day he was turned out of his garret, and wandered aimlessly through the streets, drifting over a bridge to a place where the houses grew thinner and thinner. And it was there that fulfillment came, and he met the cortege of knights come from Celephaïs to bear him thither forever.

Handsome knights they were, astride roan horses and clad in shining armor with tabards of cloth-of-gold curiously emblazoned. So numerous were they, that Kuranes almost mistook them for an army, but their leader told him they were sent in his honor; since it was he who had created Ooth-Nargai in his dreams, on which account he was now to be appointed its chief god for evermore. Then they gave Kuranes a horse and placed him at the head of the cavalcade, and all rode majestically through the downs of Surrey and onward toward the region where Kuranes and his ancestors were born. It was very strange, but as the riders went on they seemed to gallop back through Time; for whenever they passed through a village in the twilight they saw only such houses and villages as Chaucer or men before him might have seen, and sometimes they saw knights on horseback with small companies of retainers. When it grew dark they travelled more swiftly, till soon they were flying uncannily as if in the air. In the dim dawn they came upon the village that Kuranes had seen alive in his childhood, and asleep or dead in his dreams. It was alive now, and early villagers courtesied as the horsemen clattered down the street and turned off into the lane that ends in the abyss of dream. Kuranes had previously entered that abyss only at night, and wondered what it would look like by day; so he watched anxiously as the column approached its brink. Just as they galloped up the rising ground to the precipice a golden glare came somewhere out of the east and hid all the landscape in its effulgent draperies. The abyss was now a seething chaos of roseate and cerulean splendor, and invisible voices sang exultantly as the knightly entourage plunged over the edge and floated gracefully down past glittering clouds and silvery coruscations. Endlessly down the horsemen floated, their chargers pawing the ether as if galloping over golden sands; and then the luminous vapors spread apart to reveal a greater brightness, the brightness of the city Celephaïs, and the sea-coast beyond, and the snowy peak overlooking the sea, and the gaily painted galleys that sail out of the harbor toward distant regions where the sea meets the sky.

And Kuranes reigned thereafter over Ooth-Nargai and all the neighboring regions of dream, and held his court alternately in Celephaïs and in the cloud-fashioned Serannian. He reigns there still, and will reign happily forever, though below the cliffs at Innsmouth the channel tides played mockingly with the body of a tramp who had stumbled through the half-deserted village at dawn; played mockingly, and cast it upon the rocks by ivy-covered Trevor Towers, where a notably fat and especially offensive millionaire brewer enjoys the purchased atmosphere of extinct nobility.

• • • • •

"To me, Howard Phillips Lovecraft was an entity.
A most important one. And I rejoice to see that his work—
and his memory among readers and writers—endures."
—*Robert Bloch*

H.P. Lovecraft,
about 1930.

Herbert West—Reanimator

H.P. LOVECRAFT

I. From the Dark

Of Herbert West, who was my friend in college and in after life, I can speak only with extreme terror. This terror is not due altogether to the sinister manner of his recent disappearance, but was engendered by the whole nature of his life-work, and first gained its acute form more than seventeen years ago, when we were in the third year of our course at the Miskatonic University Medical School in Arkham. While he was with me, the wonder and diabolism of his experiments fascinated me utterly, and I was his closest companion. Now that he is gone and the spell is broken, the actual fear is greater. Memories and possibilities are ever more hideous than realities.

The first horrible incident of our acquaintance was the greatest shock I ever experienced, and it is only with reluctance that I repeat it. As I have said, it happened when we were in the medical school, where West had already made himself notorious through his wild theories on the nature of death and the possibility of overcoming it artificially. His views, which were widely ridiculed by the faculty and his fellow-students, hinged on the essentially mechanistic nature of life; and concerned means for operating the organic machinery of mankind by calculated chemical action after the failure of natural processes. In his experiments with various animating solutions he had killed and treated immense numbers of rabbits, guinea-pigs, cats, dogs, and monkeys, till he had become the prime nuisance of the college. Several times he had actually obtained signs of life in animals supposedly dead; in many cases violent signs; but he soon saw that the perfection of this process, if indeed possible, would necessarily involve a lifetime of research. It likewise became clear that, since the same solution never worked alike on different organic species, he would require human subjects for further and more specialised progress. It was here that he first came into conflict with the college authorities, and was debarred from future experiments by no less a dignitary than the dean of the medical school himself—the learned and benevolent Dr. Allan Halsey, whose work in behalf of the stricken is recalled by every old resident of Arkham.

I had always been exceptionally tolerant of West's pursuits, and we frequently discussed his theories, whose ramifications and corollaries were almost infinite. Holding with Haeckel that all life is a chemical and physical process, and that the so-called "soul" is a myth, my friend believed that artificial reanimation of the dead can depend only on the condition of the tissues; and that unless actual

Reprinted from *Home Brew,* (serialized) February, March, April, May, June, July 1922.

decomposition has set in, a corpse fully equipped with organs may with suitable measures be set going again in the peculiar fashion known as life. That the psychic or intellectual life might be impaired by the slight deterioration of sensitive brain-cells which even a short period of death would be apt to cause, West fully realised. It had at first been his hope to find a reagent which would restore vitality before the actual advent of death, and only repeated failures on animals had shewn him that the natural and artificial life-motions were incompatible. He then sought extreme freshness in his specimens, injecting his solutions into the blood immediately after the extinction of life. It was this circumstance which made the professors so carelessly sceptical, for they felt that true death had not occurred in any case. They did not stop to view the matter closely and reasoningly.

It was not long after the faculty had interdicted his work that West confided to me his resolution to get fresh human bodies in some manner, and continue in secret the experiments he could no longer perform openly. To hear him discussing ways and means was rather ghastly, for at the college we had never procured anatomical specimens ourselves. Whenever the morgue proved inadequate, two local Negroes attended to this matter, and they were seldom questioned. West was then a small, slender, spectacled youth with delicate features, yellow hair, pale blue eyes, and a soft voice, and it was uncanny to hear him dwelling on the relative merits of Christchurch Cemetery and the potter's field. We finally decided on the potter's field, because practically every body in Christchurch was embalmed; a thing of course ruinous to West's researches.

I was by this time his active and enthralled assistant, and helped him make all his decisions, not only concerning the source of bodies but concerning a suitable place for our loathsome work. It was I who thought of the deserted Chapman farmhouse beyond Meadow Hill, where we fitted up on the ground floor an operating room and a laboratory, each with dark curtains to conceal our midnight doings. The place was far from any road, and in sight of no other house, yet precautions were none the less necessary; since rumors of strange lights, started by chance nocturnal roamers, would soon bring disaster on our enterprise. It was agreed to call the whole thing a chemical laboratory if discovery should occur. Gradually we equipped our sinister haunt of science with materials either purchased in Boston or quietly borrowed from the college—materials carefully made unrecognizable save to expert eyes—and provided spades and picks for the many burials we should have to make in the cellar. At the college we used an incinerator, but the apparatus was too costly for our unauthorized laboratory. Bodies were always a nuisance—even the small guinea-pig bodies from the slight clandestine experiments in West's room at the boarding-house.

We followed the local death-notices like ghouls, for our specimens demanded particular qualities. What we wanted were corpses interred soon after death and without artificial preservation; preferably free from malforming disease, and certainly with all organs present. Accident victims were our best hope. Not for many weeks did we hear of anything suitable; though we talked with morgue and hospital authorities, ostensibly in the college's interest, as often as we could without

exciting suspicion. We found that the college had first choice in every case, so
that it might be necessary to remain in Arkham during the summer, when only
the limited summer-school classes were held. In the end, though, luck favored us;
for one day we heard of an almost ideal case in the potter's field; a brawny young
workman drowned only the morning before in Sumner's Pond, and buried at the
town's expense without delay or embalming. That afternoon we found the new
grave, and determined to begin work soon after midnight.

It was a repulsive task that we undertook in the black small hours, even
though we lacked at that time the special horror of graveyards which later experiences brought to us. We carried spades and oil dark lanterns, for although electric
torches were then manufactured, they were not as satisfactory as the tungsten
contrivances of today. The process of unearthing was slow and sordid—it might
have been gruesomely poetical if we had been artists instead of scientists—and
we were glad when our spades struck wood. When the pine box was fully uncov-
ered West scrambled down and removed the lid, dragging out and propping up the
contents. I reached down and hauled the contents out of the grave, and then both
toiled hard to restore the spot to its former appearance. The affair made us rather
nervous, especially the stiff form and vacant face of our first trophy, but we managed to remove all traces of our visit. When we had patted down the last shovelful
of earth we put the specimen in a canvas sack and set out for the old Chapman
place beyond Meadow Hill.

On an improvised dissecting-table in the old farmhouse, by the light of a
powerful acetylene lamp, the specimen was not very spectral looking. It had been
a sturdy and apparently unimaginative youth of wholesome plebeian type—large-
framed, grey-eyed, and brown-haired—a sound animal without psychological
subtleties, and probably having vital processes of the simplest and healthiest sort.
Now, with the eyes closed, it looked more asleep than dead; though the expert test
of my friend soon left no doubt on that score. We had at last what West had always
longed for—a real dead man of the ideal kind, ready for the solution as prepared
according to the most careful calculations and theories for human use. The tension on our part became very great. We knew that there was scarcely a chance for
anything like complete success, and could not avoid hideous fears at possible grotesque results of partial animation. Especially were we apprehensive concerning
the mind and impulses of the creature, since in the space following death some of
the more delicate cerebral cells might well have suffered deterioration. I, myself,
still held some curious notions about the traditional "soul" of man, and felt an
awe at the secrets that might be told by one returning from the dead. I wondered
what sights this placid youth might have seen in inaccessible spheres, and what he
could relate if fully restored to life. But my wonder was not overwhelming, since
for the most part I shared the materialism of my friend. He was calmer than I as
he forced a large quantity of his fluid into a vein of the body's arm, immediately
binding the incision securely.

The waiting was gruesome, but West never faltered. Every now and then
he applied his stethoscope to the specimen, and bore the negative results philo-

sophically. After about three-quarters of an hour without the least sign of life he disappointedly pronounced the solution inadequate, but determined to make the most of his opportunity and try one change in the formula before disposing of his ghastly prize. We had that afternoon dug a grave in the cellar, and would have to fill it by dawn—for although we had fixed a lock on the house we wished to shun even the remotest risk of a ghoulish discovery. Besides, the body would not be even approximately fresh the next night. So taking the solitary acetylene lamp into the adjacent laboratory, we left our silent guest on the slab in the dark, and bent every energy to the mixing of a new solution; the weighing and measuring supervised by West with an almost fanatical care.

The awful event was very sudden, and wholly unexpected. I was pouring something from one test-tube to another, and West was busy over the alcohol blast-lamp which had to answer for a Bunsen burner in this gasless edifice, when from the pitch-black room we had left there burst the most appalling and demoniac succession of cries that either of us had ever heard. Not more unutterable could have been the chaos of hellish sound if the pit itself had opened to release the agony of the damned, for in one inconceivable cacophony was centered all the supernal terror and unnatural despair of animate nature. Human it could not have been—it is not in man to make such sounds—and without a thought of our late employment or its possible discovery both West and I leaped to the nearest window like stricken animals; overturning tubes, lamp, and retorts, and vaulting madly into the starred abyss of the rural night. I think we screamed ourselves as we stumbled frantically toward the town, though as we reached the outskirts we put on a semblance of restraint—just enough to seem like belated revellers staggering home from a debauch.

We did not separate, but managed to get to West's room, where we whispered with the gas up until dawn. By then we had calmed ourselves a little with rational theories and plans for investigation, so that we could sleep through the day—classes being disregarded. But that evening two items in the paper, wholly unrelated, made it again impossible for us to sleep. The old deserted Chapman house had inexplicably burned to an amorphous heap of ashes; that we could understand because of the upset lamp. Also, an attempt had been made to disturb a new grave in the potter's field, as if by futile and spadeless clawing at the earth. That we could not understand, for we had patted down the mould very carefully.

And for seventeen years after that West would look frequently over his shoulder, and complain of fancied footsteps behind him. Now he has disappeared.

II. The Plague-Daemon

I shall never forget that hideous summer sixteen years ago, when like a noxious afrite from the halls of Eblis typhoid stalked leeringly through Arkham. It is by that satanic scourge that most recall the year, for truly terror brooded with batwings over the piles of coffins in the tombs of Christchurch Cemetery; yet for me there is a greater horror in that time—a horror known to me alone now that Herbert West has disappeared.

West and I were doing post-graduate work in summer classes at the medical school of Miskatonic University, and my friend had attained a wide notoriety because of his experiments leading toward the revivification of the dead. After the scientific slaughter of uncounted small animals the freakish work had ostensibly stopped by order of our sceptical dean, Dr. Allan Halsey; though West had continued to perform certain secret tests in his dingy boarding-house room, and had on one terrible and unforgettable occasion taken a human body from its grave in the potter's field to a deserted farmhouse beyond Meadow Hill.

I was with him on that odious occasion, and saw him inject into the still veins the elixir which he thought would to some extent restore life's chemical and physical processes. It had ended horribly—in a delirium of fear which we gradually came to attribute to our own overwrought nerves—and West had never afterward been able to shake off a maddening sensation of being haunted and hunted. The body had not been quite fresh enough; it is obvious that to restore normal mental attributes a body must be very fresh indeed; and a burning of the old house had prevented us from burying the thing. It would have been better if we could have known it was underground.

After that experience West had dropped his researches for some time; but as the zeal of the born scientist slowly returned, he again became importunate with the college faculty, pleading for the use of the dissecting-room and of fresh human specimens for the work he regarded as so overwhelmingly important. His pleas, however, were wholly in vain; for the decision of Dr. Halsey was inflexible, and the other professors all endorsed the verdict of their leader. In the radical theory of reanimation they saw nothing but the immature vagaries of a youthful enthusiast whose slight form, yellow hair, spectacled blue eyes, and soft voice gave no hint of the supernormal—almost diabolical—power of the cold brain within. I can see him now as he was then—and I shiver. He grew sterner of face, but never elderly. And now Sefton Asylum has had the mishap and West has vanished.

West clashed disagreeably with Dr. Halsey near the end of our last undergraduate term in a wordy dispute that did less credit to him than to the kindly dean in point of courtesy. He felt that he was needlessly and irrationally retarded in a supremely great work; a work which he could of course conduct to suit himself in later years, but which he wished to begin while still possessed of the exceptional facilities of the university. That the tradition-bound elders should ignore his singular results on animals, and persist in their denial of the possibility of reanimation, was inexpressibly disgusting and almost incomprehensible to a youth of West's logical temperament. Only greater maturity could help him understand the chronic mental limitations of the "professor-doctor" type—the product of generations of pathetic Puritanism; kindly, conscientious, and sometimes gentle and amiable, yet always narrow, intolerant, custom-ridden, and lacking in perspective. Age has more charity for these incomplete yet high-souled characters, whose worst real vice is timidity, and who are ultimately punished by general ridicule for their intellectual sins—sins like Ptolemaism, Calvinism, anti-Darwinism, anti-Nietzscheism, and every sort of Sabbatarianism and sumptuary legislation. West, young despite his marvellous scientific acquirements, had scant patience with good Dr. Halsey and his erudite colleagues; and nursed an increasing resentment, coupled with a desire to prove his theories to these obtuse worthies in some striking and dramatic fashion. Like most youths, he indulged in elaborate day-dreams of revenge, triumph, and final magnanimous forgiveness.

And then had come the scourge, grinning and lethal, from the nightmare caverns of Tartarus. West and I had graduated about the time of its beginning, but had remained for additional work at the summer school, so that we were in Arkham when it broke with full daemoniac fury upon the town. Though not as yet licensed physicians, we now had our degrees, and were pressed frantically into public service as the numbers of the stricken grew. The situation was almost past management, and deaths ensued too frequently for the local undertakers fully to handle. Burials without embalming were made in rapid succession, and even the Christchurch Cemetery receiving tomb was crammed with coffins of the un-embalmed dead. This circumstance was not without effect on West, who thought often of the irony of the situation—so many fresh specimens, yet none for his persecuted researches! We were frightfully overworked, and the terrific mental and nervous strain made my friend brood morbidly.

But West's gentle enemies were no less harassed with prostrating duties. College had all but closed, and every doctor of the medical faculty was helping to fight the typhoid plague. Dr. Halsey in particular had distinguished himself in sacrificing service, applying his extreme skill with whole-hearted energy to cases which many others shunned because of danger or apparent hopelessness. Before a month was over the fearless dean had become a popular hero, though he seemed unconscious of his fame as he struggled to keep from collapsing with physical fatigue and nervous exhaustion. West could not withhold admiration for the fortitude of his foe, but because of this was even more determined to prove to him the truth of his amazing doctrines. Taking advantage of the disorganization of both college work and municipal health regulations, he managed to get a recently deceased body smuggled into the university dissecting-room one night, and in my presence injected a new modification of his solution. The thing actually opened its eyes, but only stared at the ceiling with a look of soul-petrifying horror before collapsing into an inertness from which nothing could rouse it. West said it was not fresh enough—the hot summer air does not favor corpses. That time we were almost caught before we incinerated the thing, and West doubted the advisability of repeating his daring misuse of the college laboratory.

The peak of the epidemic was reached in August. West and I were almost dead, and Dr. Halsey did die on the 14th. The students all attended the hasty funeral on the 15th, and bought an impressive wreath, though the latter was quite overshadowed by the tributes sent by wealthy Arkham citizens and by the municipality itself. It was almost a public affair, for the dean had surely been a public benefactor. After the entombment we were all somewhat depressed, and spent the afternoon at the bar of the Commercial House; where West, though shaken by the death of his chief opponent, chilled the rest of us with references to his notorious theories. Most of the students went home, or to various duties, as the evening advanced; but West persuaded me to aid him in "making a night of it". West's landlady saw us arrive at his room about two in the morning, with a third man between us; and told her husband that we had all evidently dined and wined rather well.

Apparently this acidulous matron was right; for about 3:00 a.m. the whole house was aroused by cries coming from West's room, where when they broke down the door they found the two of us unconscious on the blood-stained carpet, beaten, scratched, and mauled, and with the broken remnants of West's bottles and instruments around us. Only an open window told what had become of our assailant, and many wondered how he himself had fared after the terrific leap from the second story to the lawn which he must have made. There were some strange garments in the room, but West upon regaining consciousness said they did not belong to the stranger, but were specimens collected for bacteriological analysis in the course of investigations on the transmission of germ diseases. He ordered them burnt as soon as possible in the capacious fireplace. To the police we both declared ignorance of our late companion's identity. He was, West nervously said, a congenial stranger whom we had met at some downtown bar of uncertain location. We had all been rather jovial, and West and I did not wish to have our pugnacious companion hunted down.

That same night saw the beginning of the second Arkham horror—the horror that to me eclipsed the plague itself. Christchurch Cemetery was the scene of a terrible killing; a watchman having been clawed to death in a manner not only too hideous for description, but raising a doubt as to the human agency of the deed. The victim had been seen alive considerably after midnight—the dawn revealed the unutterable thing. The manager of a circus at the neighboring town of Bolton was questioned, but he swore that no beast had at any time escaped from its cage. Those who found the body noted a trail of blood leading to the receiving tomb, where a small pool of red lay on the concrete just outside the gate. A fainter trail led away toward the woods, but it soon gave out.

The next night devils danced on the roofs of Arkham, and unnatural madness howled in the wind. Through the fevered town had crept a curse which some said was greater than the plague, and which some whispered was the embodied daemon-soul of the plague itself. Eight houses were entered by a nameless thing which strewed red death in its wake—in all, seventeen maimed and shapeless remnants of bodies were left behind by the voiceless, sadistic monster that crept abroad. A few persons had half seen it in the dark, and said it was white and like a malformed ape or anthropomorphic fiend. It had not left behind quite all that it had attacked, for sometimes it had been hungry. The number it had killed was fourteen; three of the bodies had been in stricken homes and had not been alive.

On the third night frantic bands of searchers, led by the police, captured it in a house on Crane Street near the Miskatonic campus. They had organized the quest with care, keeping in touch by means of volunteer telephone stations, and when someone in the college district had reported hearing a scratching at a shuttered window, the net was quickly spread. On account of the general alarm and precautions, there were only two more victims, and the capture was effected without major casualties. The thing was finally stopped by a bullet, though not a fatal one, and was rushed to the local hospital amidst universal excitement and loathing.

For it had been a man. This much was clear despite the nauseous eyes, the voiceless simianism, and the demoniac savagery. They dressed its wound and carted it to the asylum at Sefton, where it beat its head against the walls of a padded cell for sixteen years—until the recent mishap, when it escaped under circumstances that few like to mention. What had most disgusted the searchers of Arkham was the thing they noticed when the monster's face was cleaned—the mocking, unbelievable resemblance to a learned and self-sacrificing martyr who had been entombed but three days before—the late Dr. Allan Halsey, public bene-factor and dean of the medical school of Miskatonic University.

To the vanished Herbert West and to me the disgust and horror were supreme. I shudder tonight as I think of it; shudder even more than I did that morning when West muttered through his bandages,

"Damn it, it wasn't quite fresh enough!"

III. Six Shots by Midnight
It is uncommon to fire all six shots of a revolver with great suddenness when one would probably be sufficient, but many things in the life of Herbert West were uncommon. It is, for instance, not often that a young physician leaving college is obliged to conceal the principles which guide his selection of a home and office, yet that was the case with Herbert West. When he and I obtained our degrees at the medical school of Miskatonic University, and sought to relieve our poverty by setting up as general practitioners, we took great care not to say that we chose our house because it was fairly well isolated, and as near as possible to the potter's field.

Reticence such as this is seldom without a cause, nor indeed was ours; for our requirements were those resulting from a life-work distinctly unpopular. Out-wardly we were doctors only, but beneath the surface were aims of far greater and more terrible moment—for the essence of Herbert West's existence was a quest amid black and forbidden realms of the unknown, in which he hoped to uncover the secret of life and restore to perpetual animation the graveyard's cold clay. Such a quest demands strange materials, among them fresh human bodies; and in order to keep supplied with these indispensable things one must live quietly and not far from a place of informal interment.

West and I had met in college, and I had been the only one to sympathise with his hideous experiments. Gradually I had come to be his inseparable assistant, and now that we were out of college we had to keep together. It was not easy to find a good opening for two doctors in company, but finally the influence of the university secured us a practice in Bolton—a factory town near Arkham, the seat of the col-lege. The Bolton Worsted Mills are the largest in the Miskatonic Valley, and their polyglot employees are never popular as patients with the local physicians. We chose our house with the greatest care, seizing at last on a rather run-down cottage near the end of Pond Street; five numbers from the closest neighbor, and separated from the local potter's field by only a stretch of meadow land, bisected by a narrow neck of the rather dense forest which lies to the north. The distance was greater than we wished, but we could get no nearer house without going on the other side of the field, wholly out of the factory district. We were not much displeased, however, since there were no people between us and our sinister source of supplies. The walk was a trifle long, but we could haul our silent specimens undisturbed.

Our practice was surprisingly large from the very first—large enough to please most young doctors, and large enough to prove a bore and a burden to students whose real interest lay elsewhere. The mill-hands were of somewhat turbulent inclinations; and besides their many natural needs, their frequent clashes and stabbing affrays gave us plenty to do. But what actually absorbed our minds was the secret laboratory we had fitted up in the cellar—the laboratory with the long table under the electric lights, where in the small hours of the morning we often injected West's various solutions into the veins of the things we dragged from the potter's field. West was experimenting madly to find something which would start man's vital motions anew after they had been stopped by the thing we call death, but had encountered the most ghastly obstacles. The solution had to be differently compounded for different types—what would serve for guinea-pigs would not serve for human beings, and different human specimens required large modifications.

The bodies had to be exceedingly fresh, or the slight decomposition of brain tissue would render perfect reanimation impossible. Indeed, the greatest problem was to get them fresh enough—West had had horrible experiences during his secret college researches with corpses of doubtful vintage. The results of partial or imperfect animation were much more hideous than were the total failures, and we both held fearsome recollections of such things. Ever since our first demoniac session in the deserted farmhouse on Meadow Hill in Arkham, we had felt a brooding menace; and West, though a calm, blond, blue-eyed scientific automaton in most respects, often confessed to a shuddering sensation of stealthy pursuit. He half felt that he was followed—a psychological delusion of shaken nerves, enhanced by the undeniably disturbing fact that at least one of our reanimated specimens was still alive—a frightful carnivorous thing in a padded cell at Sefton. Then there was another—our first—whose exact fate we had never learned.

We had fair luck with specimens in Bolton—much better than in Arkham. We had not been settled a week before we got an accident victim on the very night of burial, and made it open its eyes with an amazingly rational expression before the solution failed. It had lost an arm—if it had been a perfect body we might have succeeded better. Between then and the next January we secured three more; one total failure, one case of marked muscular motion, and one rather shivery thing—it rose of itself and uttered a sound. Then came a period when luck was poor; interments fell off, and those that did occur were of specimens either too diseased or too maimed for use. We kept track of all the deaths and their circumstances with systematic care.

One March night, however, we unexpectedly obtained a specimen which did not come from the potter's field. In Bolton the prevailing spirit of Puritanism had outlawed the sport of boxing—with the usual result. Surreptitious and ill-conducted bouts among the mill-workers were common, and occasionally professional talent of low grade was imported. This late winter night there had been such a match; evidently with disastrous results, since two timorous Poles had come to us with incoherently whispered entreaties to attend to a very secret and desperate case. We followed them to an abandoned barn, where the remnants of a crowd of frightened foreigners were watching a silent black form on the floor.

The match had been between Kid O'Brien—a lubberly and now quaking youth with a most un-Hibernian hooked nose—and Buck Robinson, "The Harlem Smoke." The Negro had been knocked out, and a moment's examination shewed us that he would permanently remain so. He was a loathsome, gorilla-like thing, with abnormally long arms which I could not help calling fore legs, and a face that conjured up thoughts of unspeakable Congo secrets and tom-tom poundings under an eerie moon. The body must have looked even worse in life—but the world holds many ugly things. Fear was upon the whole pitiful crowd, for they did not know what the law would exact of them if the affair were not hushed up; and they were grateful when West, in spite of my involuntary shudders, offered to get rid of the thing quietly—for a purpose I knew too well.

There was bright moonlight over the snowless landscape, but we dressed the thing and carried it home between us through the deserted streets and meadows, as we had carried a similar thing one horrible night in Arkham. We approached the house from the field in the rear, took the specimen in the back door and down the cellar stairs, and prepared it for the usual experiment. Our fear of the police was absurdly great, though we had timed our trip to avoid the solitary patrolman of that section.

The result was wearily anticlimactic. Ghastly as our prize appeared, it was wholly unresponsive to every solution we injected in its black arm; solutions prepared from experience with white specimens only. So as the hour grew dangerously near to dawn, we did as we had done with the others—dragged the thing across the meadows to the neck of the woods near the potter's field, and buried it there in the best sort of grave the frozen ground would furnish. The grave was not very deep, but fully as good as that of the previous specimen—the thing which had risen of itself and uttered a sound. In the light of our dark lanterns we carefully covered it with leaves and dead vines, fairly certain that the police would never find it in a forest so dim and dense.

The next day I was increasingly apprehensive about the police, for a patient brought rumors of a suspected fight and death. West had still another source of worry, for he had been called in the afternoon to a case which ended very threateningly. An Italian woman had become hysterical over her missing child—a lad of five who had strayed off early in the morning and failed to appear for dinner—and had developed symptoms highly alarming in view of an always weak heart. It was a very foolish hysteria, for the boy had often run away before; but Italian peasants are exceedingly superstitious, and this woman seemed as much harassed by omens as by facts. About seven o'clock in the evening she had died, and her frantic husband had made a frightful scene in his efforts to kill West, whom he wildly blamed for not saving her life. Friends had held him when he drew a stiletto, but West departed amidst his inhuman shrieks, curses, and oaths of vengeance. In his latest affliction the fellow seemed to have forgotten his child, who was still missing as the night advanced. There was some talk of searching the woods, but most of the family's friends were busy with the dead woman and the screaming man. Altogether, the nervous strain upon West must have been tremendous. Thoughts of the police and of the mad Italian both weighed heavily.

We retired about eleven, but I did not sleep well. Bolton had a surprisingly good police force for so small a town, and I could not help fearing the mess which would ensue if the affair of the night before were ever tracked down. It might mean the end of all our local work—and perhaps prison for both West and me. I did not like those rumors of a fight which were floating about. After the clock had struck three the moon shone in my eyes, but I turned over without rising to pull down the shade. Then came the steady rattling at the back door.

I lay still and somewhat dazed, but before long heard West's rap on my door. He was clad in dressing-gown and slippers, and had in his hands a revolver and an electric flashlight. From the revolver I knew that he was thinking more of the crazed Italian than of the police.

"We'd better both go," he whispered. "It wouldn't do not to answer it anyway, and it may be a patient—it would be like one of those fools to try the back door."

So we both went down the stairs on tiptoe, with a fear partly justified and partly that which comes only from the soul of the weird small hours. The rattling continued, growing somewhat louder. When we reached the door I cautiously unbolted it and threw it open, and as the moon streamed revealingly down on the form silhouetted there, West did a peculiar thing. Despite the obvious danger of attracting notice and bringing down on our heads the dreaded police investigation—a thing which after all was mercifully averted by the relative isolation of our cottage—my friend suddenly, excitedly, and unnecessarily emptied all six chambers of his revolver into the nocturnal visitor.

For that visitor was neither Italian nor policeman. Looming hideously against the spectral moon was a gigantic misshapen thing not to be imagined save in nightmares—a glassy-eyed, ink-black apparition nearly on all fours, covered with bits of mould, leaves, and vines, foul with caked blood, and having between its glistening teeth a snow-white, terrible, cylindrical object terminating in a tiny hand.

IV. The Scream of the Dead

The scream of a dead man gave to me that acute and added horror of Dr. Herbert West which harassed the latter years of our companionship. It is natural that such a thing as a dead man's scream should give horror, for it is obviously not a pleasing or ordinary occurrence; but I was used to similar experiences, hence suffered on this occasion only because of a particular circumstance. And, as I have implied, it was not of the dead man himself that I became afraid.

Herbert West, whose associate and assistant I was, possessed scientific interests far beyond the usual routine of a village physician. That was why, when establishing his practice in Bolton, he had chosen an isolated house near the potter's field. Briefly and brutally stated, West's sole absorbing interest was a secret study of the phenomena of life and its cessation, leading toward the reanimation of the dead through injections of an excitant solution. For this ghastly experimenting it was necessary to have a constant supply of very fresh human bodies; very fresh because even the least decay hopelessly damaged the brain structure, and human because we found that the solution had to be compounded differently for different types of organisms. Scores of rabbits and guinea-pigs had been killed and treated, but their trail was a blind one. West had never fully succeeded because he had never been able to secure a corpse sufficiently fresh. What he wanted were bodies from which vitality had only just departed; bodies with every cell intact and capable of receiving again the impulse toward that mode of motion called life. There was hope that this second and artificial life might be made perpetual by repetitions of the injection, but we had learned that an ordinary natural life would not respond to the action. To establish the artificial motion, natural life must be extinct—the specimens must be very fresh, but genuinely dead.

The awesome quest had begun when West and I were students at the Miskatonic University Medical School in Arkham, vividly conscious for the first time of the thoroughly mechanical nature of life. That was seven years before, but West looked scarcely a day older now—he was small, blond, clean-shaven, soft-voiced, and spectacled, with only an occasional flash of a cold blue eye to tell of the hardening and growing fanaticism of his character under the pressure of his terrible investigations. Our experiences had often been hideous in the extreme; the results of defective reanimation, when lumps of graveyard clay had been galvanished into morbid, unnatural, and brainless motion by various modifications of the vital solution.

One thing had uttered a nerve-shattering scream; another had risen violently, beaten us both to unconsciousness, and run amuck in a shocking way before it could be placed behind asylum bars; still another, a loathsome African monstrosity, had clawed out of its shallow grave and done a deed—West had had to shoot that object. We could not get bodies fresh enough to shew any trace of reason when reanimated, so had perforce created nameless horrors. It was disturbing to think that one, perhaps two, of our monsters still lived—that thought haunted us shadowingly, till finally West disappeared under frightful circumstances. But at the time of the scream in the cellar laboratory of the isolated Bolton cottage, our fears were subordinate to our anxiety for extremely fresh specimens. West was more avid than I, so that it almost seemed to me that he looked half-covetously at any very healthy living physique.

It was in July 1910, that the bad luck regarding specimens began to turn. I had been on a long visit to my parents in Illinois, and upon my return found West in a state of singular elation. He had, he told me excitedly, in all likelihood solved the problem of freshness through an approach from an entirely new angle—that of artificial preservation. I had known that he was working on a new and highly unusual embalming compound, and was not surprised that it had turned out well; but until he explained the details I was rather puzzled as to how such a compound could help in our work, since the objectionable staleness of the specimens was largely due to delay occurring before we secured them. This, I now saw, West had clearly recognized; creating his embalming compound for future rather than immediate use, and trusting to fate to supply again some very recent and unburied corpse, as it had years before when we obtained the Negro killed in the Bolton prize-fight. At last fate had been kind, so that on this occasion there lay in the secret cellar laboratory a corpse whose decay could not by any possibility have begun. What would happen on reanimation, and whether we could hope for a revival of mind and reason, West did not venture to predict. The experiment would be a landmark in our studies, and he had saved the new body for my return, so that both might share the spectacle in accustomed fashion.

West told me how he had obtained the specimen. It had been a vigorous man; a well-dressed stranger just off the train on his way to transact some business with the Bolton Worsted Mills. The walk through the town had been long, and by the time the traveller paused at our cottage to ask the way to the factories his heart had become greatly overtaxed. He had refused a stimulant, and had suddenly dropped dead only a moment later. The body, as might be expected, seemed to West a heaven-sent gift. In his brief conversation the stranger had made it clear that he was unknown in Bolton, and a search of his pockets subsequently revealed him to be one Robert Leavitt of St. Louis, apparently without a family to make instant inquiries about his disappearance. If this man could not be restored to life, no one would know of our experiment. We buried our materials in a dense strip of woods between the house and the potter's field. If, on the other hand, he could be restored, our fame would be brilliantly and perpetually established. So without delay West had injected into the body's wrist the compound which would hold it fresh for use after my arrival. The matter of the presumably weak heart, which to my mind imperiled the success of our experiment, did not appear to trouble West extensively. He hoped at last to obtain what he had never obtained before—a rekindled spark of reason and perhaps a normal, living creature.

So on the night of July 18, 1910, Herbert West and I stood in the cellar laboratory and gazed at a white, silent figure beneath the dazzling arc-light. The embalming compound had worked uncannily well, for as I stared fascinatedly at the sturdy frame which had lain two weeks without stiffening I was moved to seek West's assurance that the thing was really dead. This assurance he gave readily enough; reminding me that the reanimating solution was never used without careful tests as to life; since it could have no effect if any of the original vitality were present. As West proceeded to take preliminary steps, I was impressed by the vast intricacy of the new experiment; an intricacy so vast that he could trust no hand less delicate than his own. Forbidding me to touch the body, he first injected a drug in the wrist just beside the place his needle had punctured when injecting the embalming compound. This, he said, was to neutralize the compound and release the system to a normal relaxation so that the reanimating solution might freely work when injected. Slightly later, when a change and a gentle tremor seemed to affect the dead limbs, West stuffed a pillow-like object violently over the twitching face, not withdrawing it until the corpse appeared quiet and ready for our attempt at reanimation. The pale enthusiast now applied some last perfunctory tests for absolute lifelessness, withdrew satisfied, and finally injected into the left arm an accurately measured amount of the vital elixir, prepared during the afternoon with a greater care than we had used since college days, when our feats were new and groping. I cannot express the wild, breathless suspense with which we waited for results on this first really fresh specimen—the first we could reasonably expect to open its lips in rational speech, perhaps to tell of what it had seen beyond the unfathomable abyss.

West was a materialist, believing in no soul and attributing all the working of consciousness to bodily phenomena; consequently he looked for no revelation of hideous secrets from gulfs and caverns beyond death's barrier. I did not wholly disagree with him theoretically, yet held vague instinctive remnants of the primitive faith of my forefathers; so that I could not help eyeing the corpse with a certain amount of awe and terrible expectation. Besides—I could not extract from my memory that hideous, inhuman shriek we heard on the night we tried our first experiment in the deserted farmhouse at Arkham.

Very little time had elapsed before I saw the attempt was not to be a total failure. A touch of color came to cheeks hitherto chalk-white, and spread out under the curiously ample stubble of sandy beard. West, who had his hand on the pulse of the left wrist, suddenly nodded significantly; and almost simultaneously a mist appeared on the mirror inclined above the body's mouth. There followed a few spasmodic muscular motions, and then an audible breathing and visible motion of the chest. I looked at the closed eyelids, and thought I detected a quivering. Then the lids opened, shewing eyes which were grey, calm, and alive, but still unintelligent and not even curious.

In a moment of fantastic whim I whispered questions to the reddening ears; questions of other worlds of which the memory might still be present. Subsequent terror drove them from my mind, but I think the last one, which I repeated, was: "Where have you been?" I do not yet know whether I was answered or not, for no sound came from the well-shaped mouth; but I do know that at that moment I firmly thought the thin lips moved silently, forming syllables I would have vocalized as "only now" if that phrase had possessed any sense or relevancy. At that moment, as I say, I was elated with the conviction that the one great goal had been attained; and that for the first time a reanimated corpse had uttered distinct words impelled by actual reason. In the next moment there was no doubt about the triumph; no doubt that the solution had truly accomplished, at least temporarily, its full mission of restoring rational and articulate life to the dead. But in that triumph there came to me the greatest of all horrors—not horror of the thing that spoke, but of the deed that I had witnessed and of the man with whom my professional fortunes were joined.

For that very fresh body, at last writhing into full and terrifying consciousness with eyes dilated at the memory of its last scene on earth, threw out its frantic hands in a life and death struggle with the air; and suddenly collapsing into a second and final dissolution from which there could be no return, screamed out the cry that will ring eternally in my aching brain:

"Help! Keep off, you cursed little tow-head fiend—keep that damned needle away from me!"

V. The Horror from the Shadows

Many men have related hideous things, not mentioned in print, which happened on the battlefields of the Great War. Some of these things have made me faint, others have convulsed me with devastating nausea, while still others have made me tremble and look behind me in the dark; yet despite the worst of them I believe I can myself relate the most hideous thing of all—the shocking, the unnatural, the unbelievable horror from the shadows.

In 1915 I was a physician with the rank of First Lieutenant in a Canadian regiment in Flanders, one of many Americans to precede the government itself into the gigantic struggle. I had not entered the army on my own initiative, but rather as a natural result of the enlistment of the man whose indispensable assistant I was—the celebrated Boston surgical specialist, Dr. Herbert West. Dr. West had been avid for a chance to serve as surgeon in a great war, and when the chance had come he carried me with him almost against my will. There were reasons why I would have been glad to let the war separate us; reasons why I found the practice of medicine and the companionship of West more and more irritating; but when he had gone to Ottawa and through a colleague's influence secured a medical commission as Major, I could not resist the imperious persuasion of one determined that I should accompany him in my usual capacity.

When I say that Dr. West was avid to serve in battle, I do not mean to imply that he was either naturally warlike or anxious for the safety of civilization. Always an ice-cold intellectual machine; slight, blond, blue-eyed, and spectacled; I think he secretly sneered at my occasional martial enthusiasms and censures of supine neutrality. There was, however, something he wanted in embattled Flanders; and in order to secure it he had to assume a military exterior. What he wanted was not a thing which many persons want, but something connected with the peculiar branch of medical science which he had chosen quite clandestinely to follow, and in which he had achieved amazing and occasionally hideous results. It was, in fact, nothing more or less than an abundant supply of freshly killed men in every stage of dismemberment.

Herbert West needed fresh bodies because his life-work was the reanimation of the dead. This work was not known to the fashionable clientele who had so swiftly built up his fame after his arrival in Boston; but was only too well known to me, who had been his closest friend and sole assistant since the old days in Miskatonic University Medical School at Arkham. It was in those college days that he had begun his terrible experiments, first on small animals and then on human bodies shockingly obtained. There was a solution which he injected into the veins of dead things, and if they were fresh enough they responded in strange ways. He had had much trouble in discovering the proper formula, for each type of organism was found to need a stimulus especially adapted to it. Terror stalked him when he reflected on his partial failures; nameless things resulting from imperfect solutions or from bodies insufficiently fresh. A certain number of these failures had remained alive—one was in an asylum while others had vanished—and as he thought of conceivable yet virtually impossible eventualities he often shivered beneath his usual stolidity.

West had soon learned that absolute freshness was the prime requisite for useful specimens, and had accordingly resorted to frightful and unnatural expedients in body-snatching. In college, and during our early practice together in the factory town of Bolton, my attitude toward him had been largely one of fascinated admiration; but as his boldness in methods grew, I began to develop a gnawing fear. I did not like the way he looked at healthy living bodies; and then there came a nightmarish session in the cellar laboratory when I learned that a certain specimen had been a living body when he secured it. That was the first time he had ever been able to revive the quality of rational thought in a corpse; and his success, obtained at such a loathsome cost, had completely hardened him.

Of his methods in the intervening five years I dare not speak. I was held to him by sheer force of fear, and witnessed sights that no human tongue could repeat. Gradually I came to find Herbert West himself more horrible than anything he did—that was when it dawned on me that his once normal scientific zeal for prolonging life had subtly degenerated into a mere morbid and ghoulish curiosity and secret sense of charnel picturesqueness. His interest became a hellish and perverse addiction to the repellently and fiendishly abnormal; he gloated calmly over artificial monstrosities which would make most healthy men drop dead from fright and disgust; he became, behind his pallid intellectuality, a fastidious Baudelaire of physical experiment—a languid Elagabalus of the tombs.

Dangers he met unflinchingly; crimes he committed unmoved. I think the climax came when he had proved his point that rational life can be restored, and had sought new worlds to conquer by experimenting on the reanimation of detached parts of bodies. He had wild and original ideas on the independent vital properties of organic cells and nerve-tissue separated from natural physiological systems; and achieved some hideous preliminary results in the form of never-dying, artificially nourished tissue obtained from the nearly hatched eggs of an indescribable tropical reptile. Two biological points he was exceedingly anxious to settle—first, whether any amount of consciousness and rational action be possible without the brain, proceeding from the spinal cord and various nerve-centres; and second, whether any kind of ethereal, intangible relation distinct from the material cells may exist to link the surgically separated parts of what has previously been a single living organism. All this research work required a prodigious supply of freshly slaughtered human flesh—and that was why Herbert West had entered the Great War.

The phantasmal, unmentionable thing occurred one midnight late in March 1915, in a field hospital behind the lines at St. Eloi. I wonder even now if it could have been other than a demoniac dream of delirium. West had a private laboratory in an east room of the barn-like temporary edifice, assigned him on his plea that he was devising new and radical methods for the treatment of hitherto hopeless cases of maiming. There he worked like a butcher in the midst of his gory wares—I could never get used to the levity with which he handled and classified certain things. At times he actually did perform marvels of surgery for the soldiers; but his chief delights were of a less public and philanthropic kind, requiring many explanations of sounds which seemed peculiar even amidst that babel of the damned. Among these sounds were frequent revolver-shots—surely not uncommon on a battlefield, but distinctly uncommon in an hospital. Dr. West's reanimated specimens were not meant for long existence or a large audience. Besides human tissue, West employed much of the reptile embryo tissue which he had cultivated with such singular results. It was better than human material for maintaining life in organless fragments, and that was now my friend's chief activity. In a dark corner of the laboratory, over a queer incubating burner, he kept a large covered vat full of this reptilian cell-matter; which multiplied and grew puffily and hideously.

On the night of which I speak we had a splendid new specimen—a man at once physically powerful and of such high mentality that a sensitive nervous system was assured. It was rather ironic, for he was the officer who had helped West to his commission, and who was now to have been our associate. Moreover, he had in the past secretly studied the theory of reanimation to some extent under West. Major Sir Eric Moreland Clapham-Lee, D.S.O., was the greatest surgeon in our division, and had been hastily assigned to the St. Eloi sector when news of the heavy fighting reached headquarters. He had come in an aëroplane piloted by the intrepid Lieut. Ronald Hill, only to be shot down when directly over his destination. The fall had been spectacular and awful; Hill was unrecognizable afterward, but the wreck yielded up the great surgeon in a nearly decapitated but otherwise intact condition. West had greedily seized the lifeless thing which had once been his friend and fellow-scholar; and I shuddered when he finished severing the head, placed it in his hellish vat of pulpy reptile-tissue to preserve it for future experiments, and proceeded to treat the decapitated body on the operating table. He injected new blood, joined certain veins, arteries, and nerves at the headless neck, and closed the ghastly aperture with engrafted skin from an unidentified specimen which had borne an officer's uniform. I knew what he wanted—to see if this highly organized body could exhibit, without its head, any of the signs of mental life which had distinguished Sir Eric Moreland Clapham-Lee. Once a student of reanimation, this silent trunk was now gruesomely called upon to exemplify it.

I can still see Herbert West under the sinister electric light as he injected his reanimating solution into the arm of the headless body. The scene I cannot describe—I should faint if I tried it, for there is madness in a room full of classified charnel things, with blood and lesser human debris almost ankle-deep on the slimy floor, and with hideous reptilian abnormalities sprouting, bubbling, and baking over a winking bluish-green spectre of dim flame in a far corner of black shadows.

The specimen, as West repeatedly observed, had a splendid nervous system. Much was expected of it; and as a few twitching motions began to appear, I could see the feverish interest on West's face. He was ready, I think, to see proof of his increasingly strong opinion that consciousness, reason, and personality can exist independently of the brain—that man has no central connective spirit, but is merely a machine of nervous matter, each section more or less complete in itself. In one triumphant demonstration West was about to relegate the mystery of life to the category of myth. The body now twitched more vigorously, and beneath our avid eyes commenced to heave in a frightful way. The arms stirred disquietingly, the legs drew up, and various muscles contracted in a repulsive kind of writhing. Then the headless thing threw out its arms in a gesture which was unmistakably one of desperation—an intelligent desperation apparently sufficient to prove every theory of Herbert West. Certainly, the nerves were recalling the man's last act in life; the struggle to get free of the falling aëroplane.

What followed, I shall never positively know. It may have been wholly an hallucination from the shock caused at that instant by the sudden and complete destruction of the building in a cataclysm of German shell-fire—who can gainsay it, since West and I were the only proved survivors? West liked to think that before his recent disappearance, but there were times when he could not; for it was queer that we both had the same hallucination. The hideous occurrence itself was very simple, notable only for what it implied.

The body on the table had risen with a blind and terrible groping, and we had heard a sound. I should not call that sound a voice, for it was too awful. And yet its timbre was not the most awful thing about it. Neither was its message—it had merely screamed, "Jump, Ronald, for God's sake, jump!" The awful thing was its source.

For it had come from the large covered vat in that ghoulish corner of crawling black shadows.

VI. The Tomb-Legions

When Dr. Herbert West disappeared a year ago, the Boston police questioned me closely. They suspected that I was holding something back, and perhaps suspected graver things; but I could not tell them the truth because they would not have believed it. They knew, indeed, that West had been connected with activities beyond the credence of ordinary men; for his hideous experiments in the reanimation of dead bodies had long been too extensive to admit of perfect secrecy; but the final soul-shattering catastrophe held elements of demoniac phantasy which make even me doubt the reality of what I saw.

I was West's closest friend and only confidential assistant. We had met years before, in medical school, and from the first I had shared his terrible researches. He had slowly tried to perfect a solution which, injected into the veins of the newly deceased, would restore life; a labor demanding an abundance of fresh corpses and therefore involving the most unnatural actions. Still more shocking were the products of some of the experiments—grisly masses of flesh that had been dead, but that West waked to a blind, brainless, nauseous animation. These were the usual results, for in order to reawaken the mind it was necessary to have specimens so absolutely fresh that no decay could possibly affect the delicate brain-cells.

This need for very fresh corpses had been West's moral undoing. They were hard to get, and one awful day he had secured his specimen while it was still alive and vigorous. A struggle, a needle, and a powerful alkaloid had transformed it to a very fresh corpse, and the experiment had succeeded for a brief and memorable moment; but West had emerged with a soul calloused and seared, and a hardened eye which sometimes glanced with a kind of hideous and calculating appraisal at men of especially sensitive brain and especially vigorous physique. Toward the last I became acutely afraid of West, for he began to look at me that way. People did not seem to notice his glances, but they noticed my fear; and after his disappearance used that as a basis for some absurd suspicions.

West, in reality, was more afraid than I; for his abominable pursuits entailed a life of furtiveness and dread of every shadow. Partly it was the police he feared; but sometimes his nervousness was deeper and more nebulous, touching on certain indescribable things into which he had injected a morbid life, and from which he had not seen that life depart. He usually finished his experiments with a revolver, but a few times he had not been quick enough. There was that first specimen on whose rifled grave marks of clawing were later seen. There was also that Arkham professor's body which had done cannibal things before it had been captured and thrust unidentified into a madhouse cell at Sefton, where it beat the walls for sixteen years. Most of the other possibly surviving results were things less easy to speak of—for in later years West's scientific zeal had degenerated to an unhealthy and fantastic mania, and he had spent his chief skill in vitalizing not entire human bodies but isolated parts of bodies, or parts joined to organic matter other than human. It had become fiendishly disgusting by the time he disappeared; many of the experiments could not even be hinted at in print. The Great War, through which both of us served as surgeons, had intensified this side of West.

In saying that West's fear of his specimens was nebulous, I have in mind particularly its complex nature. Part of it came merely from knowing of the existence of such nameless monsters, while another part arose from apprehension of the bodily harm they might under certain circumstances do him. Their disappearance added horror to the situation—of them all West knew the whereabouts of only one, the pitiful asylum thing. Then there was a more subtle fear—a very fantastic sensation resulting from a curious experiment in the Canadian army in 1915. West, in the midst of a severe battle, had reanimated Major Sir Eric Moreland Clapham-Lee, D.S.O., a fellow-physician who knew about his experiments and could have duplicated them. The head had been removed, so that the possibilities of quasi-intelligent life in the trunk might be investigated. Just as the building was wiped out by a German shell, there had been a success. The trunk had moved intelligently; and, unbelievable to relate, we were both sickeningly sure that articulate sounds had come from the detached head as it lay in a shadowy corner of the laboratory. The shell had been merciful, in a way—but West could never feel as certain as he wished, that we two were the only survivors. He used to make shuddering conjectures about the possible actions of a headless physician with the power of reanimating the dead.

West's last quarters were in a venerable house of much elegance, overlooking one of the oldest burying-grounds in Boston. He had chosen the place for purely symbolic and fantastically aesthetic reasons, since most of the interments were of the colonial period and therefore of little use to a scientist seeking very fresh bodies. The laboratory was in a sub-cellar secretly constructed by imported workmen, and contained a huge incinerator for the quiet and complete disposal of such bodies, or fragments and synthetic mockeries of bodies, as might remain from the morbid experiments and unhallowed amusements of the owner. During the excavation of this cellar the workmen had struck some exceedingly ancient masonry; undoubtedly connected with the old burying-ground, yet far too deep to correspond with any known sepulchre therein. After a number of calculations West decided that it represented some secret chamber beneath the tomb of the Averills, where the last interment had been made in 1768. I was with him when he studied the nitrous, dripping walls laid bare by the spades and mattocks of the men, and was prepared for the gruesome thrill which would attend the uncovering of centuried grave-secrets; but for the first time West's new timidity conquered his natural curiosity, and he betrayed his degenerating fiber by ordering the masonry left intact and plastered over. Thus it remained till that final hellish night; part of the walls of the secret laboratory. I speak of West's decadence, but must add that it was a purely mental and intangible thing. Outwardly he was the same to the last—calm, cold, slight, and yellow-haired, with spectacled blue eyes and a general aspect of youth which years and fears seemed never to change. He seemed calm even when he thought of that clawed grave and looked over his shoulder; even when he thought of the carnivorous thing that gnawed and pawed at Sefton bars.

The end of Herbert West began one evening in our joint study when he was dividing his curious glance between the newspaper and me. A strange headline item had struck at him from the crumpled pages, and a nameless titan claw had seemed to reach down through sixteen years. Something fearsome and incredible had happened at Sefton Asylum fifty miles away, stunning the neighborhood and baffling the police. In the small hours of the morning a body of silent men had entered the grounds and their leader had aroused the attendants. He was a menacing military figure who talked without moving his lips and whose voice seemed almost ventriloquially connected with an immense black case he carried. His expressionless face was handsome to the point of radiant beauty, but had shocked the superintendent when the hall light fell on it—for it was a wax face with eyes

118

WINDY CITY PULP STORIES

of painted glass. Some nameless accident had befallen this man. A larger man guided his steps; a repellent hulk whose bluish face seemed half eaten away by some unknown malady. The speaker had asked for the custody of the cannibal monster committed from Arkham sixteen years before; and upon being refused, gave a signal which precipitated a shocking riot. The fiends had beaten, trampled, and bitten every attendant who did not flee; killing four and finally succeeding in the liberation of the monster. Those victims who could recall the event without hysteria swore that the creatures had acted less like men than like unthinkable automata guided by the wax-faced leader. By the time help could be summoned, every trace of the men and of their mad charge had vanished.

From the hour of reading this item until midnight, West sat almost paralysed. At midnight the doorbell rang, startling him fearfully. All the servants were asleep in the attic, so I answered the bell. As I have told the police, there was no wagon in the street; but only a group of strange-looking figures bearing a large square box which they deposited in the hallway after one of them had grunted in a highly unnatural voice, "Express—prepaid." They filed out of the house with a jerky tread, and as I watched them go I had an odd idea that they were turning toward the ancient cemetery on which the back of the house abutted. When I slammed the door after them West came downstairs and looked at the box. It was about two feet square, and bore West's correct name and present address. It also bore the inscription, *"From Eric Moreland Clapham-Lee, St. Eloi, Flanders."* Six years before, in Flanders, a shelled hospital had fallen upon the headless reanimated trunk of Dr. Clapham-Lee, and upon the detached head which—perhaps—had uttered articulate sounds.

West was not even excited now. His condition was more ghastly. Quickly he said, "It's the finish—but let's incinerate—this." We carried the thing down to the laboratory—listening. I do not remember many particulars—you can imagine my state of mind—but it is a vicious lie to say it was Herbert West's body which I put into the incinerator. We both inserted the whole unopened wooden box, closed the door, and started the electricity. Nor did any sound come from the box, after all.

It was West who first noticed the falling plaster on that part of the wall where the ancient tomb masonry had been covered up. I was going to run, but he stopped me. Then I saw a small black aperture, felt a ghoulish wind of ice, and smelled the charnel bowels of a putrescent earth. There was no sound, but just then the electric lights went out and I saw outlined against some phosphorescence of the nether world a horde of silent toiling things which only insanity—or worse—could create. Their outlines were human, semi-human, fractionally human, and not human at all—the horde was grotesquely heterogeneous. They were removing the stones quietly, one by one, from the centuried wall. And then, as the breach became large enough, they came out into the laboratory in single file; led by a stalking thing with a beautiful head made of wax. A sort of mad-eyed monstrosity behind the leader seized on Herbert West. West did not resist or utter a sound. Then they all sprang at him and tore him to pieces before my eyes, bearing the fragments away into that subterranean vault of fabulous abominations. West's head was carried off by the wax-headed leader, who wore a Canadian officer's uniform. As it disappeared I saw that the blue eyes behind the spectacles were hideously blazing with their first touch of frantic, visible emotion.

Servants found me unconscious in the morning. West was gone. The incinerator contained only unidentifiable ashes. Detectives have questioned me, but what can I say? The Sefton tragedy they will not connect with West; not that, nor the men with the box, whose existence they deny. I told them of the vault, and they pointed to the unbroken plaster wall and laughed. So I told them no more. They imply that I am a madman or a murderer—probably I am mad. But I might not be mad if those accursed tomb-legions had not been so silent.

• • • • •

"The Copernicus of the horror story."
—*Fritz Leiber, commenting on Lovecraft*

H.P. Lovecraft,
1915.

"Five stars!"—Amazon

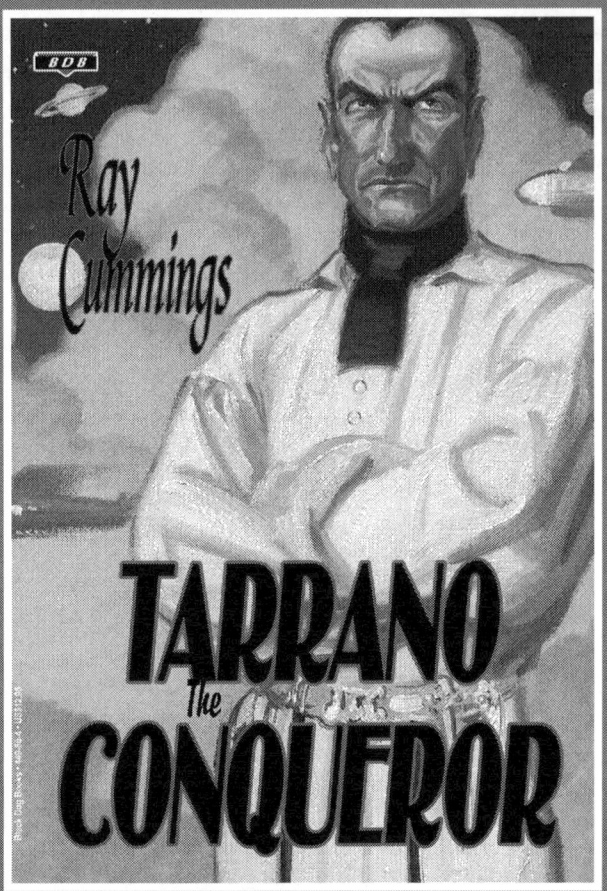

The year is 2430. The Earth awakens to find its
leaders murdered! All major cities are in turmoil. It is
rumored an interplanetary plot is underway. When the same
situation arises on Mars, panic ensues. Who is responsible?
The ruler of Venus sends word that he will protect the Earth if
all its citizens will recognize and honor his supreme authority.

A defiant Earth Council refuses to submit to such blatant
tyranny. Then a second message arrives from the stars:

Tarrano the Conqueror declares war on the Earth!

Tarrano the Conqueror by Ray Cummings.
With a new introduction by Tom Roberts.

BLACK DOG BOOKS
1115 Pine Meadows Ct.
Normal, IL 61761-5432

www.blackdogbooks.net I info@blackdogbooks.net

Follow us!

Twitter.com/blackdogbooks1

Facebook.com/blackdogbooks1

Lovecraft: A Lasting Influence

TOM ROBERTS

Editor's note: Within a few years of Lovecraft's death, other authors began to write tales of the Cthulhu Mythos, particularly August Derleth, with a series of stores running in *Weird Tales* and later collected as the Arkham House volume, *Tales of Cthulhu* in 1962.

Since that time many authors have passed through the halls of Miskatonic University or trod the foggy, river-shrouded paths of Arkham, Innsmouth or Dunwich weaving their own stories for numerous anthologies. Award-winning author Robert Weinberg has generously offered up two Lovecraft-inspired short tales to share with readers of *Windy City Pulp Stories.*

Lovecraft in Florida, 1934.

Chant

ROBERT WEINBERG

It was nearly 2:00 a.m. and I was out of ideas. Sprawled across the living room sofa, I stared with bleary eyes at the TV screen, searching for inspiration. My agent had been hounding me for weeks, begging me to put together a proposal for a novel dealing with the millennium. *Something scary and yet totally believable,* she had demanded in our last phone conversation. *Write a book filled with paranoid conspiracies about the end of the world. You're good at that type of stuff.*

Believable yet paranoid. Lori knew exactly what she was talking about. I was good at writing that type of stuff. Six novels, three of them best-sellers, proved that statement the old fashioned way. With money. Lots of money. But, now, my publisher wanted a new book focusing on the millennium. My agent had assured them I would deliver a proposal in just a few weeks. And my mind was as empty as a congressman's promise.

Whenever I came up blank, I channel surfed the cable TV networks for ideas. To me, television represented vast unexplored jungles of modern American thought. Cable channels were filled with the most outlandish and bizarre dreams of the working man. And woman. TV was the place where reality and fantasy merged and nothing was too outrageous to be dramatized or sold.

My books were hits because they took the most familiar imaginings of television and gave them new and unexpected twists. I thrust the pop icons of modern culture into crazy-quilt adventures filled with manic suspicions, half-truths, and urban mythology. The larger-than-life heroes and heroines of my novels fought a desperate, never-ceasing, battle against the huge, many-headed beast known as the System. Sometimes they won, sometimes they lost. But, they never quit. And just like the television shows from which they came, my plots always came to a satisfactory conclusion on the last page of the book. My audience, like television viewers across the country, preferred their stories nice and tidy. All plot threads were resolved, with no loose ends. My novels imitated drama, not real life. Cable was God for Middle-America and I was its humble prophet. For the right price, of course.

Thus, *Gilligan's Island* served as the basis for *Castaways,* a paranoid thriller about secret genetic testing on a Pacific atoll. *The Dukes of Hazzard* was transformed into the ghoulish *Hell's Night Riders.* And, *Lassie* underwent a startling metamorphosis into *The Dog from Hell.*

Eyes weary, I stared at Rhoda and toyed with the idea of making her into a vampiric creature, feeding off Mary Tyler Moore's goodness. It seemed plausible enough, but how then would I explain Lou Grant? As Nickelodeon switched to

Reprinted from *Song of Cthulhu: Tales of the Spheres Beyond Sound,* September 2001 commercials, I reached for the remote control. My thoughts were going goofy. Time for bed and rest. Tomorrow, a full day's schedule of reruns and cartoons hopefully would provide the impetus necessary for my new plot. And keep those fat royalty checks coming.

My eyes were turned from the set, so I heard the voices before I saw the singers. Deep, powerful, sonorous tones filled the living room. A chorus of men's voices, chanting in some unknown tongue. Harmonizing together, repeating again and again; a phrase like no other I had ever before heard. *"Ph'nglui mglw'nafh Cthulhu R'lyeh wgah'nagl fhtagn."* Stark, dramatic, intense singing, the sound sent chills racing up my spine. It felt as if someone, to use the old folk expression, was walking across my grave. I shivered, wondering the identity of the language of the chant. It was definitely not Latin, the usual tongue of such invocations.

I turned my head and stared at the TV screen. A dozen men, dressed in hooded crimson robes, stood clustered in a semi-circle around a large stone altar. A diverse group, white, black, brown and yellow, they stared at the camera with serene, composed expressions. No question that these were monks of deep, abiding faith. Behind them, though mostly blocked out by the singers' bodies, stood the walls of a massive stone church. Obviously, the commercial had been filmed on location, at some out-of-the-way cloister or abbey in Europe.

"Cthulhu, Cthulhu," sang the men a second time, but this repetition the sound was much softer, as a voice-over provided the expected product pitch.

"From the ancient halls of Exham Priory comes the most enthralling, the most captivating CD you will ever hear," declared the unseen announcer. "The voices of the Brothers of the EOD raised in harmony in their magnificent rendering of the old tongue religious litanies, *Cthulhu R'lyeh.*"

The announcer droned on, listing the dozen chants on the CD, while the red-clad monks, each now shown holding a long yellow wax candle, continued their chants in a language that was not Greek. There was no background music of any kind, no accompaniment, and yet the sound of the dozen voices was enough. The joyful sound of their singing was complete in itself. The strange words seemed to take on a meaning all their own, as if sending a message to me directly from the singers. The chant was more than a chant. It was a summoning, a calling, an urging for completion. As I watched the pictures on the TV screen, my body swayed almost hypnotically in time with the mystical adoration. It was a spooky, unexplainable feeling.

I knew without question, I had found my story.

"Send for your copy of *Cthulhu R'lyeh* today," urged the unseen announcer as the voices swelled once again in song. "Available on CD for only $6.95, on cassette tape for only $3.95. All shipping and handling charges included."

A fulfillment company's name and address flashed on the screen. Hurriedly, I copied the words on my scratchpad. A post office box in New Orleans. A guarantee of complete satisfaction or your money back from The Starry Wisdom Association, located in Los Angeles. My thoughts were racing as I wrote. It was an incredibly low price for a CD, half of what such recordings usually cost. No extra charges for shipping or state sales tax. The offer was an unbelievable bargain. Almost too good to be true. A perfect opening for my novel.

"An insidious cult of devil worshippers scheming to control the world through the use of subliminal messages planted on a seemingly innocent CD," I murmured to myself as Valerie Harper shrilly returned to my TV screen. "Disguising their hidden commands in lines of otherwise meaningless babble." Yawning, I put down the pad and pencil and clicked off the television set. Enough for tonight. I had my idea. Already, my mind was racing through dozens of possible scenarios and plot devices. Writing this book was going to be a snap.

It was time for sleep. Tomorrow, I'd begin my research. A smart writer left nothing to chance. I wanted to know the real reason the CD was so cheap. And what actual language was being sung by the monks.

Who were the Brothers of the EOD? Ditto, the Starry Wisdom Association? The Los Angeles address hinted at some fringe group, possibly one of the innumerable cults that dotted the southern California landscape. Maybe the language they used was some sort of pseudo-Atlantean tongue. Or based on supposed Lemurian thought records. It didn't matter to me. In my years as a writer, I had learned long ago that despite claims to the contrary, truth was not stranger than fiction.

In my novel, EOD would stand for the Exotic Order of Darkness. The Starry Wisdom Association would be a cabal of black magicians, seeking to rule the world for their master, an unspeakable entity from another dimension. Much different, I felt certain, than the guiding principles of the real organization. Fortunately, libel laws did not apply to religious groups.

Still, I fully intended to learn all I could about the EOD and their beliefs. The last thing I wanted was to offend some oddball religious cult. Devils and demons made good copy but they didn't frighten me. I wasn't superstitious. I worried more about real horrors-lawyers and libel suits. Though I was always extremely careful disguising the source of inspiration for my books, it never hurt to take an extra step. Tomorrow, I'd make some phone calls. And find out the truth about the EOD and Starry Wisdom Association.

I slept the sleep of the satisfied author and woke the next morning feeling the best I had in weeks. After a hearty breakfast, I dialed my agent, Lori Smith in New York, with the good news. Proposal humming, it would be on the way to her in a week. Paranoid but believable. Based on current news. Without any question, the best book I had yet written.

She sounded quite pleased and promised to relay the news to my publisher that afternoon. "If the book's as good as you say," Lori declared "we'll ask for double the advance we got for your last novel. Millennium books are hot."

"Sounds fine to me," I answered, grinning. Considering that I had received $500,000 for the previous book, we were talking big money. A million dollar advance put me in the company of King, Koontz and Rice, the superstars of horror fiction. "Let me know what they say."

"Definitely," said Lori. "You have a name for this epic? Something catchy?"

I did: It had come to me in my sleep. The perfect title, mystical and enticing, yet simple and familiar. A one-word title that I felt certain would resonate in the minds of my readers long after they finished reading my story. *"Chant,"* I told Lori.

"The book's titled *Chant.*"

"There's a popular CD by that name," she said. "The one by those monks. . . ."

"Can't copyright a title," I replied. "Besides, my book's about a pretty similar group. Only they're not priests. Just the opposite."

"The opposite of monks?" said Lori. "Pagans?"

"Devil worshippers," I replied, then said goodbye.

Now, firmly committed to the book, it was time for me to do my research. And hope that I hadn't stuck my head into a noose. As always, I went first to the most complete encyclopedia and reference guide in the world. The Internet. Logging on, I called up Infoseek and punched in the words, "Starry Wisdom." In seconds, the search engine displayed 847 sites on the subject.

Number one on the list was "The Starry Wisdom Association Home Page." I clicked on the address and waited for my computer to make the connection. The site was a large one but downloaded fast. In less than a minute I was staring at the same dozen red robed monks from last night's commercial. In dark black headlines, the page's banner proclaimed THE STARRY WISDOM SITE. Beneath, in smaller letters, were two lines in italics.

That is not dead which can eternal lie,
And with strange eons even death may die.

"Nice work if you can get it," I murmured and scrolled down the page. The Starry Wisdom Association obviously had money and knew how to use it. Their web page was totally professional, done with panache and style. Reading it answered most of my questions. But the information raised new queries, equally troublesome.

Under "Frequently Asked Questions," the language of their *Cthulhu R'lyeh* CD was listed as *the old tongue.* I assumed it was a cross between Lemurian thought records and Atlantean gibberish. The chant used in the commercial translated into "In his house in R'lyeh, dead Cthulhu waits dreaming." How someone could be dead and dream, I didn't understand. But, then again, religion was never one of my real interests.

The Starry Wisdom Association was described as a non-denominational freethinking religious order, dedicated to spreading the Gospel of the Ancient Ones. Little was actually said about what those beliefs might be, nor was there any mention of their background or past history. To me, it all sounded very New Age, very California. The organization came across as the usual scam, a pseudo-religious cult aimed primarily at leeching money from unsuspecting members.

None of my business. I was no crusader. If the idle rich wanted to pay big bucks for their chance at heaven, who was I to say no? The preamble to the

Constitution guaranteed everyone the right to "life, liberty, and the *pursuit of happiness.*" Not happiness, just the *pursuit* of happiness. I wasn't looking to save my fellow man. Just sell them a book.

At the bottom of the page was a phone number and post office box number for those who wanted more information about the association. I copied both. While contacting the group would probably be a big mistake—no cult likes to hear a writer is interested in their activities—it was better to be prepared than not.

There were no links connecting the Starry Wisdom page to any other sites on the net. So, I went back to my search engine list of all sites that mentioned the two key words. Patiently, I scanned through each page. While I had my basic concept and plot for my novel, I was hoping to find a few juicy details that would round out the story, give it some needed depth. Somewhere on the Internet, there had to be some dirt on the Starry Wisdom Association. And I wanted to find it.

The first two dozen entries were worthless. Home pages for people who were entranced by the music CD. A few sites for very strange people, filled with gibberish phrases like "The Hounds of Tindalos," "The Book of Eibon," and "The goat with a thousand young." California cult silliness. There was even one page of photographs of the night skies, with the words "The stars are right," in big bold red letters superimposed over the pictures. Since when were the stars ever wrong? Maybe the Starry Wisdom Association was involved in astrology. I didn't know, but vowed to check on the possibility later.

I was intrigued by the title of the twenty-ninth page in the web search listing. "They're All Actors." The actual contents of the site proved equally interesting. A die-hard fan of singers who worked for commercials had reproduced the photo of the Brothers of the EOD on his page, and beneath each red-clad monk had posted the man's real name. Evidently, none of the Brothers were actually monks at all. They were professional background singers, men with melodic voices who did backup work for soundtracks, commercials, and music videos.

Further down the page were biographies of each singer, along with a list of other credits and in some cases, even a contact phone number. Shaking my head in amazement, I copied down several of the names and numbers. So much for the sincerity and deep religious feeling shared by the Brothers.

I bookmarked the search page on the Starry Wisdom Association and exited the net. My eyes were starting to hurt from staring at the computer screen. It was time for me to make a few phone calls.

In my novel, all of the people who worked for the demon worshippers of EOD would be dead, killed in the most gruesome manner I could imagine. Of course, those murders would be the clue that would convince my hero that something terrible was happening. It was a melodramatic happening that made for a good story but was otherwise totally illogical. In real life, a cult would never do anything so foolish. The best disguise for evil was boring normalcy. I had no trouble contacting any of the singers in the commercial.

Larry Daniels answered on the third ring. His voice was rich and mellow, silky smooth. He was not the least bit reticent to discuss his work for the Starry

Wisdom Association.

"Great job," he told me. "Nice people, good money, wonderful production facilities. Wish I could say the same about most of my other assignments. You wouldn't believe the crap I have to put up with sometimes."

"Didn't bother you to dress up like a monk?" I asked. "You weren't concerned about deceiving the public?"

Daniels laughed, a full rich sound. "Deception? In a music CD commercial? You must be joking, right? We're talking television, son. Nothing's real on TV. So what if we dressed up in those silly red cassocks? Nobody's come looking for me to tell me their confession. No worse than those old geezer actors suckering people about health insurance for the elderly. Or the faded rockstars promoting those oldie CDs. The music's the only thing that matters. And that wasn't faked. It was us singing. We recorded the entire CD, then did the video commercial."

"Then you have no idea what the Starry Wisdom Association is all about?" I said.

"Not a clue," said Daniels. "They put an ad in *Variety* looking for commercial artists with experience in religious and choral music, Interviewed hundreds of people. Wanted men who looked the part. I was lucky enough to be one of those chosen. Spent six weeks in a studio, working on the CD. Paid well with no hassles. Best job I've had in years."

"In a studio," I repeated. "What about Exham Priory, that huge stone church behind you?"

Daniels' deep sigh was audible even over the telephone. "Son, you're awfully naive for a professional writer. We recorded the CD in a studio in Los Angeles. The commercial was shot in a studio fifteen minutes off of Sunset Strip. They backdropped in photos of that old abbey. I think I heard someone mention it was located in England. Nice touch." The singer laughed. "Candles were real, though."

"Thanks," I said, feeling stupid. "You have a contact name, someone from the Association I could talk to, find out a little more about the group? I'd make sure not to mention your name, keep it secret how I found him."

"No worry on my end " said Daniels. "After all, those people are members of a religious organization. Try Charlie Newsome," and he gave me a phone number in Los Angeles. "He directed the whole commercial. Nice guy. Though I doubt if he'll be able to tell you much more than me. Got the impression he was being paid to do a specific job. Nothing more."

"Nobody on the set from the EOD?" I asked. "Watching to make sure everything was strictly accurate?"

"Not a soul," answered Daniels.

I thanked the singer, hung up, and dialed Charlie Newsome. He proved as cooperative as Daniels and equally ignorant.

Newsome had been hired by the CD manufacture to produce the music infomercial. They selected him on the basis of previous commercials he had done for similar products. He had never met anyone from the EOD or the Starry Wisdom

Association. He did what he was told and collected his paycheck. It had been an easy job.

Newsome put me in touch with the recording company who actually produced the CD. The woman I spoke to was cool at first, until she connected my name with my books. Turned out she was a fan. A promise to send her an autographed copy of my last book and she gave me all the dirt on *Cthulhu R'lyeh*. There wasn't much.

The entire CD had been arranged by a legal firm in the Valley. The lawyer, Norman Marsh, had sent the music, lyrics, and a dreadful tape of a man singing the strange words using the correct pronunciation.

"Dreadful meaning unearthly or horrifying?" I asked.

"Dreadful as meaning the singer was tone deaf," said my fan, Rita Gladney. "My boss later told me he was convinced it was the lawyer Marsh singing. Crazy, huh?"

"Definitely," I answered. From the story, it seemed likely that Marsh was the man behind the Starry Wisdom Association. That the entire CD was his baby.

The cheap price was a marketing gimmick. Or so Marsh had claimed. The singers were relatively cheap, the studio didn't cost a lot, and the video was done in one shot. With little overhead and minimal charges, the CD was supposed to make money on volume sales, not markup. "Marsh said he wanted to sell more than a million CDs," said Rita. "That the Starry Wisdom Association was convinced that with the right promotion they'd get national attention and make headlines. Personally, I think the whole project's a tax dodge."

It seemed quite possible to me as well. After a few more minutes chatting with Rita, I hung up and tried to locate the tone-deaf Mr. Marsh. And ran into a blank wall.

There was no lawyer named Norman Marsh practicing in the San Fernando Valley. According to a call to the California Bar Association, there was no one by that name practicing law in the entire state.

I debated calling back Rita but decided it would be a waste of time. She had been quite specific on the name, even spelling it for me. Someone named Marsh had paid for the CD to be produced, advertised and distributed. He might not be a lawyer, but plenty of people weren't what they seemed to be in California. As best as I could tell, Marsh had done nothing illegal. Besides, I was no cop, just an author.

Keeping that thought in mind, I dialed the phone number for the Starry Wisdom Association. An answering machine took the call, telling me to leave my name and phone number and someone would get back to me shortly with information on the group. The message suggested in the meantime, I buy a copy of their first CD release, *Cthulhu R'lyeh*. "Play it often," the message concluded. "All truths can be found in its words."

"Modest," I said, breaking the connection. The entire scenario stank like three-day-old fish. An organization looking for publicity who answered their calls with a machine? A CD priced so cheap that it barely broke even? Why run a swindle that lost money? I didn't know the answer, but I intended to find out.

After a quick lunch, I was back searching the Internet. I hunted through a hundred entries on the Starry Wisdom Association, most of them filled with pseudo-religious babble about Old Ones, Deep Ones, Ancient Ones, and *De Vermis Mysteriis,* which sounded like something I had ordered by mistake at a French restaurant once. There was no mention of a lawyer named Marsh. There were six more pages mentioning that the stars were right, three stating that the stars were almost right but not quite yet, and one page saying that the stars were definitely wrong and would not be right for another 347 years.

Growing bored, I switched back to my search engine and ran a new search for the word "chants." As expected, in seconds, I had over a thousand locations. Hoping against hope, I scanned the long list, searching for some mention of the Starry Wisdom Association. Or *Cthulhu R'lyeh.*

I was ready to conclude there was nothing to be found on the net about the mysterious EOD and their CD when I came across entry two hundred and forty-seven. The title was intriguing. Pulling up the article, I read it carefully. I knew I had found something important. But I wasn't sure exactly what. Four times I read the article. The words remained unchanged. As I stared at them, the feeling I had about someone walking across my grave returned. But this time, the mysterious stroller was doing an Irish jig.

The page was titled "Chants: Opening Strange Doors." It was written by some guy named Murray Wills from Massachusetts. There was no mention of the *Cthulhu R'lyeh* CD from the Starry Wisdom Association. It wasn't necessary.

"A chant is merely another name for an invocation," began Wills. "Despite the rash of recordings and concerts centered around chants as entertainment, one should never forget such melodies are actually religious prayers set to music. A chant is an invocation, a magic spell, using sound and repetition. Such words can be dangerous."

I liked that line, wondered if I could use it in my novel. "There are worlds parallel to Earth, separated only by rates of atomic vibration. Quite possibly they are home to life forces, beings totally and completely alien to humanity. Monstrous creations, these things are glimpsed only in nightmares or visions. Heaven and Hell are most likely based on such psychic revelations.

"Fortunately, the quantum boundary separating our dimension from another is almost impossible to cross. But, there is a way. Vibrations keep the universes separate. Therefore, vibrations can also be used to form a gateway, a dimensional door."

I wasn't much on quantum mechanics or rates of atomic vibrations. But I had read plenty of science fiction novels about parallel universes and passages from one plane of reality to another. Not that I believed in such stuff. But Wills' writings were convincing.

"Broken down to simplest terms, music is a vibration. A chant is nothing more than an invocation, a summons. The right chant, the right words, sung in a specific manner, can open a gate between worlds. Reading the truth behind the legend, we can surmise that solitary mages in the Middle Ages were able to use such spells to bring demons, minor denizens of other realities, into our world."

The next few lines were the ones that worried me.

"If one voice, chanting the correct phrases, sung in the proper manner, pronounced exactly the right way, could accomplish this act, imagine the incredible power of a dozen such voices, blending together in perfect harmony. Ponder that. Then, consider the use of modern technology. Postulate copying that sound, that *chant,* so that each duplicate is an exact replica of the original. Imagine what a *million* chants, played at the same time, might do. The vibrations would be enough to bend space and time. *Think of the size of the gateway that would be opened.* Tremble at the thought of what could enter our world from a place outside our universe."

There were no more words. Just a number.

1,257,831.

How Wills had determined the figure I had no idea. But I had no doubts as to his meaning.

I logged off the Internet suddenly feeling very nervous. Dialing the Starry Wisdom Association gave me the same machine, the same plug. "Play it often."

I hung up.

If everyone who owned a copy of the CD played it at the same time, would those chants blend together, merge together into one immensely powerful invocation? Become a summoning that could reach outside of our universe and into another? I didn't know. But somehow I suspected that the Starry Wisdom Association wasn't the least bit concerned about publicity or a profit. That they only wanted to distribute as many copies of *Cthulhu R'lyeh,* their chant, as possible.

I emailed Murray Wills. My letter was short and to the point. *What is dead Cthulhu dreaming about? And where exactly is R'lyeh?*

That was three days ago. I still haven't received a reply. I suspect I won't.

Maybe I'm worried about nothing. Dimensional doors and forgotten languages and chants used to summon monsters. Maybe I'm letting my paranoid fantasies finally get under my skin. I'm truthfully not sure. It could all be a crazy coincidence. Still, I'm scared.

I bought *Billboard* today. To check on *Cthulhu R'lyeh.*

According to a brief mention, sales of the CD are climbing, due to the low price and flashy commercial. It's moving up the charts fast.

Number 57 with a bullet.

· · · · ·

Sydney Taine vs. The Slime God

ROBERT WEINBERG

I.

"That's it," said Vic to no one in particular. "Hawaii's gone."

"What?" said Herm Melville, Vic's immediate superior and de facto boss of the White House Ready Room. "Hawaii's gone? What do you mean, *gone?*"

"Gone, as in vanished, disappeared, out of contact, no response," replied Vic. Normally, he never got angry or upset, but the past few days had been hard on everyone's temper. That Herm didn't grasp the magnitude of the disaster they were dealing with made life even more difficult for everyone else in his crew.

Vic gestured at computer nerds two, three, and four, manning the Crays that instantly read and analyzed satellite feeds from all over the globe. "Ask them. They'll tell you the same thing. The last signal from Hawaii blinked off in the middle of transmission. All of the islands are silent. Not a peep from anyone. Army, Navy, Air Force, even the damned Coast Guard is quiet. TV and radio stations aren't broadcasting. No phone calls. No emails. We got nothing."

"What about the view from space?" asked Melville. He sounded desperate. Vic didn't blame him. It was Herm's job to keep the President informed when things got rough. The past three days had been plenty rough. And there was no doubt that life was going to get rougher.

"What view from space?" said nerd number one with a brief, harsh laugh. "The entire north Pacific is covered by an immense black storm cloud. It's the same storm cloud that's hovered over the region the past three days. A storm that size and magnitude is impossible; it's virtually impossible. But there it sits! Blocking our vision, keeping all that scenery out of sight."

"Airplanes?" asked Herm. They had gone over this list time after time during the past few days, always with the same answers. But the chief didn't want to bring anything minor to the attention to the President. Calling bad weather an emergency could have dire effects on a career. "How about sending in some unmanned drones?"

"Along with generating the storm covering its movements, the monster's also exerting a powerful magnetic field that disrupts any electrical devices within a twenty mile radius. Planes and missiles crash long before they reach it. Same is true for cars and trucks and trains. Nothing mechanical can get too close. The creature's been awake for over three days and we still don't have one photo of it. We're limited to crayon pictures drawn by survivors of its attack. Incredible, horrible pictures, but nothing more."

"We better tell the President about Hawaii," said nerd number three. "He should know when one of our states goes missing."

"He's not going to like the news," said nerd number four. "Hawaii voted for him in the last election."

"Well, better he hears the story from us rather than cable news," said Herm. "You know he hates learning stuff from TV. Vic, you're with me. For some reason I don't fully understand, the President seems to like you. No accounting for taste. Let's you and I go find him and lay out the whole mess. Maybe he'll have an idea what to do next."

Locating the President wasn't difficult. He was in the Oval Office, in the midst of a meet-and-greet with the new President of Brazil. Persuading the Secret Service to let them interrupt the meeting wasn't difficult. Getting past the Chief Executive's executive secretary proved to be much tougher. She adamantly refused to let them in to see her boss.

"Whatever it is, it can wait till after the photo shoot and the joint press conference," said Mrs. Daley. "The President's working on a global warming deal and he needs Brazil's participation. He can't just blow off Señor Gomez because you two need to bend his ear about some wacko conspiracy or something." Mrs. Daley was notorious about maintaining the President's schedule. She defined the word inflexible. It was Vic who came up with the solution to their problem.

"Turn on CNN," he told the diminutive white-haired old lady. "Go ahead, listen to what they're saying about Hawaii."

Frowning, Mrs. Daley clicked the power on the portable TV on her desk. She kept the sound on low, as if worried the voices might travel past her office into the President's chamber. Keeping his features neutral, Vic watched the old woman's face as she stared at the TV. In less than ten seconds, her lips were pressed tightly together. The passage of twenty seconds saw her eyes narrow to pinpoints. At thirty seconds, she showed her teeth, clenched together in horror. In all, a minute passed before she raised one skinny claw-like hand and pointed at the door leading to the Oval Office.

"Tell him," she declared, her voice trembling. "Tell him right now."

The President was sitting behind the Lyndon Baines Johnson desk, with Señor Gomez, the President of Brazil, sitting in a black leather chair across from him. The two leaders of their countries were engaged in a deep conversation when Vic and Herm entered. Both leaders looked up and across the room in surprise. The President grimaced when he saw who it was.

"Melville, this better be god-damn important for you to interrupt my meeting with Señor Gomez," declared President Jefferson C. Calhoun. "On the level of Russians invading Alaska or something worse."

"Mr. President," said Herm, nodding at Calhoun. "Mr. President," he repeated, nodding to the President of Brazil, "needless to say I would never have barged in your meeting if not for a crisis of international importance. Sir, it's best if we discuss this matter in private. I assure you that it's news you need to hear right now. It concerns Hawaii."

Vic couldn't help but laugh at Herm's understatement. It was a short, staccato sound that barely left his lips, but it obviously was enough to convince the President that something was amiss.

"Señor Gomez," said Calhoun politely, "we will continue our most important conversation about global warming later today. Excuse me now, but I must deal with this immediate crisis." The President's eyes slowly surveyed the room until they focused on what he had obviously hoped to find. "Here's Mrs. Daley. She'll escort you to your suite. Thank you so much for your understanding."

Once Mrs. Daley and Señor Gomez were gone, Calhoun turned to Vic and Herm with thunderclouds in his face. "This better be good," he declared in the same voice he used to order firing squads to shoot deserters.

Herm nodded at Vic. Vic cleared his throat, "Hawaii's gone, sir."

"Gone?" repeated the President. "What do you mean, gone?"

Not anxious to repeat his entire conversation with Herm, Vic decided to spell things out in straightforward fashion. "Three days ago, we told you there was an earthquake in the Pacific. What we didn't know at the time was that the stars in the sky were aligned in a certain pattern they hadn't assumed in twenty-seven thousand years. We did a computer simulation just in case you wonder how we know that. Whatever; to put it simply, the stars were definitely right."

"Earthquake in the Pacific," repeated the President. "The stars were right. Meaning—?"

"The earthquake signaled the rising up of a volcanic island in the Northern Pacific ocean near the island nation of Ponape," continued Vic. "Located on the center of this volcanic atoll was a gigantic stone temple, with walls set in very unusual geometric patterns, almost four-dimensional, if such arrangements were possible in three-dimensional space. When a boatload of sailors and tourists went exploring on the island, they evidently set off some sort of silent alarm in the building.

"Fifteen minutes after they landed, a five-hundred foot tall green globular monster emerged from inside the structure and devoured most of the tourists and sailors. Since then, the creature has been on a rampage across the Pacific, chomping up people, smashing ships, and destroying property. Today it reached Hawaii. Needless to say, that was a bad scene."

"Yes sir," added Melville. "A very bad scene, indeed. Before we lost communication with the islands, we received reports of hundreds of people being eaten or crushed alive beneath the creature's gigantic feet."

"You're not telling me that this monster ate the entire population of Hawaii?" said the President. "That's millions of people."

"No sir," answered Herm. "A Navy cruiser landed at Ponape shortly after the creature left. Evidently, the monster emitted some sort of psychic wave force that paralyzed every living thing within twenty miles of its location. The inhabitants of the island weren't dead, just flash frozen in place. The thing left them immobile, so it could harvest them later. They're something like a TV dinner, but with unmoving humans as the main course."

"A human TV dinner? A gigantic cyclopedian temple? Tell me, Melville, does this monster have a name?"

"Well, sir, according to the Navy, the natives on the islands surrounding Ponape called the thing, C-thul-hu; accent on the first and third syllable, sir."

"Cthulhu," said the Chief Executive. He suddenly began to chuckle. "All right now. Did the first lady put you up to this? Are there some doctored photos with a gigantic green monster stepping on buildings I'm supposed to see? Or maybe a film clip? C'mon now, Melville. You could have been more original. Sure I read Lovecraft in college. Everyone did. But the Old Gent's been dead for more than seventy years now. At least you could have made up a new name for the monster?"

"Lovecraft, sir?" said Melville. "Who's Lovecraft?"

The President stared at Melville. Then his gaze shifted to Vic. Slowly, all the good cheer disappeared from his face, and the laughter died on his lips. "You're not making up this whole story? It's really happening? There really is a five hundred foot tall green monster named Cthulhu?"

"Five hundred feet tall with dozens of long, slimy rope-like tentacles, sir," said Vic, feeling he needed to put things in perspective. "The creature has a dozen mouths filled with huge teeth and at least fifty eyes spread in rings across its body. There's nothing like it on Earth."

"Who's Lovecraft?" repeated Melville. "Some lunatic flying saucer cultist?"

"Howard Phillips Lovecraft," said President Calhoun. "He was a horror writer who worked in the 1920s and 1930s. I was a fan of his fiction when I was a teenager. His most famous stories were about ancient demon gods who rose after tens of thousands of years of slumber to ravage the Earth. Chief among these horrific entities was a gigantic monster known as Cthulhu."

"Amazing," said Vic. "Somehow this Lovecraft dude must have been channeling the future and using modern events as the basis for his stories. How cool is that?"

"Wonderful," said the President. "That's *just wonderful.* Lovecraft claimed that much of the inspiration for his stories came to him in dreams. He never once realized he was foreseeing the future."

"Well, then, did he visualize how to destroy the monster, sir?" asked Melville. "That thing, Cthulhu, is heading towards San Francisco. If it continues at the speed it's traveling, it will arrive there approximately four days from now. Best we stop the creature in the middle of the Pacific, before it reaches California and paralyzes the entire west coast. And then starts moving cross country."

"Lovecraft's heroes never defeated the monster," said the President. "A storm came up and Cthulhu retreated inside its temple. Then the entire island sank beneath the sea. End of story, curtain closed."

"Somehow, sir, I have the bad *bad* feeling that's not going to happen," said Vic. There were days in life that he was thrilled to be part of the White House staff. There were other days when he wished he had never signed on for the job. Today was one of the latter days.

"Atomic bombs?" asked the President. "Nuclear warheads?"

"We thought of them," said Melville. "No luck. The firing mechanisms require electricity. Nothing electric works within miles of the monster. Atomic energy's not like dynamite. You need a trigger. There's no method of setting off the bomb. Damn thing can't be killed by conventional weapons."

"Gentlemen," said the President. "It appears to me that we are faced with a problem that can't be solved by ordinary means. Plus, it's a threat not only to our country but to all nations. Do you agree with my assessment of the situation?"

"Yes sir," said Herm.

"Yes sir," said Vic. "You're not planning to call the United Nations, are you sir? I doubt if they could be of much help and you know how much time they take arguing about everything. Remember, we only have days, not weeks before the monster reaches California."

"No, no," said Calhoun. Reaching into his pants, he pulled out a key ring with two keys on it. Vic wondered why a man who was chauffeured everywhere and had doors always opened for him by the Secret Service needed keys. He soon found out as the President bent over and inserted one of keys into a lock on the lowest drawer on the LBJ desk. A moment later, the President sat up, holding in both hands a gray metal box approximately twelve inches long by six inches wide and four inches high. Carefully, almost cautiously, the President inserted the second key into the slot on the box. He turned it then looked up at Herm and Vic.

"Gentlemen, you may have heard stories about the Harry Truman box," said Calhoun. "Well, here it is."

Vic, who had never heard a word about any sort of box, felt obligated to say so. "I never heard of any box, sir. Should I?"

"It's one of those legends of the White House that gets more and more elaborate as the years pass by," said the President. "Like the story about the ghost of Lincoln knocking on the door of the bedroom that bears his name. But, in this case, the box is real."

As if to emphasis his point, the President rapped the knuckles of his right hand on the metal box top. "The first atomic bomb was dropped on the Japanese city of Hiroshima on August 6, 1945 at 8:15 in the morning. That night President Truman went to sleep certain that the war in the Pacific was about to end. He awoke the next morning to find this box on his nightstand. No one had access to his bedroom and the Secret Service had been on guard right outside his door all night. Yet, somehow, someone had left the box and inside it, a handwritten note. *This note."*

Calhoun opened the box and took out a small sheet of white stationary. He handed it to Vic, who read it and passed the note on to Herm.

"If you are ever confronted by an enemy who cannot be stopped by the power of nuclear weapons," read Herm out loud, "press the button."

"What button?" asked Vic.

"This one," said the President and turned the box around so that Vic and Herm could see inside the thin steel walls. Resting on a thick piece of purple cloth was a small slab of metal. On its center was a raised bubble on which was positioned a small red button. It looked like a doorbell.

"No president has ever pushed the button," said Calhoun, "though I'm sure that every one of them has been tempted. Then again, no president has ever faced a five-hundred foot tall green monster with bone-crushing tentacles, a dozen or so mouths, and a physical form that can't be nuked."

"I think—" said Vic.

"—it's time—" said Herm.

"—to press the button," said the President.

With those words, President Jefferson Clay Calhoun pressed the button contained in the Harry Truman box. And then waited with Vic and Herm to see what happened next.

II.

It didn't take long. The air in the Oval Office softly began to buzz. Looking around, Vic soon found the cause of the noise. In the center of the room about four feet off the floor, the air was spinning around and around a solitary point of nothingness. It was like a vortex in a pool of water, or an open drain. The air swirled and swirled, faster and faster, and the tiny hole in space grew bigger and bigger.

The hole continued to grow and as it did, the inside of it turned cloudy. Not dark, not unworldly, merely cloudy. A gray mist filled the ever-expanding circle. And expand it did, getting larger and larger by the minute. The bigger the hole got, the faster the air swirling around it seemed to move. In less than ten minutes, the swirl had transformed into a gigantic hole seven feet in diameter and a thousandth-of-an-inch in width. Staring closely into the grayness, Vic spotted something moving. He raised a hand as if warning the other two men of the anonymous figures. Vic need not have bothered for a second later, a tall woman with stunning features stepped out of the mist and on to the floor of the Oval Office. Following her a few seconds later was a short fireplug of a man, nearly as wide as he was tall. Then, with a whoosh like the sound of air deflating from a balloon, the whirl in the center of the room vanished, leaving the two figures transported from somewhere else standing in the middle of the room.

From outside the office came the sound of someone knocking on the door. "Mr. President," called one of the Secret Service agents, "is everything alright in there?"

"Yes, Roscoe," replied the President. "Everything's fine. If I need you, I'll call. Nothing to worry about. Nothing at all."

The nothing-to-worry-about was a tall, slender, very good-looking woman dressed entirely in black. She wore black boots with six-inch stiletto heels, a black leather jumpsuit with long black sleeves, and a black choker around her neck. On her hands were long black leather gloves. Her hair was jet black, combed in a punk-rock style up into the air with traces of purple interwoven in the locks. Her eye shadow, lip gloss, and cheek shimmer were various shades of the same color. Looking at the woman, Vic was reminded of a well-known female movie star. He couldn't remember her name but he did recall she had starred in some movies about the masked bandit, Zorro.

Standing a few feet behind the woman was a man who looked like an ape. He was a head shorter than the woman, but was twice as wide. With broad shoulders, a barrel chest and arms that hung almost to the floor, he resembled a hairless gorilla. Dressed in faded jeans and a black muscle T, the man had no visible neck and a bullet, shaved head. His black eyes were recessed deep in his face beneath brooding brows, and his mouth was twisted in what Vic could only assume was a grin.

"I'm Sydney Taine, Cross/Time & Space/Multiverse agent, and this is my assistant, Ape Largo," said the woman. "We're here because someone pressed *the button*. We battle unusual threats against humanity. Hopefully, this isn't a case of showing off in front of friends?"

"No, no," said President Calhoun, the first of them to regain his composure. "There's a real emergency. We do need your help. You're a Cross/Time & Space/ Multiverse agent? Like the characters H. Beam Piper wrote about? Or the Eternal Champion?"

"How nice," said the woman called Sydney, smiling. "You're actually a well-read button pusher. That's a first. Usually, we spend the first hour or two of our mission explaining who we are and why we're there."

"I'm Jefferson Clay Calhoun, President of the United States of America," said the President. He waved a hand towards Vic and Herm. "This is Vic and that's Herm. They're two of my best; they work in the White House ready room. We're dealing with a five hundred foot tall slimy green monster that's obliterated Hawaii and is headed for the West Coast. I'm really, *really* hoping you can be of some help sending this thing straight to hell."

"Hundreds of feet tall, slimy and green?" said the short man Sydney Taine had identified as Ape Largo. His voice was as deep as he was short. "Give the thing a bunch of tentacles, mouths and a few dozen eyes and you've got something straight out of Lovecraft."

"You guessed it," said the President. "It's Cthulhu."

Vic couldn't help but wonder why he had never heard of this Lovecraft character before? When this situation was over, he'd have to look up his books on Amazon.com.

"Hot damn," said Ape. "We've never fought a Lovecraftian monster before. You think maybe good old HPL was channeling the spirit of Abdul Alhazred?"

"Nothing would surprise me at the moment," said the President. "You aren't carrying some sort of disintegrator ray on you by chance? We're pretty anxious to kill this thing before it reaches California."

Sydney Taine spread her arms, showing off her svelte figure tightly clad in black leather. "Sorry. This outfit isn't tailored for guns. Can't you just drop an atomic bomb on Cthulhu? Or send the Pacific fleet after it?"

"If only," said the President. "I best explain. Vic, tell them what you told me."

Vic, who had been resting his feet, leaning on the LBJ desk, stood up, ready to tell his story. But the President wasn't finished speaking.

"Sydney, why don't you and Ape have a seat?" said the President, turning on the legendary Calhoun charm. "Would either of you care for a beer? Perhaps a sandwich or two? I don't know much about traveling through space and time but I suspect there's no refreshments available during the trip. Let's have a nibble and do some serious listening. Maybe we'll come up with a plan. Herm, you want to tell Mrs. Daley to arrange a working lunch for the five of us? Thanks. Vic, you go right ahead with your story. Tell them everything, from the beginning."

An hour and five tuna finger sandwiches later, they had still not settled on any sort of plan to destroy the monster. The satellite photos of Hawaii had come in, showing a path of destruction a half-mile wide stretching from one end of the islands to the other. Stopping Cthulhu was going to take major artillery. Unfortunately, since the development of missiles, big guns had been abandoned. Nor were there any shells large enough to damage a 500-foot tall monster.

"What I want to know," said Vic, sitting in one of the Roosevelt chairs and swigging a Coke, "is how does a monster bigger than most skyscrapers, walk? Doesn't this thing's size violate every principle of the Square-Cube law?"

"Good question," said Sydney. "I was wondering myself how a digestive system copes with ten mouths? Not to mention, the problems associated with fifty sets of eyes scattered in rings all over Cthulhu's body."

"It ain't natural," said Ape Largo. "Nothing like that exists in our universe. Damned thing violates all sorts of laws of physics and nature."

"Exactly," said Sydney. "Ape, I'm thinking Cthulhu's a refugee from M-space."

"M-space?" said the President. "I don't believe I'm familiar with that term. Is it something out of science fiction?"

"No," said Sydney. "It's actually the hot new idea in science. At least it is in our reality. It's a result of work done in Superstring theory."

"Not one of ours, either," said the President. "Since I'm the chief executive, I get briefed on all the latest scientific advances made at all our major research institutes each week. You're not ringing any bells, Sydney."

"Fair enough," said the leather-clad vixen. "M-theory requires pages and pages of advanced math to demonstrate, so I'll just simplify and summarize. The theory states that every universe has ten dimensions of space and time, and that all the laws of physics are constant throughout it. Thus, if water freezes at 32 degrees Fahrenheit on Earth, it freezes at the same temperature on a planet a billion light years from Earth. The entire universe is called a "brane," a short version of 'membrane.'

"According to physicists," continued Sydney, "there are an infinite number of branes. Supposedly, you can't travel from one to another, though the collision of two of them accounts for the Big Bang. The key point is that while the laws of physics must be consistent in each brane, they don't have to be the same as the laws in another brane. Taking our example of water freezing, in another brane water might freeze at 12 degrees or 50 degrees. All M-theory says is that it will freeze at the same temperature anywhere in the brane."

"I still don't understand why this stuff matters to us?" said Herm. The team boss knew how to get out the vote but was weak on science. Or he just liked watching Sydney Taine move her body as she talked. Vic wasn't sure which.

"In our universe," answered Taine, "a creature like Cthulhu breaks all the laws of physics. However, in another brane, it might be perfectly normal form of life. For all we know, everything in the universe it comes from might be 500-feet tall and have multiple sensory organs. Somehow, it's crossed from its universe into ours. What we need to do is send it back."

"I thought you said travel between universes is impossible?" said Herm. "That intersections between two of them causes disasters?"

"That's what M-theory states," said Sydney. "Cthulhu proves otherwise. If that monster can travel to Earth, I should be able to use my dimensional pogo-stick to travel to its home."

"That sounds dangerous," said the President.

"That's what makes the job interesting," said Sydney, rising to her feet. "Ape will stay here, and try to coordinate some sort of defense against Cthulhu in case I don't get back before it reaches San Francisco. I'll do my best to return in time."

Using the pointer finger of her left hand, Sydney drew a six-foot high circle in the air. Instantly, the outline filled with gray fog. The hole had a front but no back. With a smile and a wave, the woman in leather stepped into the two-dimensional passageway and was gone. A second later, the hole in space vanished too.

"Amazing," said the President. "That woman is absolutely amazing."

"Tell me about it," rumbled Ape.

III.

For a monster five hundred feet tall and weighing several million tons, Cthulhu made astonishing good time traveling across the Pacific. The creature's progress was followed with bated breath by hundreds of millions of Americans and several billion other people around the globe. After the disaster in Hawaii, keeping the monster secret proved to be no longer feasible. The cable news channels all sent their major anchors to San Francisco to await the arrival of the monster, while un-fortunate stringers reported from sailboats on the creature's day to day progress. All in all, it became a media circus that rivaled the glory days of OJ's ride and the Clinton sex scandal.

Vic tried with limited success to avoid the throngs of reporters that crowded around the White House gates day and night. He hated doing interviews and did not think he looked very good on television. Some people craved the spotlight and made the rounds of all the early and late night talk shows. Not Vic. When cornered, he resorted to the familiar but effective "No comment," again and again un-til the newshounds grew tired of pestering him and chased down someone else.

Two nights after Hawaii, the President called the entire Ready Room crew into the Oval Office for a major announcement. Vic hoped it wasn't going to be a resignation speech. If the President suddenly left office, his staff would be blamed. It was always the little people who were blamed for mistakes made by their superiors. Nixon became an elder statesman but none of his crew ever again found work. Chuck Colson, Nixon's hatchet man, found religion and spent the rest of his days converting prisoners. Vic swore to himself that he would commit suicide rather than preach the Gospel. Fortunately, he didn't need to face that choice.

At the meeting, President Calhoun announced that he was flying on Air Force One to California and that he was taking the entire staff of the Ready Room along for the ride. Once in San Francisco, Calhoun was hoping that his "team" would come up with some innovative ideas for stopping Cthulhu before the creature stomped the city flat. Not only were the President's re-election chances riding on how he handled this crisis, but the fate of the world might depend on it also.

Relieved that he wouldn't have to find a new job, Vic slept through most of the flight to San Francisco. He woke up shortly before Air Force One landed. It was nice to see the Golden Gate Bridge from the air. It was not so nice to be reminded by the pilot over the plane loudspeaker that unless they acted fast, Cthulhu would destroy the bridge in approximately five hours.

Deplaning, Vic ran into Ape Largo. It was the first time Vic had seen Taine's assistant since the night of revelations in the Oval Office. The short man was carrying several boxes filled with loose papers with both hands. The covers of the boxes weren't taped on and Largo was having a difficult time keeping the contents of the boxes from flying away in the stiff afternoon breeze.

"Here, let me take one of those," said Vic as he grabbed the upper box from Largo's arms. "Secret diagrams for some sort of gigantic disintegrator ray?"

"I only wish," said Largo. His voice rumbled like the inside of a live volcano. "They're sketches for a gigantic catapult. It's designed to throw huge fireballs at Cthulhu. Somehow, I suspect they won't slow him down."

"A giant catapult?" repeated Vic. "Who's crazy idea was that?"

"The President," said Largo.

"It might work," said Vic. "Catapults don't use electricity."

"Anything might work," said Largo. "But excuse me if I keep a bicycle nearby."

Mentally, Vic made a note to check on the availability of bicycles. He had planned on a motorcycle himself, but thinking about it, a bicycle was a safer bet. Though when dealing with a five-hundred foot tall monster, there were no safe bets.

Four and a half hour later found him standing at Christmas Tree Point located on the Twin Peaks at the center of the city. The Point was over 900 feet above sea level and offered a good view of the ocean west of the city. President Calhoun stood nearby, flanked by Ape Largo and Herm Melville. The four computer nerds, each armed with an extremely powerful hand-held computer, were tracking the movement of Cthulhu on Goggle.Earth. The creature was only a few miles away from the city and approaching fast.

Building a giant catapult had proven, alas, to be an impossible task in the time remaining. As had every other attack plan advanced by the desperate population of San Francisco. Some fled, others prayed, but the vast majority just waited for a miracle.

"Estimated time of arrival is seven minutes," said nerd number one. "The floating mines didn't slow it down much."

"Newsperson seventy-two just disappeared into the monster's lower mouth," said nerd number two.

"There it is," said nerds three and four, both looking up from their computers and pointing to a green dot on the horizon.

"Mr. President, sir," said Herm Melville. "I think it's time for you to leave the Twin Peaks and head for a secure shelter. We're pretty exposed up here, and there's a good chance the monster will stomp us flat."

"Herm, I appreciate your concern," said the President. "But our country needs a leader who's not a coward. I'm staying here."

"Sydney," said Ape Largo. "If you're going to show up, now would be a good time to reappear, bringing a miracle along."

"Have I ever failed to deliver?" asked Sydney Taine, stepping out of a hole in the air where no hole had been an instant before. The Cross/Time & Space/Multiverse agent was dressed in a charcoal gray cat-suit. Crimson streaks highlighted her black hair and her nails, eyebrows, and lip gloss were equally red.

"Ms. Taine," said President Calhoun, a note of relief in his voice, "am I to assume you visited the home world of this monster? And you've returned with some aid?"

"Yes to both questions, Mr. President," said Sydney. "Sorry to be so late but it took time to initiate communication. Once I made contact, the aliens proved quite friendly. The results of my mission should be apparent in about two minutes."

"Cthulhu will reach the harbor in three minutes," said all four computer nerds. For the first time Vic could recall, the geeks sounded worried. Not that he blamed them. A five-hundred foot tall green tentacle monster that had eaten thousands of Hawaiians and seventy-two news journalists was a major cause for alarm. He hoped Sydney Taine hadn't cut things too close.

The green glob on the horizon had taken shape and size. It was moving with astonishing speed for such an immense being. In the sky around the Twin Peaks, thousands of birds were cawing. Somewhere, someone had hooked up an ipod to a loudspeaker system and was playing Metallica's Heavy Metal anthem, "Enter Sandman." Cthulhu loomed larger and larger in the distance.

"Two minutes till it reaches Fisherman's Wharf," said nerd number one.

"Cthulhu refers to its species," said Sydney Taine. "We should have realized what it was from the legends, but its size deceived us."

"The legends?" said Ape.

"The stories that it hibernated for long periods," said Sydney. "That it devoured everything in its path. That it's green and extremely ugly. No god is so stupid that it eats all of its worshippers. Nor does a demonic entity allow itself to be trapped in a stone temple, no matter how confusing the architecture."

"Boss, you're not implying—?" asked Ape Largo.

"One minute," said nerd number two.

"Damn, that thing is huge," said the President.

Though Cthulhu was still several miles distant, Vic was willing to swear he could see the monster's numerous mouths gnashing huge yellow teeth in grisly hunger for human flesh. Dozens and dozens of eyes glared down hundreds of feet at the cityscape the monster was fast approaching. All seemed lost.

And then, the sky opened. From out of nowhere two pillars of living flesh, each at least five miles long and a thousand feet thick, appeared, and reaching down, snagged Cthulhu between them. The monster squirmed and squirmed but could not break free. An instant later, the two pillars squeezed together, squashing the five hundred foot monstrosity flat. It moved no longer. With that, the two immense alien *fingers* and the squashed monster held between them vanished.

"When the stars were right," said Sydney Taine, afterwards, "the passageways between universes, between branes, were open. A few monsters stumbled through. Cthulhus, Azathoths, Nyarlathoteps, and the like. Lovecraft thought because of their immense size they were Elder Gods, Lords of another dimension.

"They're not. In their universe, they're actually very tiny. In ours, they're gigantic. It's just a matter of perspective. Simply put, Lovecraft's Elder Gods, Cthulhu and company, are just ugly bugs."

• • • • •

"The oldest and strongest emotion of mankind is fear,
and the oldest and strongest kind of fear is fear of the unknown."
—*H.P. Lovecraft*

Adventure House Presents:

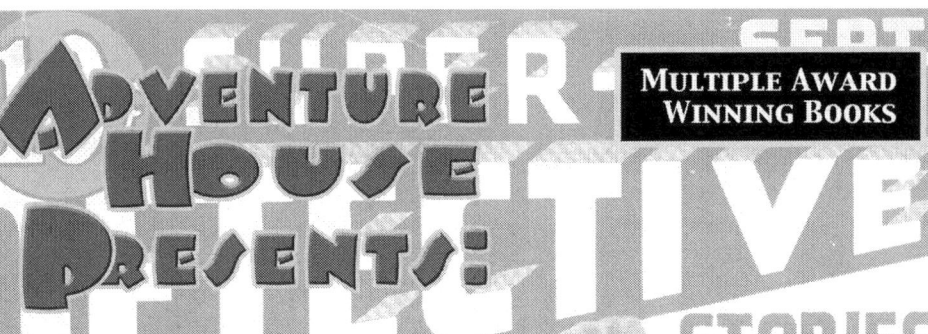

Multiple Award Winning Books

For nearly 10 years, over 300 titles, Adventure House have produced pulp reprints afordable by all. For $14.95, each reprint is packed with the lead and backup stories that really bring out the full flavor of the pulp magazine experience. Vintage ads, full color cover, we've got it all.

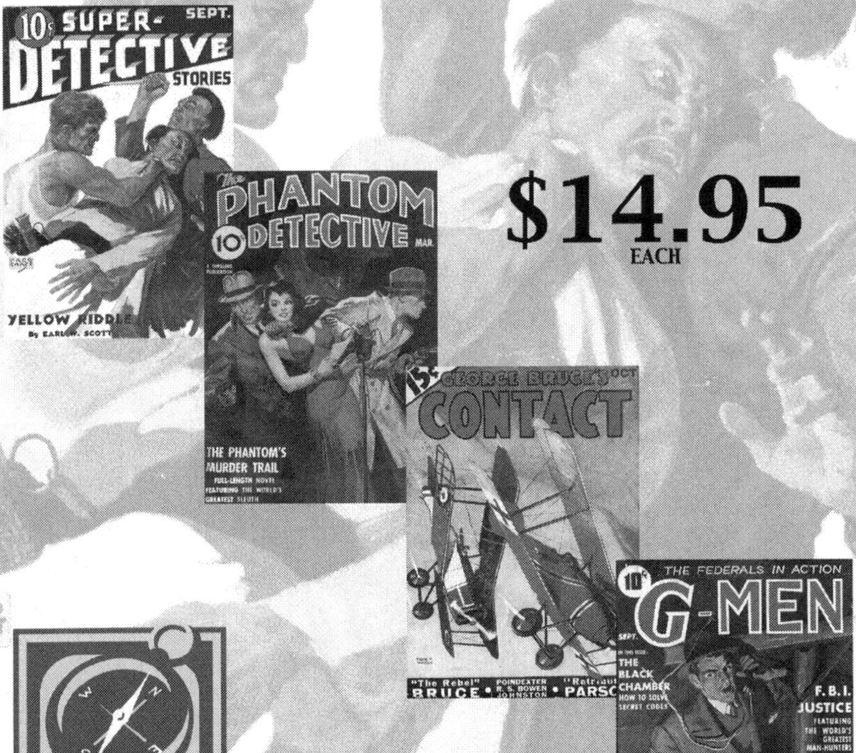

$14.95
EACH

ADVENTURE HOUSE

Adventure House - 914 Laredo Rd - Silver Spring MD 20901
www.adventurehouse.com - gunnison@adventurehouse.com

The Art of H.P. Lovecraft

WILL MURRAY

Perhaps one of the most oft-interpreted figures in fantastic literature is H.P. Lovecraft's high priest of R'lyeh, Great Cthulhu.

In the decades since "The Call of Cthulhu" was first published, countless artists working in virtually every medium have attempted to visualize Lovecraft's greatest concept. And with varying degrees of effectiveness, inasmuch as no definitive rendering has ever eclipsed any other.

But there is a definitive Cthulhu.

In a 1933 letter to Robert Bloch, himself an amateur artist at that time, HPL revealed:

"Drawing your story themes is really an excellent idea, which makes for clear-cut, concrete visualization. I have done it once or twice—notably when designing nameless monsters like Cthulhu or the denizens of the Mountains of Madness—and I always prepare maps and diagrams where complicated action occurs. Thus I made a complete chart of Innsmouth before finishing the 'Shadow.' Some day I may try to draw a map of Arkham."

It's an obscure fact that Lovecraft, story weaver, poet, and tireless letter writer, dabbled in art as well. In fact, in his youth he was known to experiment in watercolors, and one possible example of these—a plant study—seems to have survived, showing a modest and decidedly mundane talent which HPL appears to have allowed to atrophy in adulthood.

Fortunately, Lovecraft's more mature pen-and-ink work, usually executed in the margins of stories, in plot notes and huddled in his voluminous letters, have mostly survived. They run the gamut, from crudely self-conscious self-portraits to humorous caricatures of himself in periwig and 18th Century attire generating mountains of letters that pile up, threatening to engulf him—an uncannily accurate portrait of his later life when correspondence seemed to literally overwhelm the writer.

Maps seemed of particular interest to HPL. His map of Innsmouth is in truth not much more than a connect-the-dots route that the unnamed narrator takes during that novella's famous flight-and-pursuit scene, with only the critical streets indicated. If there is a fully-detailed Lovecraft map of Innsmouth, it has never been rediscovered.

However, as he told Bloch, Lovecraft from time to time worked out the physiological mechanics of some of his more ultramundane creations on paper.

Among them, Cthulhu. Although the original conception of Cthulhu seems not to have survived, no less than three drawings of the infamous soapstone

Cthulhu carving, dated May 11, 1934, were executed, apparently at the request of his friend, Robert H. Barlow, whom he was visiting at the time.

Like much of Lovecraft's pen-and-ink work, these are crude, and were conceived to elaborate design details, and not function as art.

The surviving Cthulhu drawings show a classic airplane-style "three view" (front, back and sides) of a rather portly Cthulhu squatting on a stone block covered with prehuman petroglyphs. Subsequent artists have executed more arresting and awe-inspiring versions than Lovecraft's own, but it being HPL's work, no one can gainsay that it is the most faithful depiction ever committed to paper.

Of course, it is painfully evident that Lovecraft the artist tended toward doodling, and the tentacle-visaged Cthulhus he drew, sadly, evoke no fear in the viewer. They are curiosities. The Cthulhuvian body is bloated, seemingly fungoid or scaly, as is the melon-like head. The beard of tentacles droops listlessly for such a fearsome entity, and appears vaguely wormy. On either side of the face, set fish-fashion, are a triple cluster of too-round orbs. And the clawed arms and legs, oddly enough, are reminiscent of the back legs of a lobster—probably not by accident. Except for the unimpressive tentacles, there isn't much suggestion of traditional octopi or squid.

Plainly, Lovecraft's artistic skills were not equal to realizing the awesome Cthulhu.

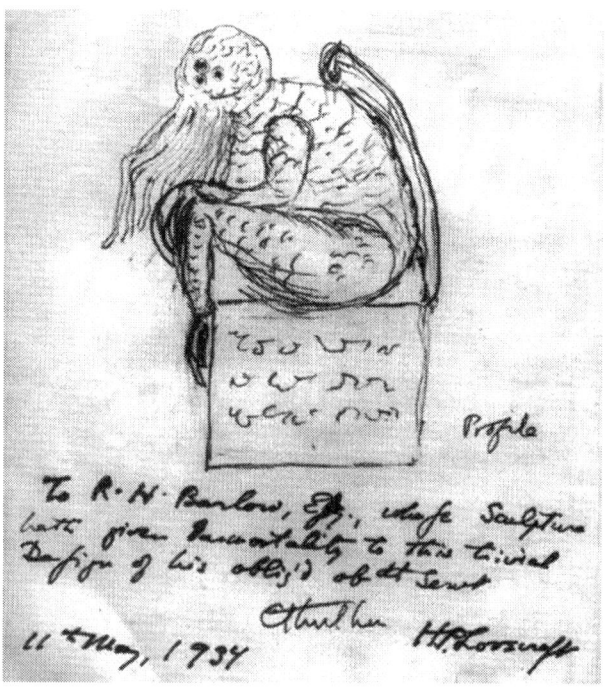

The author's own representation of the Elder God, Cthulhu.

Another drawing, made only months later, obviously not in preparation for the story (written years before) but again seemingly for Barlow's edification, visualized Pickman's Model. Here, Lovecraft committed to paper a moody graveyard scene, replete with tombstones and a lowering moon, and the dog-like ghoul lording over his charnel playground.

The bestial creature is rather muddily rendered and details are not readily discerned. Fortunately, preliminary sketches have been preserved, showing variant modelings of the canine face and other details. Showing, too, that despite their apparent crudity, these were not carelessly tossed-off scribblings. Lovecraft had definite images he wished to capture, and it was only his lack of formal training that kept him from doing so with more memorable results.

Lovecraft defines his vision of Pickman's Model.

The earliest surviving Lovecraftian concept drawings were of the star-headed Old Ones from "At the Mountains of Madness," written in 1931. Done on the back of a disassembled envelope, and crowded by story notes, the central drawing shows a highly-detailed specimen that appears part sea cucumber and part starfish, with coloration, organ functions and size ratios indicated.

Again, the execution leaves much to be desired, but for an artist interested in realizing a star-headed Old One as Lovecraft himself visualized one, this is virtually a blueprint with color notes. One noteworthy detail: the creature's starfish head lies on a horizontal plane, not a vertical one as many subsequent artists

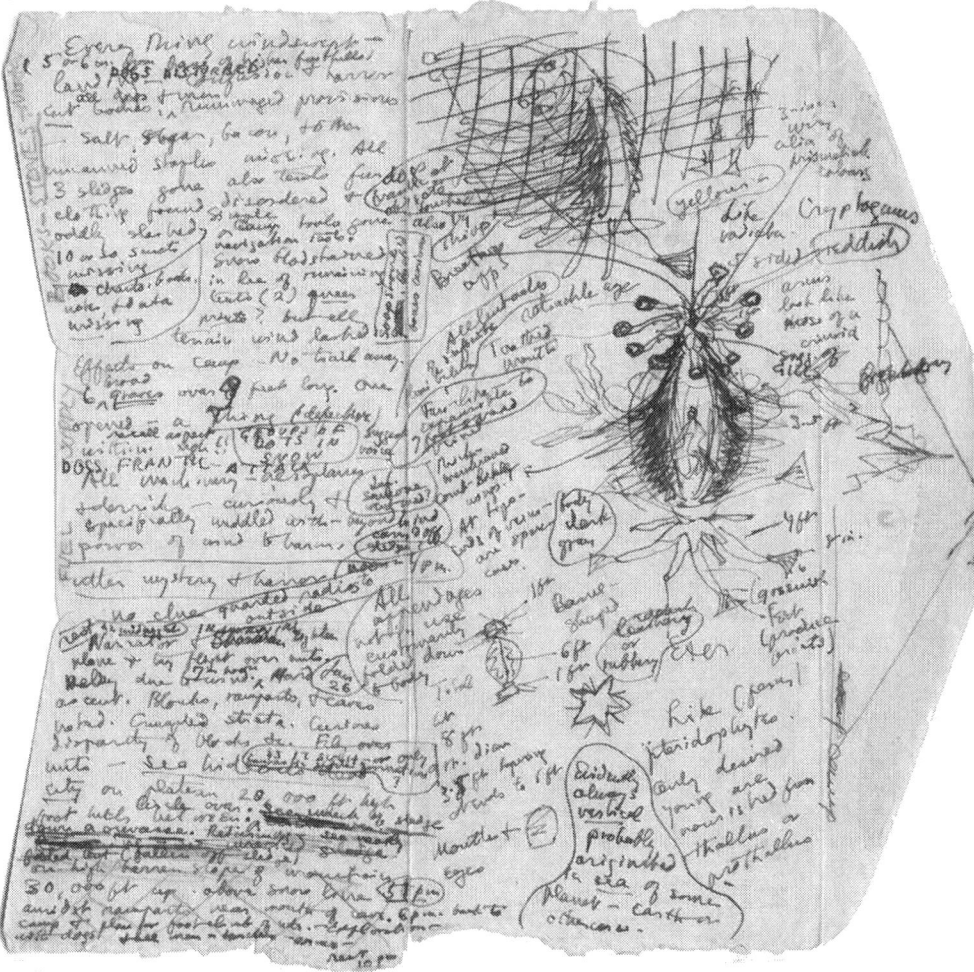

An envelope served as the canvas for Lovecraft to tangibly capture his idea of an Old One along with the story outline for "At the Mountains of Madness."

have concluded, and the flexible eye stalks actually overshadow the "arms" of the starfish-like head, essentially understating it. Too many artists have given these Old Ones an inadvertently cartoonish sunflower aspect by making the starfish function as a face.

Of particular fascination are two other creatures, both crossed out. One shows an amorphous featureless blob like a potato with two rows of flipper-like feet. A shoggoth perhaps? The other is a bizarre creature resembling a malevolent sea-horse or shrimp, with two extraordinarily long and weighty head antennae, dorsal spines, and numerous blunt-ended ventral tentacles. What this creature may be is impossible to say with certainty—an aborted Old One conceptualization, one would imagine.

In the margins of the notes is a simple sketch of what appears to be gigantic Mount Erebus and perhaps the Plateau of Leng, or a mountainous stronghold of the Old Ones. It shows the location of the Miskatonic Antarctic expedition, and was done to help HPL visualize his story setting.

Perhaps the most satisfying Lovecratian conceptualization is of a member of the Great Race as described in "The Shadow Out of Time." The drawing is simply rendered in pencil, so unnecessary shading and scratchy ink lines are pleasingly absent. Like the Old Ones visualization, this 1935 drawing includes a color key and function guide.

When "The Shadow Out of Time" was first published in *Astounding Stories*, artist Howard V. Brown choose to depict a member of the conical Great Race on the cover. The similarities between his version and the Lovecraft sketch are amazing. Lovecraft's version is squatter and makes the four neck-like apex appendages equal in size and weight, where Brown de-emphasized some to create some semblance of anthropomorphism, giving them a friendly, almost whimsical look, but otherwise they are uncannily close.

It's extremely unlikely that Brown was furnished with a Lovecraft sketch to work from. His version was no doubt executed with only HPL's excruciatingly detailed text to go on. Which, when you think about it, is one reason why Lovecraft went to all the trouble. When he wanted to merely suggest a creature, he did that with a minimum of detail, but when he wanted the reader to see with absolute clarity what he was writing about, he spared no details. If a magazine artist happened to get a perfect word picture, and produce a reasonable facsimile as a result, that was to Lovecraft's benefit, too.

Sadly, true Lovecraftian conceptualizations are rare. There are no surviving sketches of Innsmouth denizens, Brown Jenkin, Azathoth, Yog-Sothoth—or even Wilbur Whateley. And the original Cthulhu, perhaps with greater details, is sadly lost. HPL's letters make reference to a map of the Dreamland of "The Dream-Quest of Unknown Kadath," but this cartographic treasure has yet to surface. But those drawings that do survive enable us to see some of Lovecraft's concepts in ways even his painstaking words cannot. And for that, we can be grateful.

Lovecraft did, by the way, get around to his map of Arkham. Virtually every

Artist
Howard V. Brown
1878–1945

Astounding Stories, June 1936

street is named, and the Miskatonic University campus is placed in the city itself. Although topographically inadequate, it shows one other interesting detail—that the Miskatonic River runs through the heart of Arkham in a fashion very, very similar to the way Providence's Seekonk River quietly slips half-submerged under that city, not far from Brown University.

Which suggests that the fabled city of Arkham was modeled, not on witch-haunted Salem as is widely believed, but on HPL's own natal city!

• • • • •

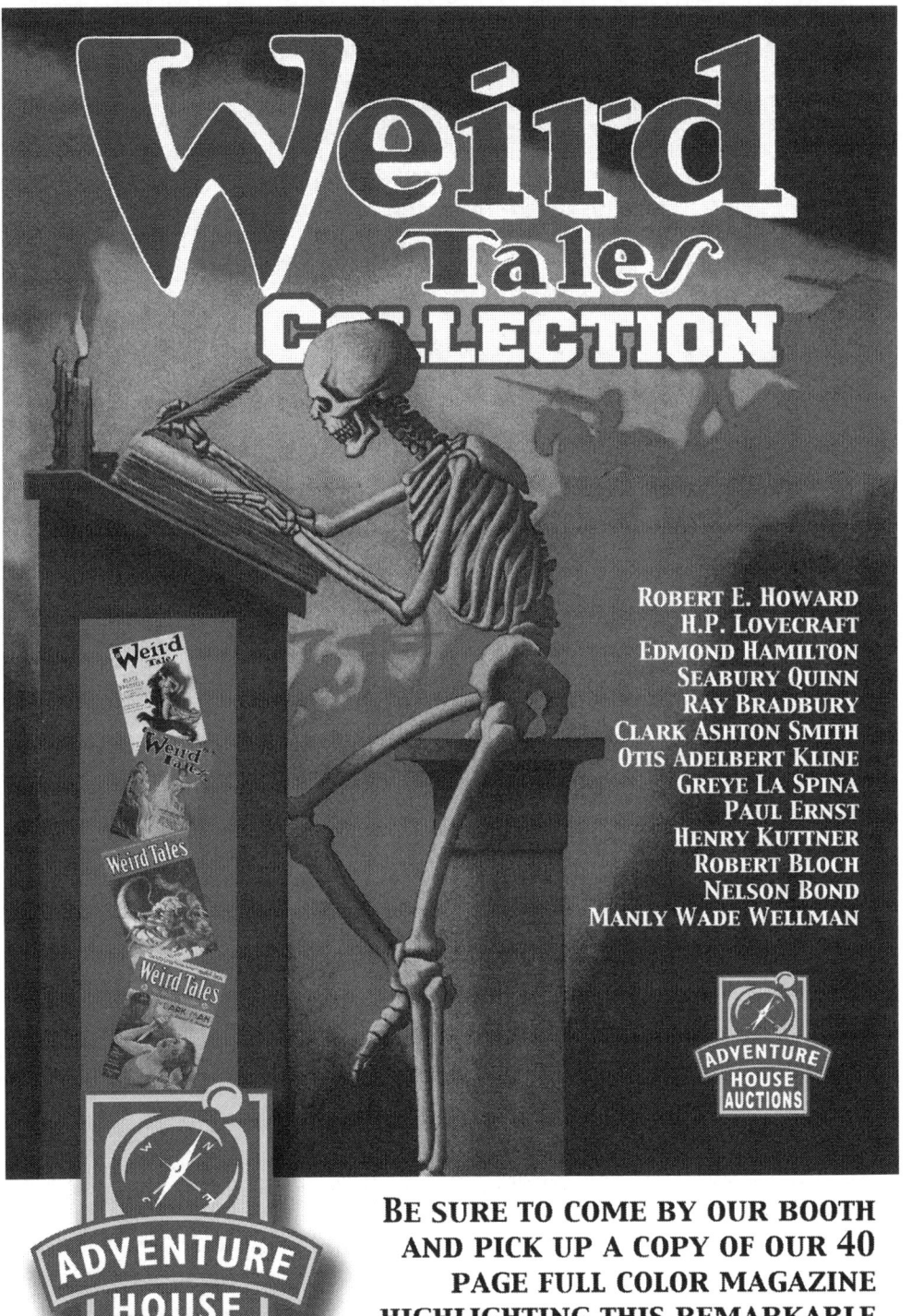

Weird Tales COLLECTION

ROBERT E. HOWARD
H.P. LOVECRAFT
EDMOND HAMILTON
SEABURY QUINN
RAY BRADBURY
CLARK ASHTON SMITH
OTIS ADELBERT KLINE
GREYE LA SPINA
PAUL ERNST
HENRY KUTTNER
ROBERT BLOCH
NELSON BOND
MANLY WADE WELLMAN

ADVENTURE HOUSE AUCTIONS

BE SURE TO COME BY OUR BOOTH
AND PICK UP A COPY OF OUR 40
PAGE FULL COLOR MAGAZINE
HIGHLIGHTING THIS REMARKABLE
WEIRD TALES SET.
ONLY $10.00

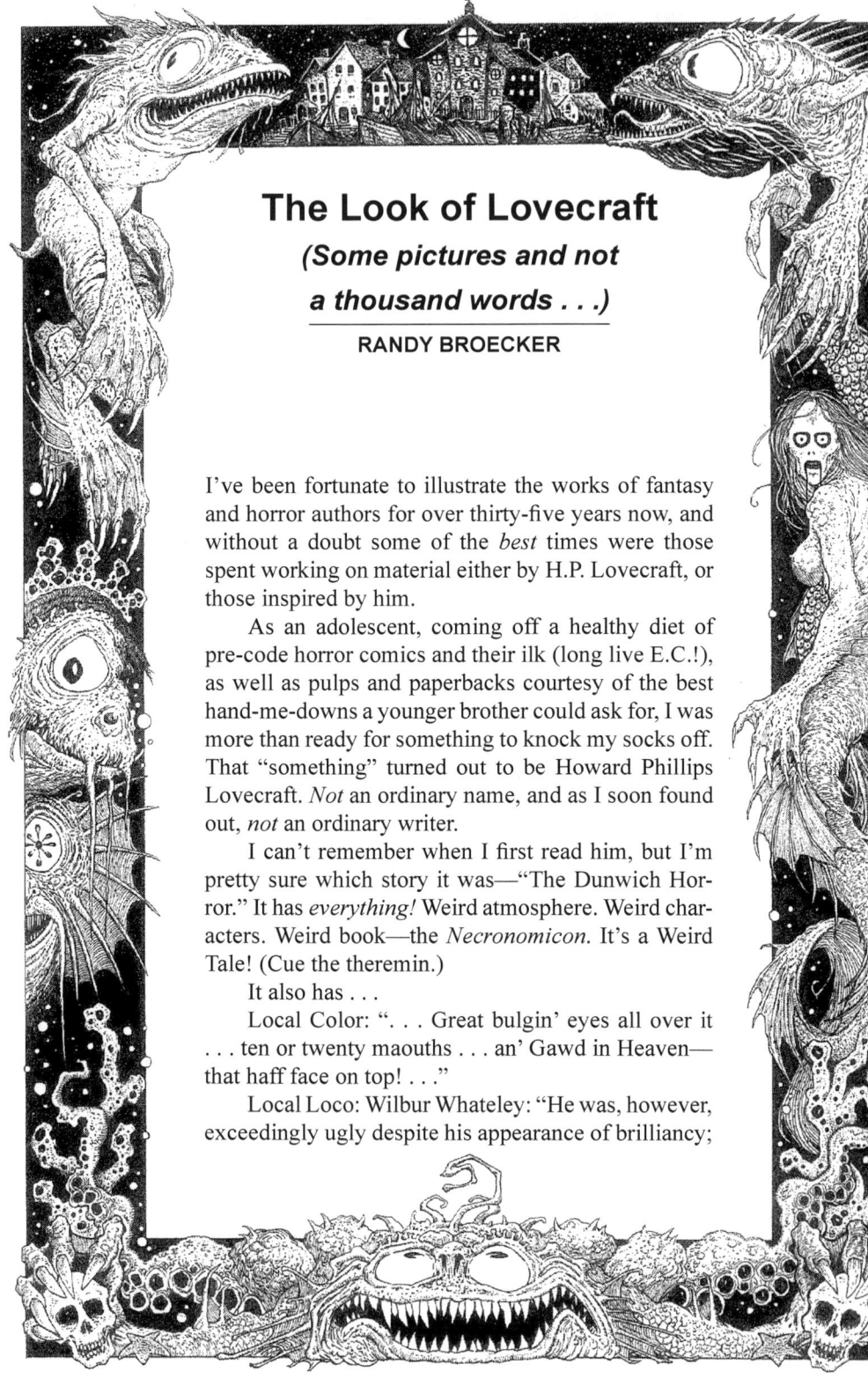

The Look of Lovecraft

(Some pictures and not a thousand words . . .)

RANDY BROECKER

I've been fortunate to illustrate the works of fantasy and horror authors for over thirty-five years now, and without a doubt some of the *best* times were those spent working on material either by H.P. Lovecraft, or those inspired by him.

As an adolescent, coming off a healthy diet of pre-code horror comics and their ilk (long live E.C.!), as well as pulps and paperbacks courtesy of the best hand-me-downs a younger brother could ask for, I was more than ready for something to knock my socks off. That "something" turned out to be Howard Phillips Lovecraft. *Not* an ordinary name, and as I soon found out, *not* an ordinary writer.

I can't remember when I first read him, but I'm pretty sure which story it was—"The Dunwich Horror." It has *everything!* Weird atmosphere. Weird characters. Weird book—the *Necronomicon*. It's a Weird Tale! (Cue the theremin.)

It also has . . .

Local Color: ". . . Great bulgin' eyes all over it . . . ten or twenty maouths . . . an' Gawd in Heaven— that haff face on top! . . ."

Local Loco: Wilbur Whateley: "He was, however, exceedingly ugly despite his appearance of brilliancy;

there being something almost goatish or animalistic about his thick lips, large-pored, yellowish skin, coarse crinkly hair, and oddly elongated ears."

Local Monster: The "Horror" itself. Anyone raised on 1950s Giant Monster Movies and pre-super hero Marvel Comics behemoths ("I Created . . . *Sporr!* The Thing That Could Not Die!") would recognize the "Horror." It smashed down houses, slaughtered cattle, left noxious pools of questionable secretions and strange odors in its wake, along with massive footprints, devoured locals, and, oh yes . . . it was *invisible too!*

I recently re-read it, and let me say right now that H.P. Lovecraft's writing, like a fine wine, only improves with age. For me, in terms of sheer power and strangeness, you can't beat "The Dreams in the Witch House." And once I discovered "The Shadow Over Innsmouth," and

Randy Broecker

"The Call of Cthulhu," I was as hopelessly trapped as any of the protagonists in his stories. I am particularly fond of the "Big C" and the folks of Innsmouth, and usually try to get them to sit for me whenever the stars are right, which fortunately for us isn't too often.

This portfolio is a Pickman Sampler, so to speak, of periodic visits taken to Lovecraft country, and of *all* things *Lovecraftian.* (I love that word, don't you?) The illustrations selected here range from personal pieces to works from three different Lovecraft-inspired anthologies edited by my old friend Stephen Jones. I thank Doug Ellis for the platform to share them with you, and would like to thank the Gentleman of Providence for the inspiration. He has a helluva lot to answer for.

Randy Broecker
Born during the Boulevard Massacre.
Self-educated Illustrator and Master of Black Arts.
Once exiled to Devil's Island for Criminally Insane
Escaped.
Now at large. . . .

Left: Contents Page Design *(Weird Shadows Over Innsmouth,* 2005)

Great Cthulhu! *(Weirder Shadows Over Innsmouth*, 2013)

Night Owls (Limited edition etching,1990)

Servants of Cthulhu *(Weirder Shadows Over Innsmouth,* 2013)

Above: Brown Jenkin (personal piece, 2005)

Left: A Gentleman From Innsmouth (original 2014 remarque in
Weirder Shadows Over Innsmouth)

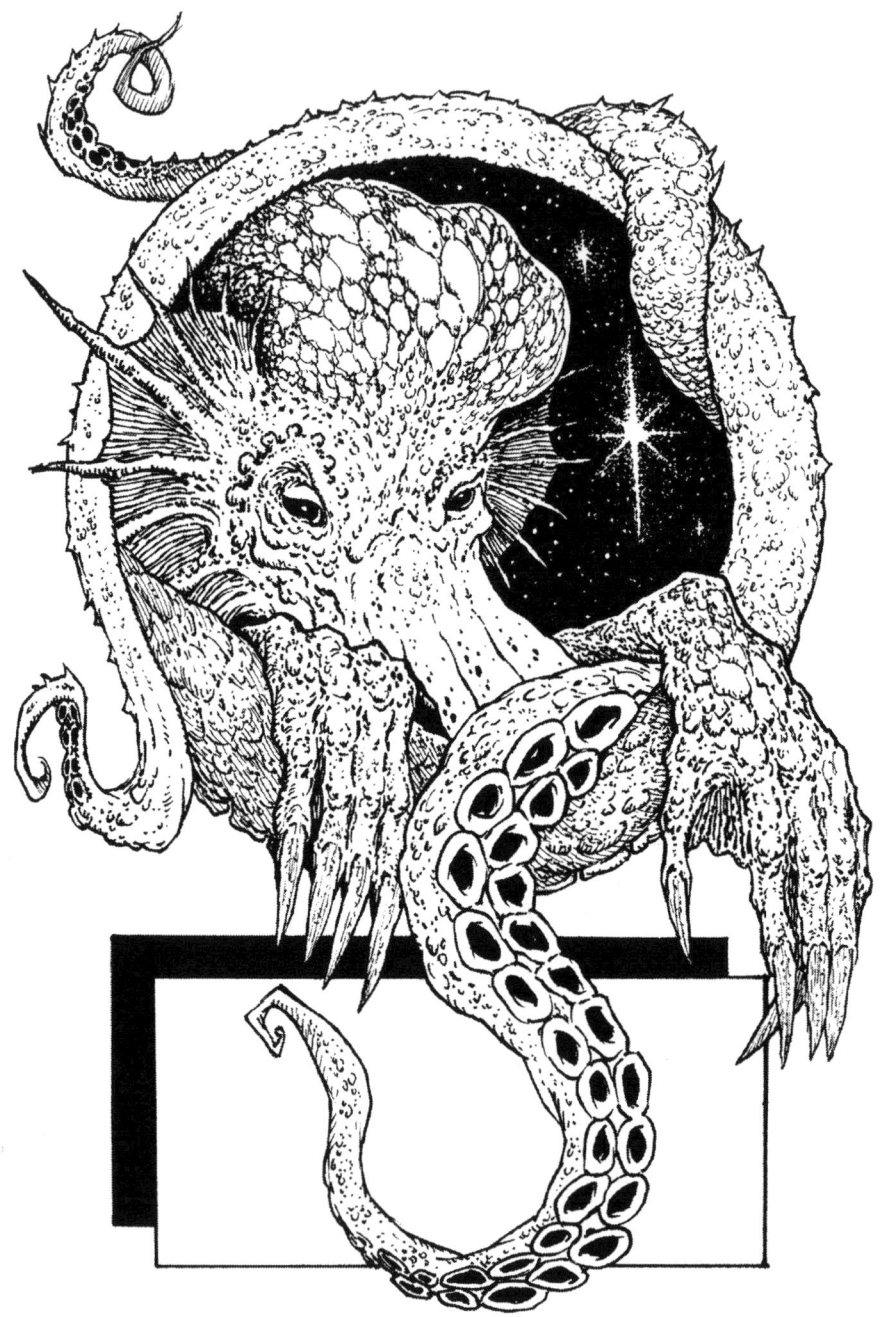

Above: Dagon *(Inhuman Magazine, 2011)*

Left: Cthulhu—His Book (original 2014 remarque in
Weirder Shadows Over Innsmouth)

HPL (personal piece, 1997)

Innsmouth Gothic *(Weirder Shadows Over Innsmouth,* 2014)

That Innsmouth Look *(Weird Shadows Over Innsmouth,* 2005)

Right: Pickman's Model (personal piece, 2008)

The Shadow Over Innsmouth
(original 2014 remarque in *Weirder Shadows Over Innsmouth*)

H.P. Lovecraft—Whisperer In Darkness *(H.P. Lovecraft's Book of the Supernatural,* 2006)

When Wakes Cthulhu *(Weird Shadows Over Innsmouth,* 2005)

"Atmosphere, not action, is the great desideratum of weird fiction. Indeed, all that a wonder story can ever be is a vivid picture of a certain type of human mood. The moment it tries to be anything else it becomes cheap, puerile, and unconvincing. Prime emphasis should be given to subtle suggestion—imperceptible hints and touches of selective associative detail which express shadings of moods and build up a vague illusion of the strange reality of the unreal. Avoid bald catalogues of incredible happenings which can have no substance or meaning apart from a sustaining cloud of color and symbolism."

—*from "Notes on Writing Weird Fiction" by H.P. Lovecraft*

INNSMOUTH
shadows & denizens

a collection of drawings of
the unlikely inhabitants of
H.P. Lovecraft's mythic town

by Mark A. Nelson

Kickstarter campaign launches
May 15, 2015

**ALAXIS
PRESS**
www.alaxispress.com

visit our table for a free bookmark

Street & Smith In Four-Colors

ANTHONY TOLLIN

Seventy-five years ago, The Shadow, Doc Savage, Nick Carter, Bill Barnes, Frank Merriwell, Iron Munro and a variety of other popular Street & Smith pulp characters made their four-color debuts in *Shadow Comics* No.1.

With the exception of *Walt Disney's Comics and Stories,* no other comic book was ever launched with as many pre-proven famous characters. The Shadow had already starred in nearly 200 pulp novels and several films, while his radio show had the highest ratings in daytime radio. *Doc Savage Magazine* was reputed to have the highest per-issue circulation of any hero pulp, while Nick Carter and Frank Merriwell had been American icons going back more than a half century to the dime novel era. *Shadow Comics* No.1 also featured adaptations of *Crime Busters'* Carrie Cashin, the Air Trails Boys and assorted dime novel characters.

In creating the earliest comic book superheroes, Superman's Jerry Siegel and Joe Shuster, Batman's Bob Kane and Bill Finger, Jack Kirby, Stan Lee, Gardner Fox and Will Eisner had taken inspiration from the supermen of their own youth: legendary pulp heroes like The Shadow, Doc Savage, Zorro and The Whisperer.

While smaller pulp publishers like Harry Donenfeld's *Spicy* line and Martin Goodman's Red Circle were quick to jump onto the comic book bandwagon, Street & Smith was slow to move into the rapidly expanding comics market. The nation's largest publisher of pulp fiction magazines had initially rejected comics because it deliberately avoided publishing material that couldn't be printed on their own in-house presses. That changed after Allen Grammer was installed as president in 1938. The former Curtis executive instituted sweeping changes, developing new publishing formats and eventually eliminating the company-owned printing plants.

During the 1930s, *The Shadow Magazine* had been a force unto itself, a groundbreaking publication that relaunched the long-dormant single hero magazine that reached its zenith with the 1940s comic book explosion. By 1937, Shadow wordsmith Walter Gibson was lobbying Street & Smith to expand The Shadow franchise into newspaper strips and the mushrooming comic book field. A veteran of newspaper syndicated features, Gibson was a lifelong fan of the comics medium: "Comics were just beginning when I was very young. The comics that we used to see in newspapers like the *Philadelphia Press* and *North American* consisted of such things as *Hairbreadth Harry, The Airship Man, Foxy Grandpa, The Yellow Kid, Happy Hooligan, Lulu and Leander* and the original *Katzenjammer Kids*. I was brought up on all of those."

Gibson attempted to interest S&S promotions manager William de Grouchy

All Street & Smith comic book images copyright ©Advance Magazine Publishers, Inc. d/b/a Condé Nast.

in a Shadow comic book after noticing that the new comic strip reprint magazines were successfully competing for newsstand space with *The Shadow Magazine.* When de Grouchy pointed out that the most popular newspaper strips had already been bought up by rival publishers, Gibson countered, "Why not get up some and sell them to syndicates and get the rights to use them in comic books? And we should begin with The Shadow." Unfortunately, the executive initially rejected Gibson's suggestion that could have resulted in The Shadow and other Street & Smith characters debuting in comics ahead of Superman and Batman.

Gibson also fielded an offer from Everett "Busy" Arnold of Quality Comics to produce a Shadow comic book supplement for Sunday newspapers, but again failed to interest Street & Smith in the prospect. Unable to license rights to The Shadow, Arnold hired writer/artist Will Eisner to create and package *The Spirit,* a weekly 16-page newspaper comic book that ran for more than a decade and featured a character similarly garbed in a dark suit, hat and gloves.

In 1939, Street & Smith executives finally bowed to the inevitable and began preparations to launch a comic book line.

Though its hero pulps were regularly being mined for plots by comics creators, Street & Smith's first attempt at a comic strip superhero wasn't the more prominent Doc Savage or The Shadow, but Aarn Munro, a science fiction superman originated by *Astounding Stories* editor John W. Campbell in his 1934 novel, "The Mightiest Machine." One of the inspirations for Jerry Siegel's Superman, it featured the exploits of a human born and raised under Jupiter's heavy gravity, who arrived on Earth to discover that his denser molecular structure gave him invulnerablity, super strength and the ability to leap huge distances. The popularity of the *Superman* and *Buck Rogers in the 25th Century* features led Street & Smith to develop a comic strip version of Campbell's pulp superman, whose childhood under the influence of Jupiter's heavy gravity had resulted in a powerful musculature and a denser physical anatomy than Earthmen's.

John W. Campbell

"The business of turning 'The Mightiest Machine' . . . into a strip has been started," Campbell wrote on September 19, 1939. "The promotion department is at work on a preliminary work-up of the thing, all agreeing that it ought to be a natural, having the best features of Superman and Buck Rogers, plus some new items of its own. Aarn Munro makes a nice superman, you know, and further, we'll make him look like a superman."

Street & Smith began developing *Astounding Comics,* an anthology title to be headlined by the renamed Iron Munro as "The Astounding Man," with The Shadow, Doc Savage and Nick Carter as supporting features. While still in the planning stage, the project was briefly renamed (and advertised as) *Street & Smith Comics* before finally arriving on newsstands as *Shadow Comics* on January 21, 1940. The eleventh hour title change was initiated to tie in with the publicity generated by the release of Columbia Pictures' *Shadow* movie serial.

Despite its title, *Shadow Comics* was an anthology series, which like DC's *Action Comics* and Timely's *Marvel Mystery* focused not only on the exploits of its titular star but a variety of supporting features. The first issue led off with a six-page Shadow adventure illustrated by Vernon Greene, followed by Iron Munro (initially scripted by Otto Binder and continued by science fiction great Theodore Sturgeon in later issues) and Doc Savage (with artist Maurice Gutwirth adapting a 1934 Lester Dent radio script into a six-page story). Eight pages were devoted to Nick Carter while seven were allotted to Bill Barnes (by veteran pulp illustrator Frank Tinsley), five to Frank Merriwell, four to Theodore Tinsley's distaff sleuth, Carrie Cashin, and three to the Air Trails Boys. The remainder of the book featured four-color versions of assorted Street & Smith dime novel properties, including Diamond Dick and Horatio Alger's Bob Burton and Mark the Match Boy.

Doc Savage and *Shadow Magazine* editor John Nanovic had little interest in the new medium, so William de Grouchy became comics editor. "De Grouchy didn't know how to get hold of artists," Gibson recalled, "so he looked for someone to do it, and ran into that guy Chiseler. His real name was Chesler, but we called him Chiseler. He was a character.

"Jack Binder was his right-hand man. So they gave Binder the first Shadow comic. They may have taken one of the radio plots. They just wanted to see what he could do with it. When I came in, they had that made up. So I said, 'Go ahead and run it.' That was the first issue. From then on, I took over and tied them in with the pulp magazine. So de Grouchy broke off with Chesler and went with Binder."

Brothers Jack and Otto Binder.

The brother of science fiction author Otto Binder, Jack Binder (1902–1988) was born in Austria-Hungary and emigrated to the United States in 1910. Binder had attended the Chicago Art Institute, studying with legendary Tarzan illustrator J. Allen St. John. Binder produced spot illustrations for *Weird Tales* and science fiction pulps including *Thrilling Wonder Stories* and *Astounding Science Fiction,* before going to work as art director of Harry Chesler's comics shop.

Binder left Chesler to organize his own comics shop in 1940, initially producing material for Street & Smith and Fawcett, and later adding Nedor and Timely to his client list. Binder recalled:

> [Comics] were a great part of my life in those days, and I took them very seriously. In fact, when I had my first staffing at Englewood, New Jersey, I invested, on the average, about $1500 per man before they could really produce what I considered quality work. And I would give [new artist assistants] demonstrations on how to really get involved in a story and to act this thing out and make believe that you are this particular character, and to give it everything the artist had. Of course, in a sense, they had to follow instructions on what I call "a Binder Shop Technique," because it was my work they were selling. And that was the reason I had to . . . develop a shop, because of the demand for my work and possibly even the need for it. I had quite a few artists—Bill Ward, and Ken Bald, and Boyajian, and the rest of them, very accomplished artists—who when they went on their own, never lost their own

The Binder Studio, circa 1941 included (clockwise from top left): Jack Binder, Ken Bald, Sam Brooks (top right), Vic Dowd, Ray Harford and Bob Boyajian.

style. I always made sure I wouldn't make machines out of them and gave them a very practical, very realistic way of approaching the Binder commercial technique without losing their own personality or their own talent and style because of working for me.

The Binder Studio soon grew to include 38 writers and artists including Bill Ward, Al Bare, André LeBlanc, Kurt Schaffenberger and John Spranger, supervised by Wendell Crowley (later the editor of *Captain Marvel)* and assistant editor Babette Rosmond, who moved on to an editorial position in Fawcett before joining Street & Smith to edit *The Shadow* and *Doc Savage* digests.

Though many Street & Smith comic features bore Jack Binder's signature, the studio owner was kept busy selling the service. "He did some art directing, initially, but I never saw him put pencil or pen to paper," recalled Ken Bald, who doubled as art director and primary cover artist. "He was like the company salesman; he got us the work. Wendell Crowley handled all the business and the numbers—he was the office manager. . . . At the beginning, Bill [Ward] did breakdowns for the rest of us. One guy would then pencil main figures, another penciled secondary figures, another did backgrounds, and then the inkers did the same thing. We'd all sign our names on the backs of the original art, detailing what we had done. It was a production line—everything was piecework."

Walter Gibson learned of Street & Smith's new line after the first issue of *Shadow Comics* had already been completed, but quickly lined up the lead scripting assignment and eventually received $10 per page, double Street & Smith's standard rate.

". . . *Shadow Comics* was intended to promote the Street & Smith magazines, which were going at full blast," Gibson recalled. "The Shadow was chosen as

Walter Gibson and Vernon Greene produced *The Shadow*
daily newspaper strip and the early comic book stories.

the leader because of its adaptability to comic treatment. *The Shadow Magazine* had already reached its two hundredth issue, so I conferred with the editor, John Nanovic, and between us we chose the magazine covers and novels that we felt would attract new readers to the magazine. I then turned out six- to eight-page scripts highlighting action scenes from such novels as 'The Crime Oracle,' 'The Salamanders' and 'Lingo.'"

His comic book assignment soon led to a syndicated *Shadow* daily strip, though its genesis actually began in November 1935 during a chance encounter between Walter and the manager of the *Ledger* Syndicate aboard a train from New York City to Philadelphia. "I gave him a copy of 'Zemba,' my latest Shadow novel, and after he read it, he called me up and said that when the time was right, he would like to start a new comic strip based on my Shadow novels," Gibson wrote in *The Shadow Scrapbook.* "That time came in 1940, when Street & Smith decided to add comic books to their magazine line, with The Shadow as the leader. I reduced excerpts from Shadow stories to short comic strips, and one was turned over to Vernon Greene, who was intrigued by the possibility of extending the continuity to cover the entire novel. I contacted the *Ledger* and they liked the idea, so Vernon finished the first week of art while I was finishing several weeks of continuity. We went to Philadelphia together and made an instant sale. Back in New York, terms were approved by Street & Smith, who arranged to have the strip remade into pages for the *Shadow Comics.*" Between 1940 and 1942, Gibson and Greene produced fourteen Shadow newspaper storylines, most of which were later reworked for Shadow Comics.

Doc Savage Comics No.1 arrived on newsstands on April 16, 1940, expanding the Street & Smith comics line with new features including Cap Fury, Pete Rice, boy sleuth Danny Garrett, The Whisperer and Walter Gibson's Norgil the Magician. The first issue led off with the second installment of "The Land of Terror" serial by pioneer African American cartoonist Elmer Stoner that had

Doc Savage Comics No.1 lead off with an adaption of "The Land of Terror" by Elmer C. Stoner.

begun in the third issue of *Shadow Comics* and concluded in the second issue of *Doc Savage Comics*. An eight-page condensation of "The Polar Treasure" by artist Jack Alderman appeared in the third issue, followed by a 17-page adaptation of "The Terror in the Navy" in the fourth issue, with art by Jack Binder's new assembly-line comic art studio which had recently broken away from Chesler's operation. With its hooded criminal mastermind and explosive plot, "The Terror in the Navy" adaptation was the longest single-issue *Doc Savage* pulp adaptation produced during the Golden Age of Comics, and the creative benchmark for the series.

Unfortunately, it was also the final comics story adapted from the original pulp novels. With the next issue, Doc Savage was re-imagined as a costumed superhero by writer Carl Formes and Jack Binder. The August 1941 edition of *Doc Savage Comics* chronicled how the Hermit of Thibar recognized the shipwrecked Savage as the "Chosen One" and presented him with a magical blue hood adorned with the Sacred Ruby, a gem that provided Doc with super strength and the power to control minds.

In the November 1942 issue of *Doc Savage Comics,* Doc's team was drawn into the investigation of a murdered cabby by his sister, Myrtle Rose, who would continue as a regular in the comic book and radio series. Arriving at a cemetery at midnight, Doc is confronted by a death's-headed fiend whom he recognizes as his former assistant, Zashu Mittory, who had been terribly burned two years earlier in a lab accident. The Skull's disfigurement left him mentally unstable and has provoked him to exact a terrible revenge against his former friend, just as Doctor Doom would be similarly motivated decades later in Marvel Comics' *The Fantastic Four.*

The Skull reappeared with an expanded origin in the May 1943 issue. "A Toast to Blood!" revealed that Doc and Mittory were childhood friends, both raised to become mental giants by Clark Savage, Sr. Writer Edward Gruskin's creation provided Doc Savage with an adversary who was truly his deadly opposite.

Doc Savage Comics never found its niche, and was cancelled after just twenty issues, at a time when wartime paper shortages also forced Street & Smith's pulps to be reduced to digest size. The Man of Bronze's four-color adventures returned to the back pages of *Shadow Comics.* However, other Street & Smith comics fared better.

Sport Comics debuted in the fall of 1940 but was retitled *True Sport Stories* with its fifth issue. Initially supervised by *Sports Story Magazine* editor Charles Moran, the comic continued through its fiftieth issue to become Street & Smith's third longest-running comic series.

Bill Barnes, Air Ace Comics ran a dozen issues before its title was shortened to *Air Ace,* under which title it continued for another twenty issues.

A suggestion from *Astounding Science Fiction* editor John W. Campbell resulted in Gibson writing a script for *Bill Barnes, Air Ace* that foreshadowed the fall of Japan due to the dropping of an American atomic bomb: "I dug into some Japanese lore, and I found out that there was a tradition that someday the whole of Japan would tilt up and flop in the Pacific deep. So that's what our bomb did to it

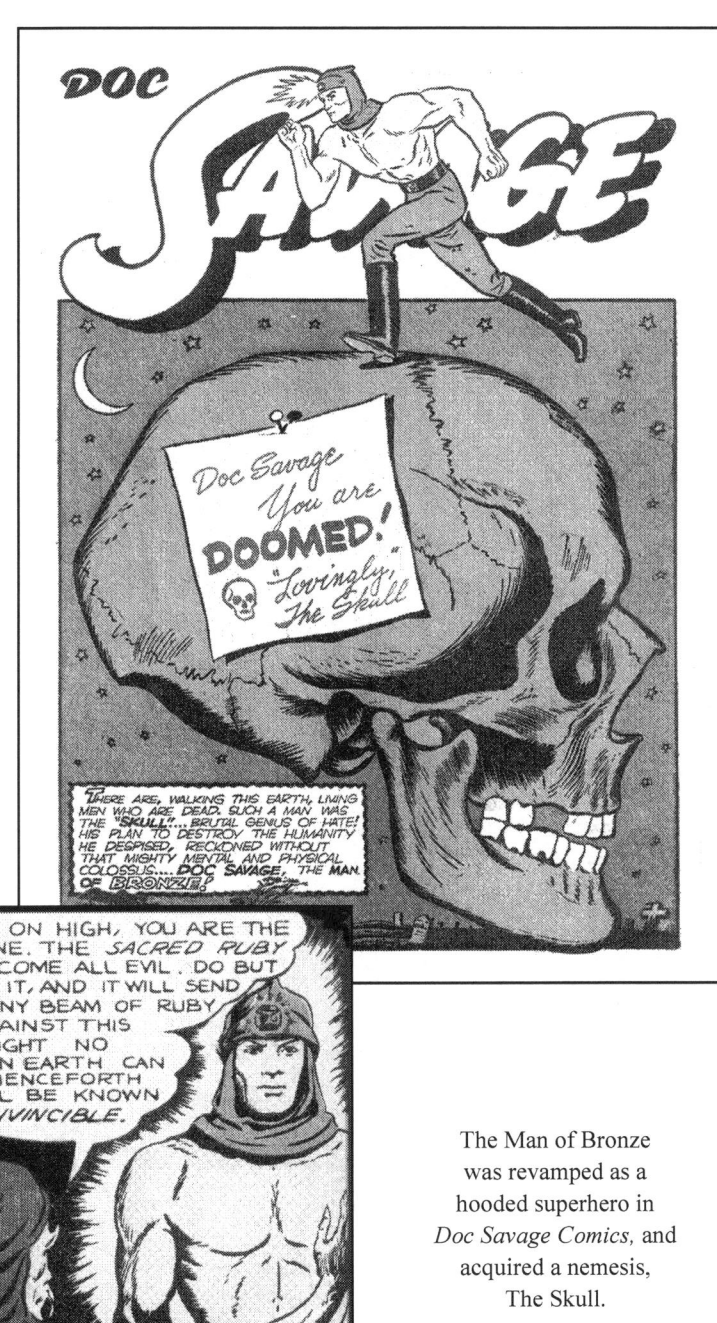

The Man of Bronze
was revamped as a
hooded superhero in
Doc Savage Comics, and
acquired a nemesis,
The Skull.

Bill Barnes Comics, No.1, Dec. 1940.
The back cover reprinted a cover from
The Shadow Magazine to promote the
new *Shadow Comics,* which had
debuted in May of that same year.

in the double-spread—it showed the whole island going over!" The comic came out just six months after Pearl Harbor. "Immediately the government wanted to know what the hell is this? . . . And on the cover it says: 'How to Actually Blow Japan Off the Map!'" When G-men descended upon Street & Smith's offices, Gibson and Campbell had to produce prewar science articles to prove there hadn't been a security leak.

Super-Magican Comics debuted in 1941, featuring adventures of stage magicians, headlined by the real-life Harry Blackstone, along with Tao Anwar, Boy Magician, and Red Dragon, who was soon spun off into his own title.

"Street and Smith were always thinking of doing new comics at that time," Gibson recalled. "So, the deal I proposed was this: The comics were selling for a dime and would they give Blackstone returns at 5 cents apiece? That meant that Blackstone could order a thousand a week, hold a matinee on Saturday and the theatre would pay 5 cents. "So I called Street and Smith and talked to William de Grouchy: 'How many do you have to print to make a comic book go over?'

"He said: 'We could get by with 50,000 returns and stash 50,000 or so.'

"I said, 'Fine, I've got your 50,000 for a year. Blackstone will buy them at a nickel a piece. At cost.' 'Oh, boy!' he says. 'That's great! You can't lose.' So we made a deal right then.

"I took a drawing room on the day train from Boston to New York and knocked out the first script to

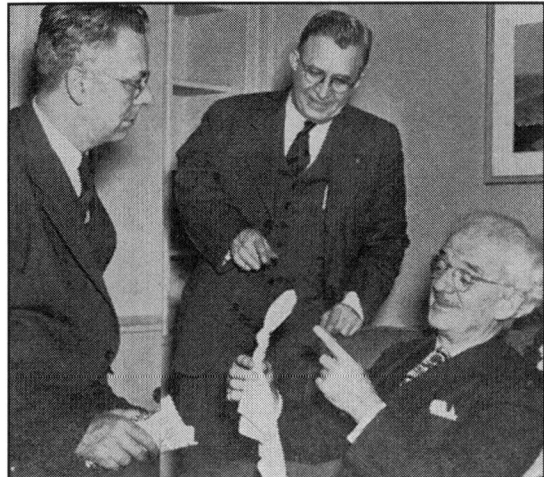 

Walter Gibson (left) wrote fictionalized adventures starring his friend
Harry Blackstone (right) in *Super Magician Comics* for Street & Smith.

Super Magician," Gibson continued. "They had some other things they could throw in the first issue. But we began to run more magic-related things as *Super-Magician* went along."

Originally titled *Super-Magic Comics,* the first issue was actually too successful. "They sold that so fast and did so well with it that they couldn't supply Blackstone with the copies he wanted."

Super-Magican Comics ran through 1947, with a 56-issue run eclipsed only by *Shadow Comics,* before being retitled *Red Dragon Comics* for its final seven issues.

With Doc Savage and Bill Barnes now headlining their own comic anthologies, a variety of replacement features debuted in *Shadow Comics* including the Dead End Kids, the Hooded Wasp, Supersnipe, the robotic Iron Ghost, Beebo the Wonder Horse and a revived Little Nemo in Slumberland feature by Robert Windsor McCay, whose father had created the legendary Sunday strip in 1905.

Sixty-five years before television's *The Big Bang Theory* made the culture of geek chic, cartoonist George Marcoux (1896–1946) launched *Supersnipe* to poke fun at the new superhero genre and its overly imaginative fans. Closely following in the creative footsteps of Sheldon Mayer's Scribbly & the Red Tornado in DC's *All-American Comics,* Supersnipe was the second comic book feature to poke fun at the recently launched superhero genre and its fans. Supersnipe debuted in the March 1942 issue of *Shadow Comics,* and returned in subsequent issues and also appeared in *Doc Savage Comics* and *Army & Navy Comics,* which became *Supersnipe Comics* with its sixth issue. A hit with 1940s comics readers, *Supersnipe Comics* continued through forty-four issues to become Street & Smith's fourth longest-running comic book series, after *Shadow Comics, Super-Magician Comics* and *True Sport Picture Stories.*

Supersnipe was Koppy McFad, "the boy with the most comic books in America." Curiously, Koppy's collection appeared to consist solely of titles published by Street & Smith. Since the pulp giant seldom published more than a half-dozen comics a month, one is forced to assume that McFad must have been hoarding huge quantities of multiple copies. Longing to be a superhero, Koppy created his makeshift costume out of his grandfather's red-flannel longjohns and his father's lodge cape. In his fantasies, Koppy wasn't an awkward ten-year-old but a dynamic superhero whose foes included Hitler himself.

By the early 1940s, The Shadow's pulp fame had been eclipsed, first by the hugely popular MBS radio series and then by Street & Smith's comic book. By 1941, *Shadow Comics* was selling 425,000 copies a month while pulp sales continued to decline. With their target audience departing to fight World War II, wartime paper rationing forced publishers to drop pulps for the more-profitable comic magazines. Since two 64-page comics could be published with the same amount of paper stock as a 128-page pulp, Street & Smith dropped *The Shadow* to monthly frequency in February 1943, and by the end of the year reduced to a half-size digest format.

"During that period, I began turning out three Shadow scripts a month, averaging ten pages each," Gibson recalled, "so when *The Shadow Magazine* went monthly, instead of twice a month, in March 1943, the comic book took up the slack, aided by *Super-Magician Comics,* which I originated and for which I was also doing thirty pages a month."

While Walter Gibson's earliest comic book scripts had adapted his earlier pulp novels, the diminishing sales of pulps and the ever-growing popularity of the Mutual radio series encouraged him to realign the comic feature with the radio series. Margo Lane, a radio creation, had made her illustrated debut in *Shadow Comics* No.1. Gibson regularly showcased the character in his daily strips and comic book stories for more than a year before The Shadow's girl Friday tentatively moved into the pages of *The Shadow Magazine.*

The radio show's expanding influence was further demonstrated when the comic book Shadow began relying on hypnotic invisibility rather than dark shadows for concealment. The cover of the eleventh issue of *Shadow Comics* proclaimed: *"The Shadow Shows In Pictures How He Becomes Invisible."* On the Editor's Page, the tenth anniversary of *The Shadow Magazine* was celebrated with an announcement that confirmed the growing influence of the radio broadcasts:

> In this issue we show The Shadow in pictures for the first time doing the "invisible man" act. The Shadow in the comics is now exactly the same as The Shadow over the radio. You'll be thrilled by it!

Shadow Comics No.11 led off with a comic adaptation of "The Leopard Strikes," a just-aired radio show. After conferring with the art department, Gibson himself suggested using blue color surprints to simulate The Shadow's invisibility. Original art was now prepared with The Shadow inked in on a separate vellum overlay, a technique continued throughout the run of the comic magazine.

Gibson also introduced two new aides in his comic strip continuities. The teenaged Skeet Harley was obviously intended to appeal to young fans of Milton Caniff's Terry Lee and Superman's radio pal, Jimmy Olsen. Valda Rune was first introduced as an aide of the villainous Althor, but quickly reformed and joined The Shadow's team. The sultry blonde was cut from the same bad-girl cloth as Burma in *Terry and the Pirates* and the sky-pirate Sala in *The Phantom*. Better suited as a crimefighting partner than Margo, the blond adventuress was portrayed as a potential romantic rival for Cranston's affections.

In 1943, Street & Smith received a notice from the Bell Syndicate threatening a lawsuit if Valda wasn't immediately dropped from the pages of *Shadow Comics*. The syndicate insisted that Valda was a blatant imitation of Tarpé Mills' Miss Fury, a feature appearing in newspaper comic pages and a Timely comic book. When de Grouchy confronted Gibson with the accusation, the writer responded, "Let 'em sue," explaining that the *Shadow Comics* tale was a reprint of an earlier newspaper story, and producing syndicate proofs that predated Miss Fury.

Shadow Comics No.11, 1941

Evidence suggests that Gibson preferred his own creation to radio's Margo Lane, often contrasting Valda's competency and athleticism with Margo's bumbling antics. Valda took center stage in stories requiring quick wits or provocative cheesecake. She went undercover as a scantily clad nightclub singer in "The Shadow and the Crime Wizard," and confronted a Shadowy doppelganger in "The Shadow at Ghost Manor." In "The Shadow Meets the Spy Master," a 1943 comic-book story adapted from the 1939 "Smugglers of Death," the swimsuited Valda (standing in for an earlier pulp heroine) comes to the rescue of the unconscious Shadow, appropriating his cloak, slouch hat and automatic to battle a spy ring.

"The Shadow comic strip's life was all too brief, because of circumstances beyond even The Shadow's control," Gibson explained. "Following Pearl Harbor, newspapers were so full of war news that they stopped adding new features such as comic strips; and when the paper shortage threatened, they began to discontinue those that they had most recently taken on. . . . I felt it was just as well, as Vernon Greene had joined the Air Force and was no longer able to provide his inimitable artwork."

Following Greene's departure, the lead feature in *Shadow Comics* was continued by the Binder Studio and Al Bare. Gibson reintroduced major pulp villains including Shiwan Khan and the Voodoo Master, and also created an array of new superfoes including Devil Kyoti, Solarus, the Crime Wizard and the Talon.

Walter Gibson adapted many of his *Shadow* pulp novels into the comic book format, but the process appears to have been reversed with "The Devil Monsters;" the novel's plot almost certainly originally developed as a comic book storyline. Monstrodamus and his Devil Monsters battled The Shadow in a groundbreaking 126-page serial that continued through eight consecutive issues of *Shadow Comics* in 1943. The Monstrodamus epic held the record as the longest comic book story, until displaced by Otto Binder's 232-page "Monster Society of Evil" serial in *Captain Marvel Adventures* (which concluded in 1945).

The World War II draft led to a severe manpower shortage in the young comic book industry. Beset by constant staff turnovers, Jack Binder closed his shop in early 1943 to become sales manager for the C.C. Beck studio. The artist shortage threatened Street & Smith's comics line until Walter Gibson came to the rescue. The Shadow's raconteur knew that his former employer, the *Philadelphia Ledger,* was cutting staff, including its Sunday magazine art department. Gibson recruited the out-of-work illustrators to staff Penn-Art, a new comics shop that de Grouchy set up in Philadelphia. Charles Coll (the cousin of illustrator Joseph Clement Coll) served as art director, while George Carney handled Penn-Art's business affairs and Gibson himself worked as copy editor.

"We had very unusual artists," Gibson recalled. "We had one fellow named Russell Henderson. He did Blackstone. There was Al Bare. Our art director was Charlie Coll. He was Jack Binder's right-hand man. Charlie Coll was an old *Ledger* artist from Philadelphia. He came to New York and did a lot of comics work. He wanted to stay in Philadelphia, so we opened the studio there. Some of the artists were excellent. They were illustrators and put a real dash in the comics."

Charles Coll also provided spot illustrations for Street & Smith's pulp line and cover paintings for the 1947 *Shadow Annual* and a pair of *Shadow* digests. Coll and Gibson introduced a youthful invisible protégé of The Shadow in 1946. The Tibetan-trained Shadow Jr. returned in two 1947 solo stories before the feature was cut short when Gibson departed in a contract dispute.

Not everyone shared Walter Gibson's fondness for Penn-Art's product. "They had some pretty grubby artwork back then," comic artist Howard Nostrand insisted: "Street and Smith published out in Elizabeth, New Jersey. This Bill de Grouchy . . . had a little studio he ran called Penn-Art. I think he must have been paying these guys about $10 a page to turn out finished artwork. The stuff was really just miserable. . . . This Bill de Grouchy was taking kickbacks and the whole bit."

After returning from World War II military duty, Edd Cartier resumed illustrating the digest-sized *Doc Savage, Astounding Science Fiction* and *The Shadow* magazines, and also tried his hand at drawing comic book stories for Street & Smith's *Super-Magician* and *Red Dragon Comics*. Just as it had on the pages of pulp magazines, Cartier's artistry attracted the praise of his fellow artists. Howard Nostrand who, teamed with Bob Powell, Marty Epp and George Siefringer, would follow Edd on the Red Dragon feature, recalled that Cartier "was one of the main-

 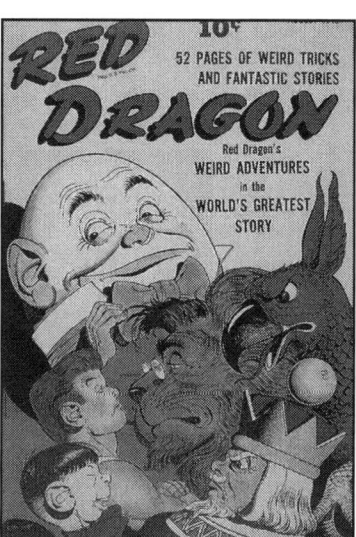

Edd Cartier illustrated several stories and covers for *Red Dragon Comics.*

stays in the science fiction jazz back then, too. He was doing comics . . . but the stuff was like blueprints, you know. I mean the stuff was tighter'n a tick. Really great. I don't see how he could make any money doing it, 'cause it looked like he used a ruling pen and compass on everything."

Shadow Comics reached its greatest heights soon after Gibson's abrupt departure when Street & Smith's comic features were assigned to Bob Powell, a veteran of Will Eisner's early comics shop and the co-creator of Blackhawk. Widely recognized as the best artist to draw The Shadow's adventures during the Golden Age of Comics, Powell's dark visions and superb placement of blacks created as stylish a world for the comic book Shadow as Edd Cartier's illustrations had for *The Shadow* pulps. Howard Nostrand recalled:

> There were three of us working for Powell when I started with him; at one point he had five assistants, but his best work was done when he had the original three. There were George Siefringer, who did backgrounds; Martin Epp, who inked, lettered and helped George on backgrounds. I started out inking and then got into doing backgrounds (when George was too hung over or just AWOL) and then penciling.

Powell also turned out spot illustrations for *The Shadow* digest along with its final cover before the title reverted to its original prewar pulp size. In stark contrast to Jack Binder, Bob Powell was personally involved with all the art produced by his shop. As Nostrand explained:

> The way the drill went was as follows: Powell would pencil the story; it

would then be sent to the publisher to be lettered, have the borders inked in and have any changes the art director deemed necessary. When we got it back Bob would ink in the faces, I would ink in the figures and George and Marty would do the backgrounds. If the story was particularly heavy as far as backgrounds were concerned, and I finished inking the figures first, I would then help out on backgrounds. Marty generally took care of the cleaning up, erasing and whiting out mistakes and brushstrokes that went over borders. Powell would then give it a final onceover and it would then be mailed to the client.

From 1946 on, Bob Powell's art shop produced the lead features for most of the Street & Smith comic titles, including *Ghost Breakers,* a Red Dragon spinoff that presented fictionalized adventures of Dr. Neff, a real-life magician famous for his midnight haunted house shows. Backup features were illustrated by future comics great Joe Maneely and Richard Waring Rockwell (nephew of legendary *Saturday Evening Post* cover artist Norman Rockwell). During his tenure, Powell produced superb adaptations of many outstanding *Shadow* radio broadcasts including "Spider Boy," "Bayou" and "The Curse of the Cat." Ironically, the audio dramas adapted more successfully to the visual medium than the pulp novels.

Shadow Comics reached a milestone 100th issue, but ended with the following number, when Street & Smith canceled all its pulp-paper magazines with the single exception of *Astounding Science Fiction.* The final issue of *Shadow Comics* appeared in the spring of 1949, along with the last issues of *Doc Savage* and *The Shadow magazines*.

ANTHONY TOLLIN is a noted expert on comics, pulps and old-time radio. He was a prominent colorist and assistant production manager for DC Comics, contributing to *The Shadow* (1970s) with articles and *Shadow Strikes* (1990s) as a colorist. As the editor-publisher of Sanctum Books, Anthony has issued nearly 200 Shadow novels and hopes to eventually bring all 325 Shadow pulp novels back into print in uniform non-flaking editions. He has also published authorized editions of nearly 170 Doc Savage novels, plus reprints of The Avenger and The Whisperer, and will soon be publishing a deluxe hardcover reprinting the entire two-year run of The Shadow newspaper strip.

In addition to his skills as a writer and historian, Anthony Tollin participated in the comic book revivals of Tarzan, Korak, The Shadow, Justice, Inc., John Carter, Carson of Venus and Doc Savage, and in 1979 co-authored *The Shadow Scrapbook* with Walter B. Gibson.

During his decade-long association with Radio Spirits, Anthony Tollin wrote more than 70 historical booklets for OTR cassette and CD releases, including many collections of pulp-related radio programs that further promoted this bygone era, and helped introduce its classic characters to new generations of fans. He also scripted more than a thousand episodes of the nationally syndicated *When Radio Was* hosted by Stan Freberg and two historical scripts narrated by Walter Cronkite, and served as Historical Consultant on the television documentary *Martian Mania: the True Story of the War of the Worlds* hosted by James Cameron.

Anthony was the 2011 recipient of the Munsey Award.

THE SHADOW KNOWS!

DWIGHT FUHRO

IS SIMPLY THE TOP BUYER OF HIGH GRADE SHADOW PULPS AND VINTAGE SHADOW COLLECTIBLES "IN THE WORLD"

PAYING TOP DOLLAR FOR

- INDIVIDUAL *HIGH GRADE SHADOW PULPS* OR AN *ENTIRE HIGH GRADE SHADOW PULP RUN.*
- *ORIGINAL SHADOW COVER PAINTINGS* BY ROZEN AND GLADNEY.
- *ORIGINAL INTERIOR SHADOW PULP ART* BY CARTIER AND LOVELL.
- *SHADOW RADIO AND PULP; PREMIUMS, TOYS,* AND *RARE* ITEMS!
- *SHADOW ADVERTISING AND PROMOTIONAL POSTERS* (BLUE COAL, STREET & SMITH, ETC.) FROM THE 1930's -1950's.
- *OTHER HIGH GRADE PULPS & RARE PULP RELATED ITEMS!*

(306) 531-2211 (C) • (306) 545-5460 (H)
EMAIL: dwightfu@yahoo.com

183

THE GARDEN OF TNT

by William J. Makin

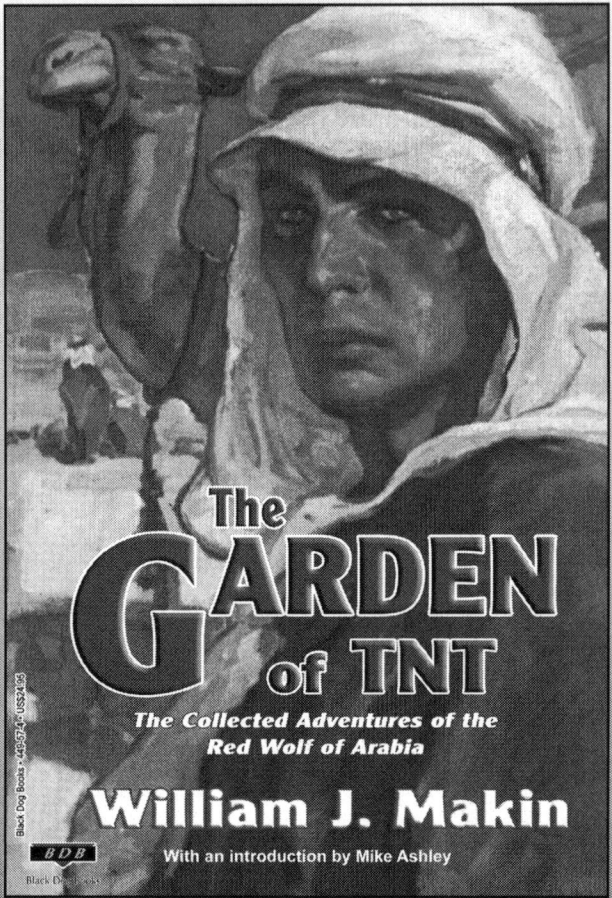

Walking a tightrope of fragile alliances, undercover British Intelligence agent Paul Rodgers, aka the Red Wolf of Arabia, faces off against revolutionaries and foreign dignitaries, trying to sway the balance of power following the Arab revolt.

Drawn from Makin's personal travels and peppered with intimate color and background, it's little wonder that the Red Wolf of Arabia stories were reader favorites when they first appeared.

Now collected for the first time in book form are the complete thrilling adventures of the Red Wolf of Arabia—over 500 pages of action and espionage excitement in the shifting sands of international intrigue!

With an introduction by Mike Ashley.

BLACK DOG BOOKS
1115 Pine Meadows Ct.
Normal, IL 61761-5432
www.blackdogbooks.net I info@blackdogbooks.net

Follow us!
Twitter.com/blackdogbooks1
Facebook.com/blackdogbooks1

The Street & Smith Comics

MICHELLE NOLAN

Only a publishing company as large, as versatile, and as well-capitalized as Street & Smith could maintain not only a decade-long monopoly on general-interest sports pulps, but also a five-year monopoly on sports comic books.

The success of *Sport Story Magazine,* which ran 427 issues from 1923–1943—and had no general-interest competitor during its first decade—no doubt inspired Street & Smith to create the first genuine sports comic book, *Sport Comics,* in 1940. Some sources cite anthology titles such as Fiction House's *Fight Comics* and what became Harvey's *Champ Comics,* but their content only partially dealt with sports.

Sport Comics, which became *True Sport Picture Stories* with Vol.1, No.5 (Feb. 1942), was one of four undated first issues released by Street & Smith in 1940. The others were anthology comics with titles based on the firm's famed hero pulps—*The Shadow, Doc Savage* and *Bill Barnes Air Ace.*

Comic books had become a commercial sensation by 1940, especially with the advent of Superman in 1938 and Batman in 1939, both smash hits that gained their own titles in the year following their debuts in anthology titles. Street & Smith, however, published only eleven issues of comic books across those first four titles in 1940, so the mighty firm was apparently not yet totally sold on four-color funny books.

Street & Smith never did become a top-tier comic book publisher. In contrast to the firm's approximately 9,000 pulps—well over one-fifth of all American pulp magazines—the company produced only 351 issues of comics through 1949. In that year, the firm abandoned its pulps and comics except for what had become the digest-size version of *Astounding Science Fiction,* the best and best-selling magazine of its type.

But Street & Smith knew all about winners, having produced by far more long-running, highly successful genre pulps than anyone else, not to mention 1,000 consecutive stories of the ultra-

All Street & Smith comic book images copyright ©Advance Magazine Publishers, Inc. d/b/a Condé Nast.

heroic Merriwell family of athletes from 1896 to 1916. *Shadow Comics* was one of the big winners in all of Golden Age comics, running 101 issues through 1949.

The other winners were the unique *Super-Magician* (56 issues from 1941–1946), the hysterically funny satire *Supersnipe* (44 issues)—and *True Sport Picture Stories*.

How big a winner was *True Sport Picture Stories,* which had a monopoly on the genre through 1945? This big: the title ran 50 issues and all other sports comics in the ten-cent era through 1961 ran only 65 issues combined! (This does not count auto racing comics, which were a genre unto themselves.) Without a doubt, *True Sport Picture Stories* dominated its genre unlike any other title ever dominated any genre, since sports was by far the smallest genre in comics to emerge from the worlds of nickel novels and pulps.

Despite the paper rationing of World War II, *Shadow Comics, Super-Magic, Supersnipe* and *True Sport Picture Stories* did not cut down on their regular runs, nor did *Air Ace,* the title that came out of the 12 issues of *Bill Barnes.* In an era when Superman and Batman were published only bi-monthly in their own titles, The Shadow's name was imposing enough to demand monthly publication from 1943 until the penultimate issue in 1949.

Several comic book publishers did well with successful "true life" comics, including Parents' Magazine with *True Comics,* Standard with *Real Life Comics* and DC with *Real Fact Comics,* along with many other publishers with less-successful true-life types. All of these titles occasionally ran sports biographies, with many featured on the covers. But only Street & Smith mastered the art of the sports comic book.

The significant publishers' sports pulps were all either cancelled, suspended or cut down in frequency during World War II, what with so many of their readers in military service. But *True Sport Picture Stories* did not count on adult readers, and thus remained a big winner.

By the end of the 1930s, the vast majority of the sports pulps focused primarily on team sports, with baseball and football by far the most popular along with boxing, which was huge in the first two thirds of the 20th Century. In the early years of *Sport Story Magazine*—and its first competitor, *The All-American Sport Story Magazine* (1933–1938) from the publisher of

True Sport Picture Stories, April 1944

Ring Magazine—all manner of sporting activities were featured on covers and on their table on contents pages.

Major League Baseball and college football, however, exploded in popularity with the blossoming of commercial radio and greatly expanded newspaper sports sections in the 1930s, so *True Sport Picture Stories* followed the emphasis of the Big Three athletic activities in the pulps. Basketball on all levels and hockey were featured nowhere near as much either in pulps or comics; there were but two basket-ball-only pulps, both one-shots, and no American hockey pulps. (Horse racing was, of course, huge in real life but not in fiction, especially with younger readers.)

That is what made *True Sport Picture Stories* successful: Street & Smith gave the youngsters what they wanted, and that was an endless emphasis on baseball, football, boxing and later basketball. In addition, while plenty of teen and young-adult sports fiction novels were available in hardcover form in the 1930s and 1940s, very few non-fiction books were available to the younger readers of comics. In fact, the primary competitor of *True Sport Picture Stories* following World War II was not another comic book but rather the beautifully illustrated and well-written *Sport Magazine,* which debuted in 1946 as the first large general-interest monthly publi-cation that covered far more than just baseball.

Until the redoubtable Bob Powell hit the post-war art scene in *True Sport*—

and created numerous highly collectible issues!—the art in *True Sport* could most charita-bly described as average at best. But the stories! Now there was some good reading, issue after issue. In recent years, with the emphasis on collecting sports nostalgia as part of Americana, *True Sport* has become signifi-cantly collectible.

Many issues of *True Sport Picture Stories,* indeed, are about as tough to find as the generally scarce 1920s issues of *Sport Story Magazine.* It took me more than 20 years—mostly in the pre-Internet era—to collect the entire 50-issue run of *True Sport Picture Stories,* including the first four issues labeled *Sports Comics.* I have often been told that it's possible no one else has ever collected them all—yet!

Sport Comics, No.1, 1940

Sport Comics hit the stands, apparently in late summer 1940, with full-page ads for *Shadow Comics* No.1 (which came out much earlier) and *Bill Barnes* No.1. *Shadow Comics* No.2 was also undated but No.3 was dated May 1940, so why *Sports Comics* featured a cover of the first issue of *Shadow Comics* is a puzzle. It is certain that no other publisher of any new comic book ever featured a cover blurb like the one for *Sport Comics* No.1: "Life Story of Lou Gehrig in 118 full-color pictures." (The story was 21 pages, then remarkable for a non-fiction comic book tale.)

The fabled "Iron Horse" was ill in 1940—he retired after playing only eight games in 1939, extending his consecutive game streak to a then-record 2,130—and passed away in 1941 at age 38. He was healthy enough to make his immortal "luckiest man" speech on the Fourth of July in 1939 at Yankee Stadium, and that may have inspired *Sport Comics* to tell the tale of Gehrig, since Babe Ruth had retired five years earlier. The cover was unique—the image of a grade-school Lou dreaming of big-league stardom—and would have had special appeal to the millions of young boys who had identical dreams.

Neither Joe DiMaggio, whose record 56-game hitting streak in 1941 still stands, nor Ted Williams, whose .406 average in 1941 remains the most recent season anyone has hit .400, was yet even remotely as heralded in 1940 as Lou Gehrig, so Street & Smith's editors, as usual, knocked it out of the park. *Sport Comics* No.1 rivals *True Sport Picture Stories* No.5 (Feb. 1942) with its Joe DiMaggio biography, plus Fawcett's *Jackie Robinson* No.1 (1949) and Eastern's scarce *Willie Mays* 1954 one-shot, as the most collectible sports comic books, depending on who your hero was.

In my book about team sports fiction in all media, *Ball Tales* (McFarland, 2010), I overlooked *Sport Comics* in my list of fictional sports heroes in newsstand comics. Street & Smith took the vast majority of its comic book features from its pulp library, and thus the baseball hero Lew Young was stolen from *Sport Story Magazine,* where he debuted in April 1940 as a series character. He also appeared in *Sport Comics* No.2 (March 1941) but thereafter was found only in the pulps. In a second fictional sports story in *Sport Comics* No.1, the old-time coach Matty Matthews tells the tale of the mythical pitcher Obadiah Centennial Holm.

Sport Comics No.3 (Aug. 1941) cover-featured "How 5 Rookies Became Stars"—Phil Rizzuto, Gerry Priddy, Lou Novikoff, Lou Stringer and Pete Reiser (who was actually a rookie in 1940). Reiser sustained numerous injuries, spoiling what might have been a Hall of Fame career, so the only one to become a genuine star was New York Yankees shortstop Rizzuto.

When *True Sport Picture Stories* became the title with No.5 (Feb. 1942), it also became the most collectible issue of all. DiMaggio and his astounding feats became the cover feature by Gus Uhlmann and a 32-page epic, truly remarkable for the era. This scarce issue commands big bucks. My personal favorite, however, is the 32-page biography of Mel Ott, credited to the shop art leader Jack Binder in *True Sport* No.7 (June 1942). The spectacular cover is by famed sports cartoonist Willard Mullin, the greatest of them all.

The last of the extra-long most memorable biographies covered Pete Reiser, 26 pages in No.9 (Oct. 1942), and the great brother battery of pitcher Mort Cooper and catcher Walker Cooper, 28 pages in Vol.2, No.2 (Aug. 1948, whole number 14). Another superb cover by Mullin featured Stan "The Man" Musial in Vol.2 No.7 (June 1944), which is likely the most under-rated of all sports comics. Also noteworthy was a four-page picture story on the Negro Leagues in Vol.2 No.9 (Oct. 1944), which likely was their first mention in comic books.

For Americana collectors, Vol.3 No.7 (June 1946) cover-features "Return of the Mighty to the Baseball Diamond," showing DiMaggio swatting headshots of returning servicemen Stan Musial, Bob Feller, Hank Greenberg and Terry Moore, all super stars. A fabulous image!

There was nothing in any 1947 issue of *True Sport* about Jackie Robinson breaking the color line with the Brooklyn Dodgers in April. Street & Smith finally featured Robinson's story in Vol.4 No.6 (April 1948), which hit the stands well before spring training started. Negro League pitching immortal Satchel Paige—a major league "rookie" at age 42 when he went 6-1 in 1948 with the World Series champion Cleveland Indians—has his story told in Vol.5 No.1 (June 1949), the penultimate issue.

Somehow, some weird way, Street & Smith's editors decided to take advantage of the new crime comics craze by including sports murder mysteries illustrated by the scorching Bob Powell covers for *True Sport* Vol.3 No.10 (Dec. 1946), Vol.3 No.11 (Feb. 1947) and Vol.3 No.12 (April 1947). These featured baseball, football and hockey, respectively, in "Murder at the World Series," "Death Scores a Touchdown" and "Danger on Ice." Other fictional accounts also appeared at that time, making sports hash of the title before returning to true tales.

Baseball was cover featured on 20 of the 50 issues, which pretty much matched the percentage of baseball covers on 1940s general interest sports pulps from all companies. Football, though, was featured on only 11 covers—four dealing with college football, three with the pro game, and four with generic scenes.

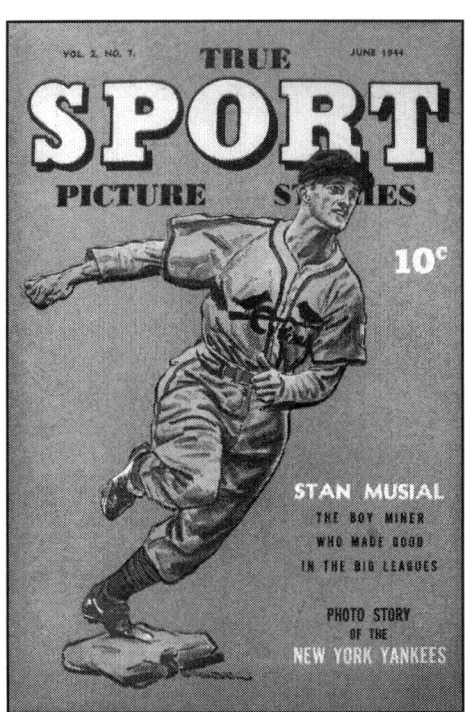

True Sport Picture Stories, June 1944, the Stan "The Man" Musial issue.

The only one of the first nine issues that cover-featured football was *Sport Comics* No.4 (Nov. 1941), which told the story of Frank Leahy, "Notre Dame's Miracle Coach." He had been first signed earlier that same year. In fact, he had likely not yet coached a game for the Fighting Irish by the time this issue hit the stands! Leahy was 33 years old in 1941, but the cover image made him look 50 or 60, a wise miracle-maker indeed. The 30-page biography told how Leahy bonded with coach Knute Rockne while Leahy played at Notre Dame, yet did not mention Rockne's death in a 1931 plane crash. The Rockne biopic from Warner Brothers in 1940 likely inspired this cover.

Another issue of interest to collectors of college football memorabilia is No.10 (Dec. 1942), which featured a 25-page account of how Georgia's Frank Sinkwich went from angry quitter to All-American rushing and passing sensation. The next issue, No.11 (Feb. 1943), features a 28-page biography of Chicago Bears founder and coach George Halas along with 1920s University of Illinois All-American Red Grange, "The Galloping Ghost." Perhaps the most noteworthy story, however, deals with how Cal's Roy Riegels ran the wrong way with a fumble recovery in the 1929 Rose Bowl, creating a safety and ultimately causing an 8-7 loss to Georgia. It's generally considered the most costly bonehead play in football history.

Willard Mullin came through with yet another remarkable cartoon cover in Vol.2 No.5 (Feb. 1944) when he illustrated Green Bay Packers receiver Don Hutson, who likely was the most noteworthy record-setter in pro football until the likes of Jim Brown and Gale Sayers emerged in the 1950s and 1960s. "Hutson holds seventeen different records, the most of any man in football history. Every time he catches a pass he sets a record, every time he scores a point it's a new mark, and every time he catches a touchdown pass it's another new standard." Can you imagine an editor today allowing such redundant verbiage?

The 27th issue of *True Sport* (Vol.3 No.3, Oct. 1945) linked the late Notre Dame heroes George Gipp, Knute Rockne and John Chevigny, who was a Fighting Irish backfield star under Rockne several years after Gipp died. Chevigny, who scored two second-half touchdowns in 1928 to help beat Army for Rockne in the famous "Win One for the Gipper" game, died in action with the Marines at Iwo Jima in 1945. That inspired the writer to end the story, "Somewhere in the volcanic ashes of Iwa Jima, Johnny threw his last block. Now he's gone to join The Gipper and The Rock. It should be quite a reunion."

THE REST OF THE STREET & SMITH COMICS

Street & Smith had its share of shorter-run pulps, but the venable firm achieved great success with its long-running big winners. Seven titles—*Detective Story, Western Story, Love Story, Sport Story, Wild West Weekly, Top-Notch* and *The Popular Magazine*—ran to more than 5,800 issues combined, surpassing the entire outputs of each of the other most prolific pulp publishers, Popular, Munsey and Standard/Thrilling. Hard to believe *The Shadow's* 325-issue run does not rank in the "Select Seven," though it's close.

Likewise, the five S&S comic book winners—*Shadow Comics, Super-*

Army and Navy Comics,
Vol.1, No.1, May 1941

Supersnipe Comics,
Vol.3, No.7, December 1946

Magician, True Sport Picture Stories, Supersnipe (originally *Army & Navy* No.1-5) and *Bill Barnes/Air Ace*—combined for 294 of the company's 351 comic book produced from 1940–1949. S&S did not fool around with low-selling comic books, although World War II paper rationing played a part, too.

The quick success of *True Comics* from Parents Magazine and *Real Life Comics* from Standard in 1941 apparently convinced S&S to begin *Pioneer Picture Stories* and *Trail Blazers,* both very much like *True Comics* (all the true life comics morphed into largely war titles for the duration). *Pioneer Picture Stories* ran 9 issues from Dec. 1941 through Jan. 1943. *Trail Blazers* lasted only 4 issues from 1941 (undated) through No.4 (Oct. 1942) and became an obscure but amusing super hero comic, *Red Dragon,* for five issues through No.9 (Jan. 1944). The first series of *Red Dragon* apparently was none too successful, and all five issues are hard to find.

The only other 1942–1943 S&S titles were the military one-shots *Remember Pearl Harbor* and *Devil Dogs* (both 1942) and *Aviation Cadets* (1943), which, despite its scarcity, is likely one of the least-sought after early S&S issues. On the other hand, *Remember Pearl Harbor* is highly sought after.

Since my father, Phil Nolan, eventually held the highest non-commissioned rank in the Navy and was a Pearl Harbor survivor, I showed my copy to him when I found it in the 1970s. He was suitably impressed by the quality of the stories and the compelling, heart-rending art. I recall during that period, when he served

Air Ace,
Vol.2 No.2, March 1944

Pioneer Picture-Stories,
Vol.1 No.1, 1941

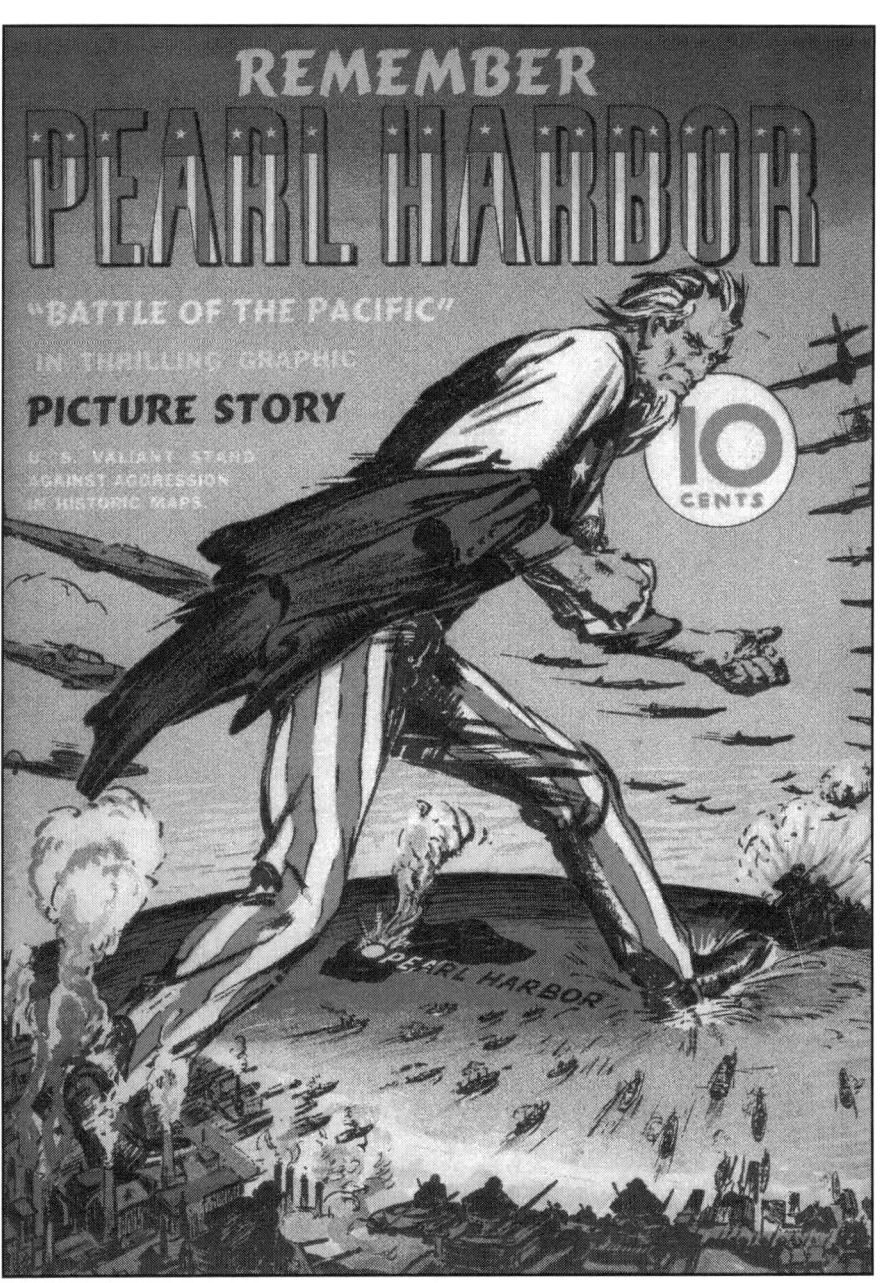

Remember Pearl Harbor, 1942

as President of a Bay Area branch of the Pearl Harbor Survivors Association, he was also impressed by two other fabulous 1942 Pearl Harbor covers and splash pages—*Spy Smasher* No.4 and *Captain America* No.13.

My copy of *Remember Pearl Harbor* has an "arrival date" penciled by the news dealer of Feb. 13, 1942, meaning Street & Smith's editors made an almost immediate decision to produce this truly remarkable piece of Americana. It's a typical S&S product in that Jack Binder was credited with most of the art (whether he did it or not) and Jack Farr and Winsor McKay, Jr., did the rest. I don't know who did the spectacular cover. It's a typical 68-page comic book with extensive text accompanied by stories with balloons, allowing both younger and older readers one of the quickest accounts of the attack. The latest date referred to is Dec. 17, 1941, so the production of this issue was obviously of the highest priority. I can't help wondering if it's the first historic-event "quick book," as we have come to call them, produced about Pearl Harbor. *Devil Dogs,* of course, deals with the heroics of the Marines and *Aviation Cadets* with the predecessor of our modern Air Force and the ever-growing popularity of aviation.

I can't recommend *Remember Pearl Harbor* enough as a truly phenomenal piece of Americana.

With the demise of *Doc Savage Comics* and *Red Dragon Comics* in 1943, Street & Smith published no new titles for nearly four years. The second series of *Red Dragon,* essentially a continuation of *Super-Magician,* ran from No.1 (Nov. 1947) through No.6 (Jan. 1949), with No.7 (July 1949) a last-gasp attempt. Art by Ed Cartier, Bob Powell and a pre-Marvel Joe Maneely makes this title highly collectible.

Likewise, S&S tried to capture part of the burgeoning crime/spy/creepy comics market with *Top Secrets* No.1 (Nov. 1947) through No.10 (July–August 1949) and *Ghost Breakers* No.1 (Sept. 1948) and No.2 (Dec. 1948). The firm's only funny animal title was the one-shot *Kid Zoo Comics* No.1 (July 1948). Apparently the editors immediately decided the anthropomorphic field was too overcrowded, what with Dell's titles leading the way among so many other funny animals at the tail end of the Golden Age. The company also tried

Kid Zoo Comics, Vol.1 No.1, 1948

Buffalo Bill Picture Stories, Vol.1 No.1 and 2, 1949, the final comics
issued from the Street & Smith line.

a Western title with *Buffalo Bill Picture Stories* No.1 (June–July 1949) and No.2
(Aug.–Sept. 1949) before giving up on comics and pulps entirely except for the
best-selling digest *Astounding Science Fiction.*

Today, only *Shadow Comics* is in exceptionally high demand among collectors of Golden Age comics. But if you like those golden oldies, check out the rest
of the often quirky, always fun Street & Smith oeuvre. There's a lot to like.

MICHELLE NOLAN has been a journalist and pop culture historian for 50 years. She started reading and collecting pop culture at age 8 in 1956. In 2014, she received the Inkpot Award at San Diego's
Comic-Con International for her body of work, which includes more than 1,000 articles in magazines,
newspapers and books on 20th Century American pop culture in several distinct disciplines. In all,
she has written more than 10,000 features and news stories, averaging about 200 articles per year, and
remains active as a prolific freelancer in the Pacific Northwest. She is the author of *Love On the Racks:
A History of American Romance Comics* (2008) and *Ball Tales* (2010), a study of team sports fiction
in all media from the 1930s through the 1960s, both from McFarland.

Michelle and longtime friend Bud Plant co-founded the first free-standing American comic book
store, in March 1968, along with several friends. Michelle wrote the first issue-by-issue indexes of
Golden Age super hero comics in 1968–1969 and provided much of the data for the first edition of the
Overstreet Comic Book Price Guide in 1970.

She lives in Bellingham, Washington.

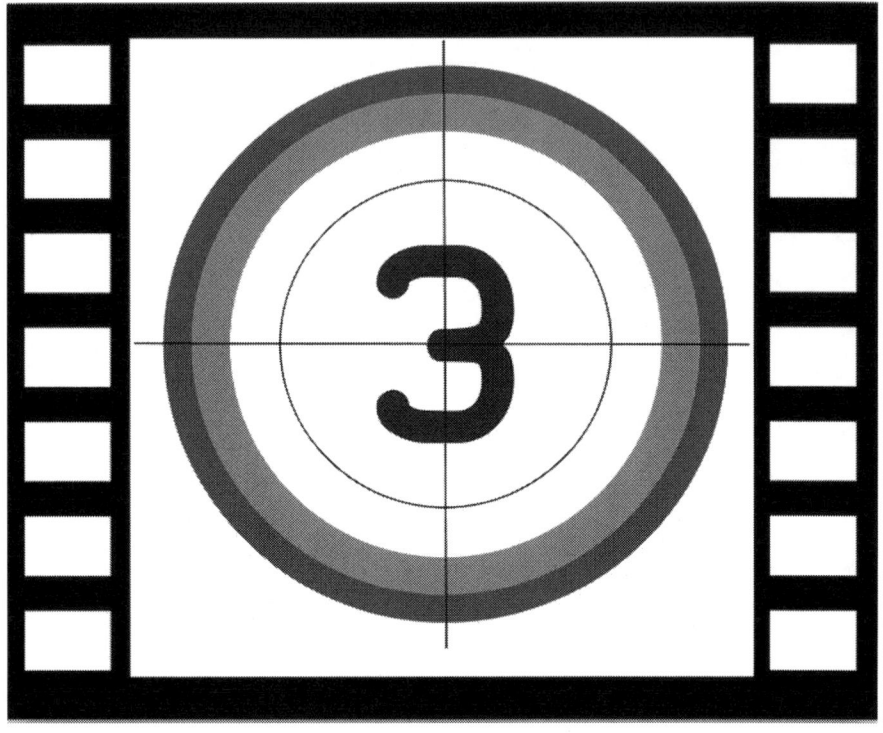

Film Schedule

Friday—

Dagon 12:00pm

Castle Freak 1:45pm

From Beyond 3:30pm

Dreams in the Witch House ....following the auction

Saturday—

The Haunted Palace 10:00am

H.P. Lovecraft's Necronomicon: To Hell and Back 11:45am

The Dunwich Horror...1:30pm

The Resurrected 3:15pm

The Call of Cthulhu ....following the auction

From Pulp to the Silver Screen, 2015

ED HULSE

Our 125th birthday tribute to H.P. Lovecraft extends to movies and TV episodes adapted from his classic pulp stories. Amazingly, it took four decades for Hollywood to discover HPL: the first Lovecraft film, 1963's *The Haunted Palace*, flashed on the nation's big screens fully 40 years after publication of his first story in *Weird Tales*. And relatively few of the Master's yarns were translated to celluloid until the late Nineties, when the floodgates opened. For this year's Windy City Film Festival we've assembled a representative sampling of HPL movies. Friday's lineup is devoted to the Lovecraft-themed output of writer-director Stuart Gordon, who brought mainstream attention to the creator of Cthulhu with his 1985 hit *Re-Animator*, nominally based on "Herbert West, Reanimator." Saturday's lineup is a cross-section of other notable adaptations.

It should be noted that most of the films we're running this weekend are either R-rated or unrated and contain occasional scenes of gore and nudity, making them potentially unsuitable for children.

Dagon (2001)

Despite the title, this Spanish-made film actually adapts HPL's "The Shadow Over Innsmouth." A boating accident off the coast of Spain finds Paul Marsh (Ezra Godden) and his girlfriend Barbara (Raquel Merono) looking for help in the ramshackle fishing village of Imboca. As night falls, people start disappearing and a shroud of unseen menace hangs over the community. Paul and Barbara, pursued by the entire town, learn Imboca's dark secret: that its residents worship Dagon, a monstrous sea god of ancient origin. The film got mixed reviews, although *AllMovie* critic Jason Buchanan said, "Lovecraft fans will most likely be willing to forgive *Dagon*'s shortcomings in favor of a film that obviously shows great respect and appreciation for its source materials." And *Film Threat*'s K.J. Doughten opined, "While not a perfect movie, *Dagon* crams its wild, over-the-top concepts down our throats with so much conviction that we can't help but get swept along for the ride."

Castle Freak (1995)

Stuart Gordon's version of HPL's "The Outsider" was produced by the father-son team of Albert and Charles Band, whose Full Moon Entertainment supplied

Barbara Crampton as the imperiled wife, Susan, in *Castle Freak* (1995).

most of the direct-to-video horror movies that flooded rental-store shelves during the Nineties. In a nod to that market, Gordon included some elements of the "splatter" school, including one surprisingly brutal sequence that Lovecraft would have abhorred. But the film is not without merit; in fact, it's more serious and mature than the lurid VHS packaging would have one believe. After inheriting a 12th-century castle that belonged to a notorious Duchess, John Reilly (Jeffrey Combs), wife Susan (Barbara Crampton), and their blind teenage daughter Rebecca (Jessica Dollarhide) relocate to Italy. The family is a troubled one: Susan blames John for the death of their son in the drunk-driving incident that also cost their daughter her sight. On the advice of the executor, the Reillys decide to stay at the castle until the estate can be liquidated. Unbeknownst to them, a freakish monster remains locked in the basement. This was the third and last HPL-inspired feature film on which Gordon, Combs, and Crampton collaborated.

From Beyond (1986)

Following the surprise success of his first Lovecraft adaptation, *Re-Animator*, Stuart Gordon was inspired to make a series of HPL films with the same stars, along the lines of American-International's Edgar Allan Poe series directed by Roger Corman. *From Beyond*, loosely based on a short story of the same title, reunited *Re-Animator* cast members Jeffrey Combs and Barbara Crampton. It centered on a pair of scientists attempting to stimulate the pineal gland with a device called "The Resonator." An unforeseen result of their experiments is the invasion of Earth by creatures from another dimension. They capture the head scientist and whisk him away to their world, returning him as a grotesque shape-changing monster that preys upon others at the laboratory. Shot in Italy to save money, *From Beyond* boosted the previous film's gore quotient and included some S&M content that the MPAA objected to. Gordon was forced to re-cut several sequences and completely eliminate some five minutes of footage. The missing scenes were restored in 2007 and we are running the original director's cut.

Dreams in the Witch House (2005)

One of Lovecraft's most memorable yarns gets fine treatment by HPL aficionado Stuart Gordon. It originally aired on American television on November 4, 2005, as the second episode of *Masters of Horror*. University student Walter Gilman (*Dagon*'s Ezra Godden) moves to a cheap room in an old boarding house. He hears shrill screaming and rushes to help his neighbor, Frances (Chelah Horsdal), when she is menaced by what appears to be a large rat. Walter becomes close with Frances and even lends her money to keep her in the boarding house. A neighbor warns the student that the house is evil—and that his room houses something unspeakably evil. Gordon's adaptation streamlines the story somewhat and gives it a contemporary setting, but the essential elements remain intact and overall *Dreams in the Witch House* is quite effective.

The Haunted Palace (1963)

We're running this American-International release starring Vincent Price because it was the first feature film that brought Lovecraft to the screen. Ostensibly another of Roger Corman's popular and profitable Edgar Allen Poe adaptations, it's actually derived from HPL's "The Case of Charles Dexter Ward." In their book *Lurker in the Lobby: A Guide to the Cinema of H.P. Lovecraft*, Andrew Migliore and John Strysik write: "*The Haunted Palace* is a seminal film for Lovecraft lovers; it is the first major motion picture to introduce [Lovecraft's] creation[s]—the *Necronomicon*, and those cosmic abominations Cthulhu and Yog-Sothoth—to a general audience. [Lovecraft's] obsession with the past is clearly presented, and in a heartfelt passage at the end of the film, so is his belief that mankind is a minor species adrift in a malevolent universe. The film strikes a good balance between narrative and action, and Vincent

Roger Corman turned to Lovecraft for the storyline of *The Haunted Place* (1963).

Vinent Price as Charles Dexter Ward/Joseph Curwen in *The Haunted Place* (1963).

Price is, well, priceless as Ward/Curwen. The supporting cast is solid and the art direction by Daniel Haller is really quite good for such a low-budget film. Roger Corman did an admirable job as the first American feature-film director to stake out some cinematic high ground for the cosmos-crushing adaptations of [H.P. Lovecraft] to follow." We're also running Dan O'Bannon's 1992 take on "Charles Dexter Ward," *The Resurrected*, but the two movies are strikingly different, though each excellent in its own right.

The tag line at the top tells you all you need to know about *The Dunwich Horror* (1970).

H.P. Lovecraft's Necronomicon: To Hell and Back (1993)

An American-made anthology film, *Necronomicon* was produced in 1993. It was directed by Brian Yuzna, Christophe Gans and Shusuke Kaneko and was written by Gans, Yuzna, Brent V. Friedman, and Kazunori Itô. It stars Bruce Payne , Richard Lynch, Jeffrey Combs (who plays Lovecraft himself in a newly devised framing story), Belinda Bauer, and David Warner. Three segments are based on a trio of Lovecraft classics: "The Drowned" comes from "The Rats in the Walls," "The Cold" from "Cool Air," and "Whispers" from "The Whisperer in Darkness." A film-festival favorite released in home-video formats, *Necronomicon* did quite well in America but was even more profitable in European and Asian markets. Truth be told, two of the film's three segments leave a little something to be desired, but we've included *Necronomicon* because it enables us to present three Lovecraft tales for the price of one, so to speak. And "The Drowned" really is quite good.

The Dunwich Horror (1970)

This drive-in favorite released by American-International Pictures attained considerable notoriety for a supposed topless scene featuring top-billed Sandra Dee, the screen's original "Gidget" and a squeaky-clean teen idol. (Actually, a body double was used for the shot.) But *Dunwich Horror* also familiarized American audiences with key elements of the Cthulhu Mythos and therefore warrants inclusion in our lineup. The film opens at the fictional Miskatonic University in Arkham, Massachusetts, where Dr. Henry Armitage (Ed Begley) has just finished a lecture on the sinister *Necronomicon*. He gives the book to his student Nancy Wagner (Dee) to return to the University library. She is followed by a stranger, who later introduces himself as Wilbur Whateley (Dean Stockwell). Using his hypnotic gaze, Whateley persuades Nancy to give him the terrible tome, with which he hopes to unleash ancient and malevolent forces. Clearly an AIP attempt to capitalize on the phenomenal success of 1968's *Rosemary's Baby,* this neatly turned out Lovecraft adaptation takes liberties with the original but replicates the oppressive, unwholesome atmosphere of timeless horror.

The Resurrected (1992)

Directed by Dan O'Bannon (screenwriter of *Alien* and long-time horror/SF filmmaker), this is an adaptation of "The Case of Charles Dexter Ward." Claire Ward (Jane Sibbett) hires private investigator John March (John Terry) to look into the increasingly bizarre activities of her husband Charles Dexter Ward (Chris Sarandon). Ward has become obsessed with the occult practices of raising the dead once practiced by his ancestor Joseph Curwen (Sarandon in a dual role). As the investigators dig deeper, they discover that Ward is performing a series of grisly experiments in an effort to actually resurrect his long-dead relative Curwen. In their book *Lurker in the Lobby: A Guide to the Cinema of H.P. Lovecraft*, Andrew Migliore and John Strysik write: "*The Resurrected* is the best serious Lovecraftian screen adaptation to date, with a solid cast, decent script, inventive direction, and excellent special effects that do justice to one of [Lovecraft's] darker tales."

The Call of Cthulhu (2005)

This lovingly crafted adaptation of the seminal Cthulhu Mythos story was produced, written, and directed by the team of Andrew Leman and Sean Branney for distribution by the HPL Historical Society. In a bold but inspired move, Leman and Branney filmed it as a black-and-white silent movie and employed for its special visual effects only such techniques as would have been available to filmmakers in 1928, when the yarn was published in *Weird Tales*. Extremely faithful to HPL's original, *The Call of Cthulhu* has found almost universal favor with Lovecraft lovers. Andrew Migliore and John Strysik write: "*The Call of Cthulhu* is a landmark adaptation that calls out to all Lovecraftian film fanatics—from its silent film form, its excellent cast, its direction, and its wonderful musical score . . . this is Cthulhuian cinema that Howard would have loved." We ran the film several years ago but feel it's worth repeating as a superb HPL adaptation.

WANTED:
Original Art

**Private collector
seeks to buy original art, both color
cover and black and white interior
illustrations. Interested in adventure,
science fiction, pin-up, Spicy
and many other genres.**

DOUG ELLIS
13 Spring Lane
Barrington Hills, IL 60010
(847) 217-4241
pulpvault@msn.com

*Artists interested
in include:*

Walter M. BAUMHOFER

Rudolph BELARSKI

Earle BERGEY

Frederick BLAKESLEE

Hannes BOK

Enoch BOLLES

Margaret BRUNDAGE

Ed EMSHWILLER

Edd CARTIER

Virgil FINLAY

Kelly FREAS

J.R. FLANAGAN

R.G. HARRIS

Roy KRENKEL

Tom LOVELL

H.W. McCAULEY

P.J. MONIHAN

Frank R. PAUL

Howard PARKHURST

Hubert ROGERS

George ROZEN

Jerome ROZEN

Norman SAUNDERS

Modest STEIN

J. Allen ST. JOHN

H.J. WARD

and many others!

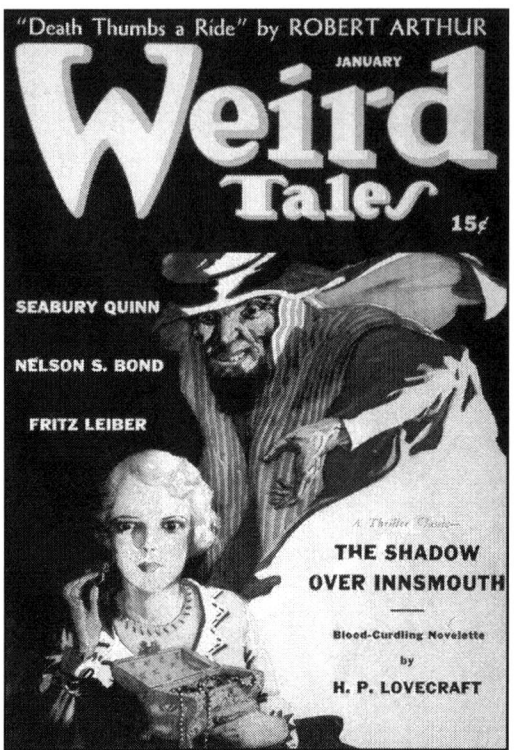

Weird Tales, January 1942

Index to advertisers

Adventure House (John Gunnison) 20, 143, 151

Alaxis Press (Stephen D. Smith) 167

Black Dog Books (Tom Roberts) 21, 27, 120, 184

Fantasy Illustrated (Dave Smith) 41

Heritage Auctions 73

Pulpfest 87

Radio Archives 144

The Shadow Knows (Dwight Fuhro) 183

Taraba Illustration 37

Wanted: Original Art (Doug Ellis) 205

68063171R00115

Made in the USA
Middletown, DE
13 September 2019